THEORY AND PRACTICE OF CLASSIC DETECTIVE FICTION

Recent Titles in
Contributions to the Study of Popular Culture

THEORY AND PRACTICE OF CLASSIC DETECTIVE FICTION

Edited by
JEROME H. DELAMATER
AND RUTH PRIGOZY

Prepared under the auspices of Hofstra University

**Contributions to the Study of Popular Culture,
Number 62**

GREENWOOD PRESS
Westport, Connecticut • London

Copyright Acknowledgment

The editors and publisher gratefully acknowledge permission for the use of excerpts from *Shake Hands Forever*, by Ruth Rendell. London: Hutchinson. Published in the United States by Doubleday, Garden City, NY, 1975. Used with permission of Random House, UK, Ltd.

Library of Congress Cataloging-in-Publication Data

Theory and practice of classic detective fiction / edited by Jerome H.
    Delamater and Ruth Prigozy ; prepared under the auspices of Hofstra
    University.
        p.   cm. — (Contributions to the study of popular culture,
    ISSN 0198–9871) ; no. 62)
    Includes bibliographical references and index.
    ISBN 0–313–30462–9 (alk. paper)
    1. Detective and mystery stories, English—History and criticism.
    2. Detective and mystery stories—History and criticism—Theory,
    etc. I. Delamater, Jerome. II. Prigozy, Ruth. III. Hofstra
    University. IV. Series.
    PR830.D4T48   1997
    823′.087209—dc21   97–1691

British Library Cataloguing in Publication Data is available.

Library of Congress Catalog Card Number: 97–1691
ISBN: 0–313–30462–9
ISSN: 0198–9871

First published in 1997

Greenwood Press, 88 Post Road West, Westport, CT 06881
An imprint of Greenwood Publishing Group, Inc.

Printed in the United States of America

The paper used in this book complies with the
Permanent Paper Standard issued by the National
Information Standards Organization (Z39.48–1984).

10 9 8 7 6 5 4 3 2 1

To the Memory of

STANLEY BRODWIN

*In honor of the 100th Anniversary of the birth
of Agatha Christie, 1891–1976*

Contents

Contents

Preface

The universally popular detective has assumed great cultural significance as modern civilization has become increasingly complex. And the detective genre seems to recreate itself every decade, finding in contemporary life the sources of inspiration that attract millions of readers worldwide. As P. D. James noted, "Detective stories help reassure us in the belief that the universe, underneath it all, is rational. They're small celebrations of order and reason in an increasingly disordered world" (*Newsweek* October 20, 1986). James's remark is particularly true of many of the earliest examples of the genre—if not of Poe's fiction with its dark, almost modernist undercurrent, then at least of the works by those eminent early practitioners of the art: Conan Doyle, Chesterton, Sayers, and, of course, the most widely read of all, Agatha Christie.

In this book, we are offering a variety of new and innovative approaches to classic detective fiction. We have organized the essays by first offering a theoretical approach to the genre, then tracing the genre back to Agatha Christie (whose centenary was the impetus for these essays) and "traditional" British detective fiction. All of these essays look at well-known and revered works from a fresh perspective, with the result that we can appreciate the complexity and dexterity involved in their creation.

Jerome H. Delamater
Ruth Prigozy

Acknowledgments

The editors wish to thank the Hofstra University Cultural Center for its support, encouragement, and unflagging work on behalf of the Agatha Christie interdisciplinary conference that inspired this volume. We are particularly grateful to Athelene A. Collins for her tireless efforts as conference coordinator. We are also appreciative of the contribution of Judy M. D'Angio, who worked so hard to prepare these essays for print.

Our editorial assistant, Keith Dallas, has been invaluable throughout the process of preparing the volume for publication. His contribution to the preparation of scholarly references and bibliographies and his help with the myriad tasks that editors face were performed with intelligence, goodwill, and generosity of spirit. We thank him.

Finally, we wish to express our thanks to all of those others at Hofstra University who helped in this endeavor and to the university itself for creating an atmosphere in which such work can be accomplished.

THEORY AND PRACTICE OF CLASSIC DETECTIVE FICTION

I

Theoretical Approaches to the Genre

In recent years the detective genre has been the site of every form of critical inquiry and theoretical postulation. Although there may still be those who disdain the mystery novel and its heirs, specialists in modern literature, film, and popular culture have clearly found the detective story a congenial object of study. Exploring the nature of the genre, its audience, and its relationship to other literary forms has become almost as much of a cottage industry as the writing of detective fiction itself. The essays in this first section give a theoretical overview of important issues about the modern detective and provide a background for subsequent essays. Fundamental to any discussion of the topic is an understanding of the classic detective, and each of these essays attempts an explanation of aspects of the classic detective to define how the genre has evolved.

In the first essay, John G. Cawelti traces the history and development of the detective story as it relates to the "canon" of English and American literature. He explores the new directions literary criticism has taken in the past decade and indicates the extent to which the detective story plot has served as a repository of important social and cultural attitudes. His essay both describes the past and points to the future of the genre.

The rise of the detective novel closely parallels the development of police forces as we know them and the reliance on scientific techniques that we deem basic to modern life. This truism is explored in Timothy Boyd and Carolyn Higbie's "Shamus-a-um," in which their play on the word *classical* centers on those recent detective novels about figures from ancient Greece and Rome who embody the "classic" characteristics of the ratiocinative or the hard-boiled schools. Using three books, one each by Margaret Doody, John Maddox Roberts, and Lindsey Davis, Boyd, and Higbie raise larger questions about historical fiction as they follow classical detectives who investigate crimes that may have little relevance in today's world within legal systems that operated so differently from our own. Nevertheless, as Boyd and Higbie conclude, Doody, Roberts, and Davis have written texts "based upon enduring motives—greed and ambition—which then spark enduring crimes—murder and theft."

Using object-relations psychology as his means of investigating the classic detective, Timothy Prchal asks questions about why people read detective fiction. Rejecting the long-held interpretations of Pederson-Krag and others that reading detective fiction links one to infantile conflicts, Prchal suggests that detective characters contribute to a reader's "psychological adaptation to the challenges and demands of day-to-day living." The "ideal imago" (in Michael Eigen's term) detectives, known more for themselves than for the actual crimes they solve, uphold the moral code in a disordered world and help explain the wide variety of mature readers who make detective fiction so popular.

The nature of narrative underlies Peter Hühn's and Ann and John Thompson's otherwise very different approaches. By analyzing three examples of mystery fiction, Hühn explores how the principle of secrecy—shared by the crime story *and* the detection story—motivates the detective plot yet is maintained even when the variations are as extreme as they are in Agatha Christie's *Curtain: Poirot's Last Case*, John Le Carré's *The Spy Who Came in from the Cold*, and Ruth Rendell's *A Judgement in Stone*. For Ann Thompson and John Thompson the concept of metonymy is an analytical tool for exploring all detective fiction, but especially that type they call the "whoizzit," in which the unmasking of a suspect in disguise is necessary to solving the crime. First exploring the relationship between resemblance/similarity (metaphor) and contiguity (metonymy), the Thompsons subsequently use Margaret Millar's *How Like an Angel* to show how contiguity can "constitute a deepening of the investigative genre."

Janice MacDonald's "Parody and Detective Fiction" and Kathleen Belin Owen's essay on the postmodern detective operate from the same base: that the seeds of the contemporary detective were sown in the first mystery stories and their earliest epigones. For MacDonald, parody, a literary device that is not just a form of ridicule, helps to define the form and its development. Noting Jacques Lacan's idea that "the detective's actions parody those of the murderer," MacDonald argues that the classic formulas established by Edgar Allan Poe, Wilkie Collins, Fergus Hume, and Arthur Conan Doyle embody parody at the outset—to some degree to distinguish their writing from others' and to establish their work as somehow superior to the genre as a whole. Owen's contention, like MacDonald's, is that "the traditional detective genre . . . possesses several traits that have equipped it with the beginnings of postmodernity," one trait indeed being parody. The genre's "game rule" structure constantly provides the opportunity to subvert the formulas so clearly set down in the form's progenitors, and subversion is basic to a postmodern detective. Douglas Adams's *Dirk Gently's Holistic Detective Agency* provides Owen's postmodern gloss on the classic attributes of the detective's eccentricity, investigation of truth, and solution arrived at by rational explanation. Owen asserts that "the detective is alive and well in the postmodern age"; these essays suggest both that detective criticism is similarly alive and well and that, pace Edmund Wilson, many people care not only who killed Roger Ackroyd but also how and why.

1

Canonization, Modern Literature, and the Detective Story

John G. Cawelti

In recent years, the far-reaching and often acrimonious debate about what has become known as the "canon" of English and American literature has dominated literary scholarship and criticism. Much of the debate has involved (a) exploring literature created by women and minorities, especially African-American, Spanish-speaking, and Native American groups and (b) giving these groups greater emphasis in the accepted literary canon. Supporters of "canon revision" have tried to generate more positive critical analyses and evaluations of literature by women and minority groups, have attacked the exclusion of these groups from the canon, and have argued that the canon itself has been strongly influenced by sexist, racist, and class ideologies. The end result of this activity has been the increasing inclusion of literary creations by women and minority groups both in literary histories and in the text anthologies that are the basis of most introductory literary courses. In this way what we know as literature is being reshaped through education and scholarship.

However, there is another important way in which our thinking about literature has been changing in the last two decades. This is the gradual assimilation into our idea of literature of popular genres that used to be sharply separated from the literary mainstream, most notably the detective story. Now, not only are certain practitioners of the detective story such as Dashiell Hammett and Raymond Chandler widely included in those classroom anthologies that effectively define the literary tradition, but the genre itself has achieved a new cultural centrality, both in America and in the world. Some of the more significant recent developments in writing by women and minorities have emerged from the detective story tradition, and the detective story has also become an important component of the new global culture that is developing around the rapid international spread of telecommunications. Finally, the basic significance of the detective story to modern culture has been reflected in the frequent use of detective story patterns by major modernist and postmodernist writers such as William Faulkner, Vladimir Nabokov, Jorge Luis Borges, and Thomas Pynchon.

ETHNIC, GENDER, AND REGIONAL DIVERSITY

When the detective story first became widely popular through the great success of Sherlock Holmes, the social values and ideologies it expressed were generally conservative. Conan Doyle's attitudes were deeply Victorian, and he strongly affirmed most of the values of traditional British culture in his stories by making Holmes and Watson embody the combination of solidity, morality, and eccentricity so central to the ideal of the British gentry while often having his criminals represent groups who threatened this traditional order. However, despite the conservatism of Doyle and most of the other successful writers of the "golden age" of the detective story, there has always been a subversive element in the genre as well, possibly going back to the ambiguous mixture of rationality and decadence that Edgar Allan Poe built into his original creation. While most of the detectives of the 1910s and 1920s were gentlemen in the mold of Holmes and Watson—one thinks immediately of such eccentric paragons as Ellery Queen, Philo Vance, Lord Peter Wimsey, Sir Henry Merrivale, Albert Campion, and Hercule Poirot—the creation of the hard-boiled detective in the late 1920s revolutionized the genre by creating a plebeian detective with subversive undertones, and the detective story increasingly moved in that direction. Recently, this subversive element has manifested itself in the genre's increasing openness to women and minority groups. Indeed, one central aspect of the recent development of the detective story has been its increasing dominance by women and other writers who, one way or another, seek to represent minority groups.

Even in the early days, the detective story strongly attracted women writers, perhaps in large part because, as an area of literature considered mere entertainment, it was more open to women than was "serious" literature.[1] In addition, since the classic detective story depended to a considerable extent on the portrayal of what used to be called "manners," it may be that women of an earlier era, trained from childhood to be exceptionally alert to social cues, had a special gift for the skillful parading of clues and suspects. Whatever the reason, women had an influence on the development of the detective story much greater than they had in any other literary genre except the romance. One of the first successful detective novelists was the American Anna Catherine Green, while the best-selling detective story writer of all time is Agatha Christie. Writers like Christie, Margery Allingham, Dorothy Sayers, Patricia Highsmith, Ngaio Marsh, and Josephine Tey were certainly as important in the so-called golden age of the detective story as their male counterparts.[2] The women writers of this early period generally expressed the same social values as their male counterparts, sometimes in so extreme a form as to be almost parodic.

Never was there a more complete model of the casual but totally competent British gentleman than Lord Peter Wimsey or Albert Campion.[3] However, the rise of the hard-boiled detective story changed all that. The hard-boiled story was initially dominated by male writers and had a distinctively antifeminist and even misogynistic animus, though, aside from this rampant sexism, the hard-boiled story had a socially liberal and even, in some ways, radical ethos.[4]

But even the hard-boiled story's misogyny proved in the long run to be only a temporary aberration. At the present time, two of the best and most popular hard-boiled writers, Sarah Paretsky and Sue Grafton, are women, who have imported into the tough-guy genre feminist values that would doubtless have put Mike Hammer into a tizzy. Paretsky's V. I. Warshawski is not only an archfeminist but also of mixed Italian and Polish parentage, so that she represents ethnic minorities as well; indeed, Warshawski is the kind of character who was typically either villain or victim in the traditional hard-boiled story, as if Brigid O'Shaughnessy or Velma Valento had become the detective. In addition, Warshawski is tough; she runs, does judo, and is able to handle herself in a fight. She bitterly resents the attempts of various men to seduce her back into a more traditional woman's style and will accept protection only from another woman, Doctor Lotty Herschel, who runs a clinic in Chicago serving Appalachian, Chicano, and other immigrant women.

In spite of her toughness and independence, Warshawski also represents many traditional "feminine" values like nurturing and family. Several of her cases develop out of her attempts to protect more vulnerable members of her family, such as her ne'er-do-well Aunt Elena in *Killing Orders*. In addition, Warshawski is presented as quite brilliant in her own right—a trained lawyer who has also developed considerable expertise in the investigation of complex financial crimes, her particular specialty as a private investigator. Paretsky has imported a whole range of feminist concerns and ideals into the detective genre; and she has, to a considerable extent, succeeded in synthesizing these with the hard-boiled world. Warshawski is a woman who has all the toughness and independence traditionally associated with men without losing the traditionally feminine concerns of family and nurturance. She is a trained professional yet has rejected the lure of bureaucratic success to become a reluctant and lonely crusader in the best hard-boiled tradition. Much the same can be said of Sue Grafton's Kinsey Millhone, and the considerable success of these writers illustrates the ability of the detective story to encourage the expression of new constellations of value and style in their relation to traditional social values.[5]

While feminism has been the most striking inspiration of new developments in the detective story, other minorities have also reached out to claim their right to a corner of the action. One of the first areas in which black actors achieved a broad success with white as well as black audiences was in the detective genre with such films as *Shaft* and *In the Heat of the Night*, though these films were, ironically, based on stories written by white writers. However, Chester Himes, a black writer, made the detective story particularly his own, and the genre continues to attract younger black writers such as the gifted Walter Mosley, who created a new kind of cool hard-boiled hero, Easy Rawlins, in his *Devil in a Blue Dress* (1990). In addition, the detective story has provided a frame for the exploration of black and white partnerships within the important Hollywood tradition of the "buddy" movie. Significantly, the first black-white "buddy" movies revolved around convicts, as if only on the illegal margins of society could a close relationship between black and white men be imagined. In this context, *48 Hours* with Nick Nolte as a white policeman and Eddie Murphy as an escaped black convict represented a transition to the full-fledged black-white detective teams of the highly successful *Beverly Hills Cop* and *Lethal Weapon* series.

While many earlier detective writers were from a Jewish-American background, they tended to suppress their Jewishness and to write about white Protestant detectives. A younger generation has more fully exploited Jewish cultural traditions, as in the Rabbi David Small stories of Harry Kemelman or in new detective types such as the schlemiel detective developed by Stuart Kaminsky, Roger Simon, and Andrew Bergmann. The Latino detective has emerged in the Luis Mendoza stories of Dell Shannon, and even Native Americans now have their detective representatives in the best-selling Navajo series of Tony Hillerman. Though Hillerman is not himself a Native American, his knowledge of Southwestern Navajo and Pueblo cultures, gained from many years of living in New Mexico, is extraordinary; and many American readers have probably gotten more insight into traditional Navajo culture from his detective stories than from any other recent books.

Sexual minorities, too, have increasingly turned to the detective story. In addition to the important feminist school of detective fiction already discussed, a thriving school of lesbian detective novels by authors such as Katherine Forrest, Lee Lynch, and Claire McNab developed in the 1980s.[6] The male homosexual detective is represented as well by the excellent Dave Brandstetter series by Joseph Hansen.[7]

The remarkable ethnic and gender diversity of recent detective stories suggests that the genre has become more than simply a popular literary entertainment. Increasingly the detective story has become a genre in which writers explore new social values and definitions and push against the traditional boundaries of gender and race to play imaginatively with new kinds of social character and human relations. The creation of representative detective heroes has become an important social ritual for minority groups who would claim a meaningful place in the larger social context.

Another related recent trend in the detective genre is the remarkable flourishing of regional and local detectives. Once most American detective stories were set in the urban centers of New York and Los Angeles. However, more and more in recent years different areas feature in detective series: There are now women detectives from Chicago, Cajun detectives from New Orleans, black detectives from Los Angeles, and Catholic detectives from Detroit in addition to "regional" detectives from Cincinnati, Denver, Minneapolis, and many other specific American locales. Many of these novels contain highly accurate presentations, in the way that Paretsky shows a keen awareness of particular neighborhoods in Chicago or Hillerman portrays the differences among Navajo, Hopi, and Zuni cultures in the Southwest. It is as if, to establish a distinctive awareness in the national consciousness, particular places must see themselves portrayed in the detective story. In this way, detective fiction is becoming our most serious and complex form of popular literature.

THE INTERNATIONALIZATION OF THE DETECTIVE STORY

Beginning as an expression of conservative, bourgeois, ethnocentric Anglo-American values,[8] the detective story has expanded to accommodate a much greater diversity of social values and ideologies until, in the aftermath of the Cold War, it seems on the verge of becoming a truly global mythos. The stages through which this transformation has occurred suggest that the genre had a dynamic that kept pushing against the seemingly rigid boundaries of the formula.

The early history of the detective story clearly displays this double impetus. On the one hand, there is a very strong emphasis on the values of Anglo-American bourgeois culture in the stories of Conan Doyle and other early masters of the genre. On the other, there is the fascination with the exotic and the strange, which even Doyle clearly felt in such stories as *A Study in Scarlet* and *The Sign of Four*. In this respect, the detective story mirrored the ambiguous mixture of fear and attraction that the English felt for cultures on the fringes of the empire and Americans had for the Native American cultures they were both exterminating and romanticizing.

This same mixture of fear and attraction toward non–Anglo-American cultures continued to dominate the detective story and its near relative the spy story well into the 1920s. The doubling of Anglo-American hero and ethnic or third-world villain so characteristic of the period is clear in some of the most compelling duos in the literature: Doyle's Sherlock Holmes and Professor Moriarty (presumably Irish), Sax Rohmer's Nayland Smyth and Dr. Fu Manchu, John Buchan's Richard Hannay and his various German, Near Eastern, and mixed antagonists. Such duos continue to appear in the literature even in the post–World War II period, as in the colorful, racially mixed figures of Dr. No, Goldfinger, and Blofeld who bedevil James Bond, but these are already showing the signs of self-parody clearly foreshadowed in the conflict between Sam Spade and the devious alliance of Joel Cairo, Caspar Gutman, and Brigid O'Shaughnessy.

Actually, in the 1930s and 1940s two important developments began to undercut the detective story's Anglo-American ethnocentricity. Writers in other countries, such as Georges Simenon in Belgium and France, Edogawa Rampo in Japan, and Arthur W. Upfield in Australia, as well as the American hard-boiled writers, began to develop important new varieties of mystery fiction, a trend that became increasingly international in the 1960s, 1970s, and 1980s.

Also in the 1930s and 1940s the quest for new kinds of detectives led to the development of a rich galaxy of non-English detectives created in large part by English and American writers: Earl Derr Biggers's Charlie Chan, John P. Marquand's Mr. Moto, Robert van Gulik's Judge Dee, Upfield's half-aborigine Napoleon Bonaparte, and Simenon's Inspector Maigret. Charlie Chan and Mr. Moto might almost have been positive transformations of Dr. Fu Manchu, which suggests that the detective story, instead of remaining an expression of ethnocentrism, was on the way to becoming a means of exploring rather than condemning other cultures. This trend continues with an increasing number of detective series dealing not only with a great variety of national cultures but also with regional cultures within large countries like America. In short, the internationalization of the detective story seems to be another major contemporary trend.

To further indicate the extent to which the detective story has expanded from its Anglo-American roots into an increasingly international genre, the *Vrij Nederland* of June 11, 1991,[9] published its annual guide of the best writers of detective novels and other kinds of thrillers, which listed seventy American and thirty-five English authors, indicating not only the national origins of the genre but also the extent to which, through the thriller, certain English and American writers have become a significant part of other cultures. In Holland, most of these authors are distributed both in the original English and in Dutch translations. In addition, the *Vrij Nederland* guide listed eight Belgian, thirty-one Dutch, one Canadian, one Dutch/Swedish collaboration, one Norwegian, one Swiss, two Swedish, one Flemish, three Russian, two French, and one Danish author of mystery novels. And this listing does not even include such international best-sellers as Umberto Eco's *The Name of the Rose* and *Foucault's Pendulum*, perhaps because they are considered more complex novels rather than thrillers, though like many modernist and postmodernist works, their basic structure is that of the detective story.

BOURGEOIS DEMOCRACY AND THE DOUBLE PLOT

The detective story is such a pervasive phenomenon of the contemporary world—not only in books but in many other media—that it is difficult both to imagine what our culture would be without it and also to understand why this is so. I offer here two tentative speculations about why the detective story has become so canonical. One of them deals with the special significance of the unique form of the detective story itself, while the second is a notion about why the theme of crime and detection has become increasingly important on a global level.

The unique formal pattern of the detective story genre lies in its double and duplicitious plot. The plot is double because the story is first narrated as it appears to the bewildered bystanders who observe the crime and are to some extent threatened by it, but who cannot arrive at its solution. Finally, through the detective's reconstruction of the crime, the true story of the events is given along with their explanation. This doubling is duplicitous because, in the first presentation of the story, the writer tries to tantalize and deceive the reader while, at the same time, inconspicuously planting the clues that will eventually make the detective's solution plausible.[10] This double plot has fascinated many major modernist and postmodernist writers because it reflects their own highly self-conscious awareness of the artificiality of narration and the ambiguity of plots.

Among major modernist writers, Faulkner was perhaps most influenced by the detective story, for the structure of the double plot not only plays an important role in the actual detective stories Faulkner wrote—the novel *Intruder in the Dust* and the stories collected in *Knight's Gambit*—but also is a major element in *The Sound and the Fury*, *Absalom, Absalom!*, and *Light in August*. For Faulkner, adapting the detective story's play with clues and successive solutions, as well as its emphasis on the testimony of different witnesses, enables him to develop some of his most important themes. For instance, in *Absalom, Absalom!* the detective story's double plot of murder and its solution is further complicated by the accounts of a number of storytellers, legend-makers, and witnesses who have their own versions of the Henry Sutpen–Charles Bon murder case. To the problem of conflicting individual truths basic to the detective story, Faulkner adds the complexities of history, memory, and myth, through which the clues of the past are communicated to the "detectives" of a later generation, Quentin Compson and Shreve McCannon. While there is no firm evidence that the solution Shreve and Quentin arrive at is the truth—the real world does not usually grant investigators the rational certainty attained by fictional detectives—the investigation leads to some devastating truths about the culture. Faulkner's complex version of the double plot dramatizes imagination and the human capacity for empathy and identification as more vital to the pursuit of truth than ratiocinative brilliance and reveals that, though truth is precarious and always elusive, its quest is the most important of human activities.

The double plot is even more pervasive in the work of postmodernist writers. In addition to the explicitly antidetective novels of Robbe-Grillet, Stanislas Lem, and others, the duplicitous parading of clues and false solutions is a pervasive element in the writing of Borges, Nabokov, and Pynchon. Two postmodernist versions of the double plot must suffice. In Borges's "Death and the Compass" the brilliant detective is lured into a trap by a series of clues planted by his archenemy. These clues lead the detective to a decaying villa filled with images of doubles ("a glacial Diana in one lugubrious niche was complemented by another Diana in another niche; one balcony was repeated by another balcony; double steps of stair opened into a double balustrade") where the detective's own murder will take place, after the criminal, in true detective fashion, carefully explains to the detective how he has set up his fatal trap.

In Nabokov's *The Real Life of Sebastian Knight* and *Pale Fire* an investigator works through a series of clues in order to uncover the "real" truth, which is, in one case, the secrets of the life of the investigator's brother and, in the other, the meaning of a poem left behind by the investigator's "friend," who has been murdered. In both these novels, as the investigator proceeds, his perversity and egotism become more and more obvious to the reader, who comes to see that, rather than discovering the hidden "truth," the "detective" is projecting his own needs and obsessions onto the clues he is examining. In the end, it is the detective's "solution" that seems totally false, while the original clues in their opacity and mystery still contain whatever there is to be known—if anything—of the "truth."

These examples suggest that twentieth-century authors find a way of artistically expressing the pervasive philosophical and cultural skepticism of modern times by using or inverting the double plot of the detective story to create a structure in which their own sense of the problems of truth and meaning can be embodied. For Faulkner, the double plot serves as a means of dramatizing the complexity and difficulty as well as the human necessity of the quest for "truth"; for Borges, the inversion of the double plot exposes the delusion of rationality fostered by the traditional detective story; finally, for Nabokov, it becomes the source of an incessant play of furtive meanings and ambivalence, a dark field in which gaudy butterflies of many different shapes and shades forever elude the lepidopterist's net.[11]

However, if the structure of the detective story has helped some of our most important writers to create fictions that seem to cast doubt on the very possibility of rational and certain truths traditionally associated with the genre, this possibility has not prevented other writers from continuing to produce more or less straight detective stories in which the clues are correctly interpreted, the conflicting solutions transcended, and the mystery resolved. The genre can apparently accommodate both the pervasive skepticism of the postmodernists and a continued belief in successful interpretation and solution. There appears to be, then, another source of the continued popularity of the detective story in its originating cultures of England and America as well as its increasing relevance on the international scene.

In essence the detective story constitutes a *mythos* or fable in which crime, as a distinctive problem of bourgeois, individualistic, and quasi-democratic societies is handled without upsetting society's fundamental institutions or its worldview. When he or she solves the crime, the detective reaffirms the fundamental soundness of the social order by revealing how the crime has resulted from the specific and understandable motives of particular individuals; the crime represents a situation that is possible but not fundamental nor endemic to the society. In other words, the detective reveals to us by his or her actions that, however corrupt or unjust society may be in some of its particulars, it yet contains the intelligence and the means to define and exorcise these evils as particular problems. Even in the more pessimistic vision of some of the hard-boiled detective stories, where the corrupt far outnumber the innocent, it is still possible for the detective to accomplish a significant act of justice or vengeance.

Of course, it is precisely this optative and optimistic view of the world that many postmodernist writers are questioning, but, because the detective story as a genre is so deeply pervaded by the bourgeois individualistic worldview, it is almost inevitable that such stories become inversions of the double structure of the detective story.

If these reflections are correct, it seems likely that the increasing internationalization of the detective story genre is related to a growing global influence of the ideologies of individualistic, bourgeois democracy. As these ideologies spread throughout the world, more and more countries seem to be developing their own detective literature. Totalitarian societies have usually shown considerable hostility toward detective stories; they were virtually banned in Nazi Germany and in the more Stalinist periods of Russia and China. The genre is apparently just beginning to flourish in the latter two countries. Furthermore, the detective story did not even exist in earlier societies and, because of its relative modernity, is one of the few major popular literary genres that can be traced to a specific date and author. Of course, we frequently compare certain myths, legends, and folktales involving mysteries, like Oedipus the King, to detective stories, but there are some basic differences, as well as obvious similarities, between the detective genre and these earlier mysteries. The tale of Oedipus does involve a kind of detecting and explaining, but the agency of the gods remains a mystery beyond investigation and solution. The true solution of the myth of Oedipus, if there is any at all, comes only much later when Oedipus is apotheosized at Colonus, again through an inexplicable action of the gods. In the detective genre, however, the key point is that every mystery can be explained not only by human agency but also by reference to the actions and motives of particular individuals. Even in *The Nine Tailors*, when Dorothy Sayers metaphysically makes God out to be the murderer, it is clear that He is acting as an individual with the clearly understandable motive of punishing the guilty.

In short, the detective story is a key *mythos* of the ideology of individualistic bourgeois democracy embodied in a unique formal pattern that ritually involves the reader in the celebration of the myth. Therefore, the detective genre has become bound up with two major trends of modern democracy: the quest for greater equality among different regional, ethnic, and gender groups and the increasing international influence of the ideologies of individualism and bourgeois democracy.

NOTES

1. Kathleen Maio lists twenty-five important mystery novels by women between 1861 and 1916 in *Murderess Ink* (47-49), while Michele Slung lists over one hundred women detectives from 1861 to 1974 in *Crime on Her Mind* (357-77).

2. Along with the continued appearance of new women writers and detectives, the literature about women mystery writers has grown considerably in the past two decades;

among the important books are Dilys Winn's *Murderess Ink*, a compendium of information on women mystery writers and other aspects of women and crime, Michele Slung's *Crime on Her Mind*, an anthology of stories featuring women detectives, and Bobbie Ann Mason's *The Girl Sleuth*, a feminist study of mysteries such as the once super-popular Nancy Drew books, featuring young girl detectives. See also Elaine Budd's *13 Mistresses of Murder*.

3. Significantly, however, both Wimsey and Campion fall in love with highly brilliant and independent women and must work very hard to understand and accept their needs as feminists. Though Wimsey defends Harriet Vane against a false charge of murder in *Strong Poison*, she is still not willing to marry him until she is sure that he has become sufficiently nonsexist to be willing to support her full independence. It takes another mystery, one of Sayers's longest and most complex, *Gaudy Night*, before the two lovers have negotiated an *entente cordiale*.

4. Dashiell Hammett, for example, was, at least in some sense, a committed Marxist and, for a time, a member of the Communist Party, though a highly individualistic and rebellious one. It is easy to read *Red Harvest* as a Marxist parable, but his best works, *The Maltese Falcon* and *The Glass Key*, largely resist that kind of interpretation. In the 1950s Hammett even went to jail for refusing to testify about other people's involvement in communist causes. Raymond Chandler was largely apolitical, though his stories express a similar critique of American society and the decadence of the rich. The only significant hard-boiled writer with a strongly conservative bent was Mickey Spillane; his views were more those of what used to be called the radical right, and his criticism of the decadence of the rich was even more strident that that of Hammett and Chandler.

5. The hard-boiled story is not the only type of detective story on which feminist writers have made their mark. There are also many women practitioners of the more ratiocinative detective story who, like Amanda Cross (Carolyn Heilbrun), are very much concerned with expressing feminist ideas in their work. Even somewhat more traditional women writers like the English P. D. James and Ruth Rendell may still use male detectives, Inspectors Dalgleish and Wexford, but these male characters are very different in their relationship to women than the traditional male detective.
Significantly, these writers are probably also the most financially successful of today's detective writers. Cf. Carolyn Heilbrun, "Gender and Detective Fiction."

6. I'm particularly grateful to Beth Heston, Ph.D. student at the University of Kentucky, for introducing me to the lesbian detective novel. See Ms. Heston's unpublished paper "'A Twice-Written Scroll': The Lesbian Detective Novel," University of Kentucky, 1991. A version of this paper was presented at the 1991 convention of the Popular Culture Association.

7. Cf. Hansen, *Nightwork, Gravedigger, Skinflick, The Man Everybody Was Afraid Of, Troublemaker, Death Claims*, etc.

8. Several studies, particularly Palmer (1979) and Knight (1980), interestingly discuss detective story ideologies.

9. This periodical is published in Amsterdam. I'm grateful to Birgit Lijmbach and Petro van der Veen for sending it to me.

10. See the discussion of this aspect of the detective story in Cawelti (1976, 87-91). For a fuller discussion of the use of the detective story plot pattern by modernist and postmodernist writers, see Cawelti, "Faulkner and the Detective Story's Double Plot."

11. For a fuller analysis of the influence of the detective story on modernist and postmodernist writers, see Michael Holquist (1971-1972), William Spanos (1972), and Stefano Tani (1984).

REFERENCES

Budd, Elaine. *13 Mistresses of Murder*. New York: Ungar, 1986.

Cawelti, John G. "Faulkner and the Detective Story's Double Plot." *Clues* 12, no. 2 (Fall/Winter 1991): 1-15.

____. *Adventure, Mystery, and Romance*. Chicago: University of Chicago Press, 1976.

Heilbrun, Carolyn. "Gender and Detective Fiction." In *The Sleuth and the Scholar: Origin, Evolution, and Current Trends in Detective Fiction*, edited by Barbara A. Rader and Howard G. Zettler. Westport, CT: Greenwood, 1988.

Heston, Beth. "'A Twice-Written Scroll': The Lesbian Detective Novel." Unpublished paper, University of Kentucky, 1991.

Holquist, Michael. "Whodunit and Other Questions: Metaphysical Detective Stories in Post-War Fiction." *New Literary History* 3 (1971-1972): 135-56.

Knight, Stephen. *Form and Ideology in Crime Fiction*. Bloomington: Indiana University Press, 1980.

Mason, Bobbie Ann. *The Girl Sleuth: A Feminist Guide*. Old Westbury, NY: Feminist Press, 1975.

Palmer, Jerry. *Thrillers: Genesis and Structure of a Popular Genre*. New York: St. Martin's, 1979.

Slung, Michele B. *Crime on Her Mind: Fifteen Stories of Female Sleuths from the Victorian Era to the Forties*. New York: Pantheon, 1975.

Spanos, William V. "The Detective and the Boundary: Some Notes on the Postmodern Literary Imagination." *Boundary* 2 (1972): 147-68.

Tani, Stefano. *The Doomed Detective: The Contribution of the Detective Novel to Postmodern American and Italian Fiction*. Carbondale: Southern Illinois University Press, 1984.

Winn, Dilys. *Murderess Ink*. New York: Workman, 1979.

2

Shamus-a-um: Having the Quality of a Classical Detective

Timothy W. Boyd and Carolyn Higbie

This has a familiar ring:

I was standing in the Forum. She was running. She looked overdressed and dangerously hot, but sunstroke or suffocation had not yet finished her off. She was shining and sticky as a glazed pastry plait, and when she hurtled up the steps of the Temple of Saturn straight towards me, I made no attempt to move aside. She missed me, just. Some men are born lucky; others are called Didius Falco. (*Silver Pigs* 3)

The Forum and the Temple of Saturn aren't at Hollywood and Vine, but there is something in that flat, self-deprecating tone that is reminiscent of:

It was about eleven o'clock in the morning, mid October, with the sun not shining and a look of hard wet rain in the clearness of the foothills. I was wearing my powder-blue suit, with dark blue shirt, tie and display handkerchief, black brogues, black wool socks with dark blue clocks on them. I was neat, clean, shaved and sober, and I didn't care who knew it. I was everything a well-dressed private detective ought to be. I was calling on four million dollars. (*The Big Sleep* 1)

The second of these quotations opens Raymond Chandler's *The Big Sleep* (1939). The first, however, is a puzzle: the Forum? the Temple of Saturn? No published Chandler novel or short story is set in such locales. Could these be cheap bars in an unfinished manuscript and this another collaboration, like Robert B. Parker's completion of Chandler's *Poodle Springs*? But what are we to do with that name—Didius Falco? The name is, in fact, the giveaway. The setting is not Chandler's Los Angeles, but Rome. The date is not in Chandler's gray 1930s to 1950s, but 70 A.D., a detail important to the story, and we are reading a recent detective novel by Lindsey Davis called *Silver Pigs*.

As *Poodle Springs* or Hiber Conteris's 1985 Chandler pastiche *Ten Percent of Life*[1] shows, setting a detective novel in the more recent past has its advantages for a writer interested in giving a little historical color to his or her tale. It is a time still fresh in many memories. Films, newsreels, newspapers, and magazines survive in great abundance to provide background. The contemporary author can garner a good deal of period detail and "feel" from detective fiction of the era. If, like Parker and Conteris, writers are operating within a single author's tradition, they can even use that author's own style as a passageway into recent history.[2] It is also helpful, of course, that the plots of such books take place in a world very like our own, in which police—and detectives—are a commonplace, in which there is a familiar legal system to which they are accountable, and in which there is an increasing array of scientific investigatory methods available to solve the forensic difficulties so common to our crimes. But what are conditions like for those daring authors, like Lindsey Davis, who would travel further into the past?

Many crime novelists have taken a step beyond Parker and Conteris into the later Victorian era, attracted in part, perhaps, because of the perennial popularity of Sherlock Holmes. Besides the growing number of continuations of the Holmes stories themselves, there are Peter Lovesey's novels about Sergeant Cribb and, more recently, about Bertie, Prince of Wales; Francis Selwyn's Sergeant Verity stories; Anne Perry's Charlotte Pitt and William Monk; John Buxton Hilton's series on Thomas Brunt; and a scattering of books by Julian Symons, among others. There are even two series set in Victorian America. The first, created by Lawrence Alexander, employs Teddy Roosevelt as his detective, during the two years that TR served as Police Commissioner in the City of New York (*The Strenuous Life, Speak Softly, The Big Stick*). The second, newly begun by William Marshall, long known for his Hong Kong police procedurals, concerns the doings of a less famous detective, although the setting and time frame are similar (*The New York Detective*).

Besides the attraction of Holmes, the Victorian period has the advantage of being an era of growing police forces and scientific techniques. These allow the modern novelist to go a little deeper into the past but to enjoy a certain comfort there in the familiarity of an age of detection just prior to our own. Holmes, after all, has a microscope and routinely seeks out and analyzes evidence like cigar ash and footprints.

Although modern techniques disappear rapidly beyond the 1880s, should a writer want to move even further back, London did have a small semblance of a constabulary in Fielding's Bow Street Runners, beginning in the mid-eighteenth century.[3] Several crime writers (notably John Dickson Carr and, more recently, J. G. Jeffreys) have availed themselves of these forerunners of the nineteenth-century Peelers.[4] Before this time, however, professional policemen are thin on the ground and private detectives nonexistent, so that those who want to place their novels before the eighteenth century must find other employ for their investigators. Leonard Tourney's Tudor Matthew Stock, for instance, is town constable, but he is also an increasingly prosperous cloth merchant (*Low Treason*, for example). Ellis Peters's early-twelfth-century Cadfael is a monk at Shrewsbury Abbey, although his best friend is the governor of Shrewsbury castle and thus the defender of law and order in the region (*The Potter's Field* among others).

In each case mentioned, it is obvious that much research has been done, the sort one would expect from the better writers of historical fiction since the time of Sir Walter Scott, for writers who accept the double challenge of history *and* mystery are, on the whole, writers who are extremely sensitive to the past and who clearly study with care the eras in which they set their stories. At least part of the fun for the reader is that sense of actually being conveyed to another time and place, and part of the fun for the writer is to make that place as vivid as possible, a vividness that comes best from the employment of careful research. This research goes towards recreating the "feel" of a past time—what might be termed its "texture," which includes everything from clothing to architecture to the objects of everyday life.[5] It also includes historical context, in which Ellis Peters seems particularly strong. Her Cadfael's Shrewsbury suffers through the civil war between Stephen and Matilda from the mid-1130s on, and often what happens in that war in the big world outside is reflected in the little world of her novels.

Texture also includes authentic period behavior—often much trickier to research and to recreate.[6] It is one of the most important elements, however, because it belongs not only to a book's texture, its feel, but also to its plot, its text. The behavior of one character toward others and the relationship between a person and society are the generators of the text. If mystery novelists who look to the past want to be as accurate in text as in texture, they need to understand just how people of an earlier time might react to a given situation. Many, if not most, human emotions might be enduring and universal, as Agatha Christie notes in her one historical mystery, *Death Comes As the End* (1944), which is set in dynastic Egypt and deals with jealousy and family feeling: "The action of this book takes place on the west bank of the Nile at Thebes in Egypt about 2000 B.C. Both place and time are incidental to the story. Any other place at any other time would have served as well" (Author's Note). But standards and the beliefs behind them can vary greatly. In the case of Dame Agatha's Egyptians, for example, the safe passage of the soul to the other world was of paramount importance, and those who could do so spent fortunes to insure that passage. If an author unintentionally depicted indifference to the afterlife in a mystery novel set in Egypt, he or she would ignore an important cultural norm and thus disturb the texture of the book, if not the text—something Dame Agatha herself takes care to avoid.

Robert van Gulik's Judge Dee, a character-based folktale about an actual seventh-century Chinese law official, must occasionally deal with supernatural forces. In context, these forces and the human reactions to them are viewed as genuine, whereas a contemporary audience might think them more likely to appear in a Stephen King thriller than in a detective novel.[7] Yet, if one may judge by van Gulik's work, to write authentically of seventh-century Chinese crime and law, one must be willing to include elements completely alien to other novels set in later times and different cultures.

To utilize beliefs alien to our culture might even prove a benefit beyond that of adding texture. Consider, for example, how many interesting varieties of crime might be possible subjects for novels in such cultures, crimes that would mean nothing to Robert Parker or Raymond Chandler. To most Americans in the late twentieth century, sacrilege has become almost an empty word. To prosecute someone for it would seem about as rational as to hang someone who has admitted sticking pins in an image in order to harm an enemy. In classical Athens, however, someone charged with sacrilege would have understood it to be an extremely serious accusation. To commit sacrilege, as Socrates was accused of doing (among other crimes), was to risk punishment from the gods for oneself and for the state as a whole, since the gods were not always discriminating in their wrath.[8] Being accused of sacrilege was tantamount to being charged with threatening the livelihood of the country.

Even our own western culture has had beliefs now no longer held. Just as sacrilege was a real crime in classical Athens, witchcraft courts here in the United States once questioned defendants severely about the use of pins and dolls. To us, witchcraft suggests Halloween. When we see that those involved in the late-seventeenth-century Salem trials were drawn both from the clergy and from the legal world, it is clear that witchcraft was deemed a grave religious *and* civil crime. To become a witch was to decide to deny and defy holy law and secular law as well—certainly good enough motives as far as Puritan courts were concerned, though such motives mean little to us now.

For such crimes to act as the motivating power in novels, they must be linked with appropriate legal, or at least retributive, structures. The problem of identifying such structures becomes increasingly difficult the further into the past and more removed from their own culture writers wish to go. We have already seen how quickly, when we look behind the Victorians, our concepts of police, detectives, and investigations disappear. If one sets a novel further in the past, however, even if the crime committed there is one still understandable to us, who will investigate and where will justice be found?

Five detective novels that deal with the ancient classical world present the opportunity to examine this question from the twin perspectives of text and texture. In chronological order, they are Margaret Doody's *Aristotle Detective* (1978), set in fourth-century B.C. Athens, John Maddox Roberts's *SPQR* (1990) and *SPQR II* (1991), set in first-century B.C. Rome, and Lindsey Davis's *Silver Pigs* (1989), which also takes place in Rome, but about a century later, in A.D. 70. Davis's second volume, *Shadows in Bronze* (1990), follows shortly after the adventures of the first. Three of these, *Aristotle Detective* and each of the first novels with Roman detectives, *SPQR* and *Silver Pigs*, can represent all the issues relevant to this examination.

Although Athens at the time of Aristotle possessed a complex legal system, complete with courts and juries,[9] the enforcement of the laws was as much a personal or family matter as it was the business of the state, which lacked an investigative police force or even public prosecutors. Should someone commit a crime, the responsibility would fall upon the injured party and his or her relatives to assemble the case and to prosecute. The same was also true for the defense. The trial of Socrates in 339 B.C. serves as illustration. Those who collected evidence against him and had him indicted were not agents of the city but private citizens. These same private citizens next appeared as the prosecution, claiming to speak for the city at large. Socrates, without the possibility of modern counsel, was then put into the position of defending himself.[10]

The Athenian system, therefore, forced Margaret Doody in *Aristotle Detective* to begin not only without the basic investigative and forensic concepts so familiar to us but also without police or detectives and without district attorneys or defense lawyers. Her hero is Stephanos, a very young man who becomes head of his family at his father's premature death. His family is small and not well-connected and thus ripe to be victimized by those with more power. When the wealthy Boutades is murdered, his real murderer, his nephew Polygnotos, accuses Stephanos's scapegrace cousin Philemon. Philemon is already in exile for accidentally killing a man, leaving Stephanos, as family head, to assume the position of defender for his absent cousin. The passage of time within the novel is thus marked off for him and for the readers each month by another appearance before the *basileus*, the officiating magistrate.

Stephanos is not completely alone in his defense, however. He has been a pupil of Aristotle, and, desperate, he takes his doubts about his cousin's guilt to his old teacher. With the shadows of Sherlock and Mycroft Holmes lurking somewhere behind a pillar, Aristotle questions Stephanos in an appropriately Aristotelian fashion, helping him to assemble and arrange in some order what he knows, what he doubts, and what he thinks. Doody has a great deal of fun at such times both with remarks about syllogistic reasoning and with Sherlock Holmes's manner of deduction and his sometimes gloating, sometimes chagrined explanation of it. Thus, after Aristotle deduces from Stephanos's face and clothing where he has been and explains how he has arrived at this conclusion, there is this exchange between them:[11] "'Oh,' I [Stephanos] said. 'That's all quite simple.' 'Yes. Isn't it wonderful when I [Aristotle] give you my reasons. Observation and logic'" (198). This action he repeats several times as Stephanos searches for proof of his cousin's innocence and of the identity of the real murderer.

Aristotle also actively investigates, helps Stephanos spirit away his newly discovered sister-in-law and nephew, and even undertakes an illegal, nighttime exhumation on Stephanos's behalf. Using bits of evidence gathered gradually and applying insights and information gained from his consultation with Aristotle, Stephanos eventually unmasks Polygnotos, who drowns while attempting to escape. Doody provides some classical Athenian texture to show the murderer's end: "No Athenian wanted the corpse back. Some official persons who knew Polygnotos went reluctantly to identify it, but no one wished to pollute the grounds of the city by harboring the corpse of such a vile murderer, a man who was, in effect, a parricide, and displeasing to the gods" (277).[12] This is a historically accurate view of what would have been Athenian reaction to Polygnotos's demise. To come to it and to Stephanos's clearing of Philemon's name, Doody has kept within the bounds of her chosen time: She has introduced nothing criminological from more recent times but has employed a period given—Aristotle's system of thinking—to solve her mystery.

Rome, like Athens, had an extensive legal system. Also, like Athens, there was no police force *per se*, although there were the *vigiles*, the watch, assigned to each of Rome's districts, whose principal job was to spot and control the fires that were such a danger in the close-packed city. The hero of John Maddox Roberts's *SPQR* and its sequel, *SPQR II*,[13] is a low-level commissioner with social and political ambitions, Decius Caecilius Metellus, one of whose duties is to oversee a district watch. In *SPQR*, when the watch captain reports a murder, Decius, as a commissioner, has an obligation to look into the victim's identity and into the crime itself. Though he does have the power to investigate, his authority can be curtailed by circumstances and the desires of those more important. This is like a policeman, for Decius himself makes it clear who actually rules the streets; to modern city dwellers, his description of life in Rome might have a familiar ring:

You must understand, whoever you are, that in those days Rome, mistress of half the world, was a place as savage as a village of Nile pygmies. Roman soldiers kept the peace in hundreds of cities around our sea, but not a single soldier patrolled the streets of Rome. Tradition forbade it. Instead, the city was controlled by street gangs, each under the protection of a powerful family or politician for whom it performed tasks liable to criminal prosecution. (2)

Decius discovers that the three murders, one break-in, robbery, and arson that he is investigating, are related and have a much more international, political flavor to them than the text based on personal greed of Doody's *Aristotle Detective*. The anxiety Greeks felt during the fourth century B.C. about the acts and intentions of the Macedonian Philip and his son Alexander serves only as a vague background to the family problems of Stephanos, but Roberts's story takes as its focus the political and military maneuvering across the Mediterranean of Rome's most powerful men. This means that, for texture, Roberts must sketch in not only information about Roman religious practices, social customs, and elite families, but also facts about Roman politics and military forces. Decius the minor magistrate finds himself pitted against the most powerful men in Rome, the two consuls for 70 B.C. (Pompey the Great and Crassus) and the politically ambitious, completely amoral P. Claudius Pulcher.

Inexplicably to his father, himself a politician of the old school, Decius decides to investigate the case, hoping to clean the corruption out of Rome. His naive idealism carries him through a wild sexual encounter with Claudia (the sister of Claudius) and her companion, numerous attempts on his life, including a riot in the Forum, and an attempt to bring charges against the Roman leaders. At the novel's end, we are privy to both the complete explanation of events and the public explanation that Decius accepts as the price for his life.[14]

Perhaps the most intriguing figure in the novel is the Greek Asklepiodes, an Egyptian-trained doctor in whom Roberts craftily brings together texture and text. Decius finds Asklepiodes at a gladiatorial school where he is studying, appropriately enough, the effects of differing kinds of wounds. As there is evidence in the Hippocratic Collection on surgery and the treatment of broken bones dating back at least to 400 B.C., such study in the Rome of 70 B.C. is quite plausible, particularly when carried out by a Greek physician, a common figure in the Roman world. Thus, Roberts can provide Decius with a certain amount of the forensic intelligence to which modern readers are accustomed without violating the borders of what was available at the time.

Although his role in Decius's investigation is more limited than Aristotle's in *Aristotle Detective*, Asklepiodes' ability to identify what kind of weapon causes what kind of wound and to make such deductions from the scars of long-healed wounds is invaluable to Decius's case. Asklepiodes reveals some of the distant haughtiness that Aristotle and Sherlock Holmes—and medical examiners in modern-day novels—sometimes can display. When Decius asks how Asklepiodes "guessed" that he—Decius—had been wounded by a Catalan javelin at some time previously, the physician replies:

"I did not guess," the Greek said smugly. "The marks are there to see, if one knows what they mean. The Catalan javelin has a serrated edge, and that scar was made by such an edge. It traveled at an upward angle. The Catalans fight on foot, and this gentleman is clearly of a rank worthy to go into battle on horseback. Furthermore, he is of the right age to have served as a junior officer in the campaigns of Generals Pompey and Metellus in Spain of a few years ago. Hence, the gentleman was wounded in Spain in recent years." (11)

Lindsey Davis provides much of the same texture—Roman life—as Roberts, but she has chosen a more questionable occupation than minor magistrate for her hero, Marcus Didius Falco, in *Silver Pigs* (1989). Didius Falco is a *delator*, or informer, of the sort who made Rome into a political hell throughout the first century A.D. Davis's choice is quite useful to her: for the sake of texture, Falco, as an informer, is logically at home in the Roman underworld, which still controlled most of the city a hundred years after the period whose activities Decius describes in *SPQR*. Davis clearly has a second, textual reason. As the language of the quotation that began this essay indicates, Falco owes more than a little to Philip Marlowe and his creator, Raymond Chandler. Language is another potential—but often neglected—part of texture. It would be very difficult to write a mystery novel in twelfth-century Norman French or Old English, as Ellis Peters would be obliged to do if she were to be strictly accurate in her reconstruction of early medieval Shrewsbury; the attempt would also drastically restrict her readership. Leonard Tourney avoids sounding like a pastiche of Shakespeare by making Matthew Stock speak a kind of common English with occasional period vocabulary, and this appears to be the general practice.[15] Both *Aristotle Detective* and *SPQR* are told in this way. Davis makes a more daring choice, for the sake of her text, in giving Falco the speech of a hard-boiled detective speaking: "He talks as the man of his age talks—that is, with rude wit, a lively sense of the grotesque, a disgust for sham and a contempt for pettiness" ("The Simple Art of Murder" 20-21).

In her "Dramatis Personae," Davis describes Falco as "a private informer with republican views" (viii). "Private informer" suggests, of course, "private detective" making Falco sound more modern than his time. As there had been an emperor in Rome, however, for nearly a hundred years by 70 A.D., the time of the novel, the phrase "with republican views" makes him sound more than a little old-fashioned.[16] This combination of yearning for the ideals of the old republic with the job of informer gives Falco speech patterns that echo those of Chandler's poignant, realist detective and stakes out new territory for historical detecting fiction. Two periods are always in play with each other—not the present and the past, but one past with another. In this first book, Davis takes it no further than to suggest a commonality of experience between the two times, however, and in the second novel, *Shadows in Bronze* (1990), she appears to have abandoned the attempt altogether.

Like Marlowe, then, Falco is an odd man for an investigator. He will ply what looks like a dingy trade, but he will show certain scruples. He will be like the detective Chandler has in mind: "He is a relatively poor man, or he would not be a detective at all. He is a common man or he could not go among common people. He has a sense of character, or he would not know his job" ("The Simple Art of Murder" 20). Decius's job is complicated by Roman politics. Rome has just endured the terrible "year of the four emperors," in which Nero was removed and generals from all over the empire attempted to try their luck as successors. By the novel's opening, Vespasian has the throne, but there are many who might still contest that. Through an attractive young upper-class girl (reflective of Chandler again), Falco becomes involved in investigating a scheme to skim off pigs of silver (ingots) from the imperial mines in Britain. The girl is killed, and Falco after a long courtship, which includes a flight through the streets of Rome, becomes involved with her cousin Helena. His clues lead him to uncover a plot, financed by the silver and led by Domitian (Vespasian's younger son), which seeks to topple Vespasian.

The language throughout is Chandler. Falco at last spends the night with Helena, and in the early morning she says to him, "Last night was wonderful. You must have realized. But I see how it is: Every case a girl, every new case a new girl—"(186). As is suggested in Chandler's novels of southern California, political convenience, if not corruption, often lies just below the surface of crime—and the law. When Falco makes his report of the plot to Titus, Vespasian's older son, there is an immediate cover-up, just as there was in *SPQR*. And the romance between Falco and Helena has a certain familiar bittersweetness to it as Falco feels it necessary to return her to her upperclass life: "Tomorrow morning everything I knew of life would start again. Tomorrow I would have to take her back. That was tomorrow. Tonight she was mine" (258). This shows both Davis's scrupulous regard for period behavior—Falco is certainly not of a social class that would ever be allowed to marry or even associate with Helena—and the linking once more of Falco with Marlowe, the loner.

Doody, Roberts, and Davis have all written highly enjoyable mysteries full of convincing classical-world texture, but their texts are based upon enduring motives—greed and ambition—that then spark enduring crimes—murder and theft. What would such novels be like if they attempted something even more radical—as Davis has with language in her first tale—going beyond the careful production of historical texture to write novels that might spring only from the beliefs and practices of the ancient past? Chandler quotes Hemingway that "the good writer competes only with the dead" ("The Simple Art of Murder" 3). Perhaps historical mystery writers with an interest in the classical past could also *speak* with the dead, learn the fears and wishes so alien to us, and, like Odysseus in his visit to the other world, gain new directions to a long-familiar place.

NOTES

1. Hiber Conteris, *Ten Percent of Life*. Originally published in Spain by Editorial Laia, S.A., 1985, under the title *El Diez Por Ciento de Vida*.

2. Although not directly derived from Chandler, Stuart Kaminsky's "Toby Peters" series works for that period flavor. See, for instance, *Murder on the Yellow Brick Road* (1977) or *The Howard Hughes Affair* (1979). See also, Ray Bradbury's *Death Is a Lonely Business* (1985) for a kind of tribute to all of the major "hard-boiled" writers of the period.

3. We have only to read P. D. James and T. A. Critchley's *The Maul and the Pear Tree* (1971), which seeks to reconstruct a series of murders that took place in London in 1811, however, to see that, Bow Street or no, crime must often have gone unsolved in pre-Victorian times.

In this sub-genre, see also John Dickson Carr's *The Murder of Sir Edmund Godfrey* (1936), which fleshes out the contemporary record of a Restoration crime with fiction-alizing. Carr also probes for a solution in his preface and conclusion. A variant of this, the historical crime, is untangled by contemporary fictional characters, as in Josephine Tey's *The Daughter of Time* (1951), in which the murder of the sons of Edward IV is removed from the door of Richard III and placed at that of his Tudor successors.

4. We might also add here the stories by Lillian Bueno McCue (under the name

Lillian de la Torre), which employ Samuel Johnson and his biographer, Boswell, as investigators. See, for example, *The Detections of Dr. Sam Johnson* (1947).

5. Although there are sometimes little slips here and there. In *Low Treason* (1982), for instance, set about the year 1600, Leonard Tourney has his hero, Matthew Stock, light a match several hundred years before they were available.

6. Does Charlotte Pitt, for instance, in Anne Perry's novels, behave rather more like an aggressive young woman of the late twentieth century than the lower-middle-class Victorian wife and mother she is supposed to be?

7. It is interesting to think here about the contrast between traditional Navajo thinking about crime and modern American law imposed on the Navajo, as revealed in *Coyote Waits*, one of Tony Hillerman's Navajo Tribal Police series. To the Navajo, one who commits crimes against others is unbalanced and needs to be healed, rather than punished.

8. Oedipus, who has inadvertently committed patricide, brings down disaster onto all of Thebes while the crime remains unsolved.

9. The seeming similarity between courts and juries in the United States and Athens disguises many fundamental differences, including size of jury. As Socrates notes in Plato's *Apology*, 221 jurors voted "not guilty" and 280 "guilty"—Athenian juries were routinely several hundred citizens in number.

10. Socrates claimed that he could have acquired a speechwriter to write his defense, but he would still have had to appear in court to deliver the speech written for him.

11. One might compare this with the opening of Conan Doyle's "The Copper Beeches." Holmes's willingness to dupe Watson, whose face and acts mirror his thoughts, for the greater good of the case is also put to use by Doody when she has Aristotle explain to Stephanos that he did not tell him everything for fear of Stephanos's giving himself away (280).

12. A special pleasure of the historical mystery lies in its ability to make knowing jokes about the period in which it is set. Doody allows Stephanos to observe that he is glad that someone has written down Aristotle's lecture on comedy so that it will survive for posterity. In fact, the lecture, a companion piece to the *Poetics*, has *not* survived.

13. The title, together with other terms, is defined in the glossary attached to the end of the novel.

14. As Doody makes ironic jokes about Aristotle, so Roberts comments on Roman politics. A street tough named Milo appears here as a minor character allied to Decius. Several decades later, he will contribute to the violent end of the Roman republic. Decius, telling his story through hindsight, can only say that, at the time, "Milo [was] just an amiable young thug on the rise" (131).

15. Jeffreys's "Jeremy Sturrock," however, recounts his detecting in a high-flown English that lacks only a profusion of capitals to look and sound like the eighteenth century at its fruitiest.

16. One thinks here of Robert Graves's Claudius, in *I, Claudius* and *Claudius the God*, who is also a closet republican, but in the generation before Decius.

REFERENCES

Alexander, Lawrence. *The Big Stick*. New York: Knightsbridge, 1991.
_____. *Speak Softly*. New York: PaperJacks, 1988.
_____. *The Strenuous Life*. New York: Knightsbridge, 1991.

Bradbury, Ray. *Death Is a Lonely Business*. 1985. Reprint. New York: Bantam, 1987.

Carr, John Dickson. *The Murder of Sir Edmund Godfrey*. 1936. Reprint. New York: International Polygonics, 1989.

Chandler, Raymond. *The Big Sleep*. New York: Vintage, 1976.

_____. "The Simple Art of Murder." *The Simple Art of Murder*. New York: Ballantine, 1987.

Christie, Agatha. *Death Comes As the End*. New York: Simon and Schuster, 1987.

Conteris, Hiber. *Ten Percent of Life*. New York: Simon and Schuster, 1987.

Davis, Lindsay. *Shadows in Bronze*. New York: Crown, 1990.

_____. *Silver Pigs*. New York: Crown, 1989.

De La Torre, Lillian. *The Detections of Dr. Sam Johnson: Told as if by James Boswell*. 1947. Reprint. New York: International Polygonics, 1984.

Doody, Margaret. *Aristotle Detective*. London: Crogi, 1983.

Hillerman, Tony. *Coyote Waits*. New York: Harper, 1990.

James, P. D., and T. A. Critchley. *The Maul and the Pear Tree*. 1971. Reprint. New York: Mysterious Press, 1987.

Kaminsky, Stuart. *Murder on the Yellow Brick Road*. New York: St. Martin's Press, 1977.

_____. *The Howard Hughes Affair*. New York: St. Martin's Press, 1979.

Marshall, William. *The New York Detective*. New York: Mysterious Press, 1989.

Parker, Robert B., and Raymond Chandler. *Poodle Springs*. New York: Putnam, 1989.

Peters, Ellis. *The Potter's Field*. New York: Mysterious Press, 1989.

Roberts, John Maddox. *SPQR*. New York: Avon, 1990.

_____. *SPQR II*. New York: Avon, 1991.

Tey, Josephine. *The Daughter of Time*. New York: Macmillan, 1951.

Tourney, Leonard. *Low Treason*. New York: 1982. Reprint. Ballantine Books, 1989.

Van Gulik, Robert. *Celebrated Cases of Judge Dee*. New York: Dover Publications, 1976.

3

An Ideal Helpmate:
The Detective Character
as (Fictional) Object and Ideal Imago

Timothy R. Prchal

There is a common—and rather weak—thread that runs through many attempts to psychoanalyze the wide appeal of detective fiction. This thread ties readers' infantile conflicts to symbols found in detective stories. Geraldine Pederson-Krag, for example, states that the genre "attempts to present a more satisfying, less painful primal scene from the standpoint of the unconscious. This fictional primal scene satisfies the voyeurs who . . . gazed with strained attention at the scene of parental coitus" (212).[1] Charles Rycroft amends this theory. He argues that reading such stories is not "analogous to a traumatic neurosis" but "a form of manic defense"; they offer self-exonerating oedipal dramas. In Rycroft's view, the reader first identifies with the criminal, who victimizes a parent figure, and then, identifying with the detective, denies feelings of guilt (230-31). Most recently, Albert D. Hutter has asserted that detective fiction does not reenact the past but reconstructs it. Still, this reconstructive act "is most gripping when it is in opposition to an equally powerful sense of mystery—not merely the mystery of the crime, but of human experience more generally" (200). The primal scene makes Wilkie Collins's *The Moonstone* gripping just as the oedipal conflict makes *Oedipus Rex* gripping, according to Hutter.

The common thread tying the appeal of detective fiction to infantile conflicts snaps under the weight of two problems, however. The first is one of applying a single universal motive or response to readers with widely variable psychological makeups. "Readers bring to the text more than . . . their fantasies," writes Aaron H. Esman; "they bring their total personalities to the reading task, and thus to suggest that there is a single right or wrong way of reading a text is a prescriptive position that ignores the diversity of human attitudes or motives" (19). Certainly some of the people who enjoy the genre have reached relatively sound psychological maturity. Indeed, Rycroft seems to regret that he has "never encountered a patient with a particular interest in detective fiction" (231). Buxbaum does discuss a case of one disturbed boy who compulsively took refuge in detective stories as an attempt to manage his real fears; however, using abnormal dependence to understand normal enjoyment of any genre is as faulty as assuming violence in film is bad for everyone because of the rare criminal cases of real-life copycatting. The many readers who may refer to themselves as "mystery addicts" are presumably speaking facetiously.

Related to this problem is the fact that different fans of the genre prefer different detective characters or different character types, such as classic British or hard-boiled. Indeed, there are rises and falls in the popularity of particular sleuths and types of sleuths over time. Universal infantile conflicts cannot explain, for instance, the longevity of Sherlock Holmes's popularity versus the meteoric rise and fall of interest in Philo Vance. This leads to the second problem. Theories emphasizing links to infantile conflicts ignore societal factors. Ernest Mandel notes that readership of detective stories soared from the 1930s to the 1950s. He warns that any psychological explanation accounting for this mass explosion while being limited "mainly or solely to factors of individual psychology is really to explain nothing of what is specific about the mystery story. Obviously, these factors of individual psychology have to be integrated, or subsumed, into the more general phenomenon of *social evolution*" (68). In other words, the psychological appeal of reading detective stories must be explained with a general scheme that accounts for socialization.

I propose that reading detective fiction can actually promote psychological adaptation to the challenges and demands of day-to-day living in a society that values intellectual prowess more than, say, spiritual or physical attributes. This is its appeal for most readers. Detective characters can serve as an embodiment of the *ideal imago*, a term Michael Eigen has coined to signify the conscious and unconscious ideal images an individual uses to uphold and enchance his or her management of reality. Eigen explains: "The mind spontaneously creates ideal images which enter into varied points of tension and harmony with representations of material reality. The ability to sustain the tension between representations of ideal and material realities is an essential condition of creative growth and work" (318). The *ideal imago* may be thought of as an exemplary portrait painted by the mind's ego-ideal. As such, it becomes an object for the self to emulate.

Detective characters serve as similar exemplary objects in their enviable ability to solve mysteries and to maintain morality when characters around them fail. The images of the detective are created by each individual reader in amiable collaboration with the author. In order for these ideal images to enter and become a viable part of the reader's mind, a reader must find a detective with whom an identification can be made. Ultimately, detectives offer characteristics to redefine and fortify ego-ideals in highly individualized ways.

THE PHILOSOPHY AND PSYCHOLOGY
OF (FICTIONAL) OBJECTS

Theorists finding parallels between fiction and developmental conflicts root their arguments in plots. However, the popularity of detective fiction appears to be based far more on the detective *characters*, who are comparable to but still distinctive from one another. What other contemporary literary genre returns so persistently to an established central character? Sherlock Holmes, Miss Marple, Mike Hammer, Spenser, and so many other sleuths are better known for themselves than for any one of their cases. Books are often sold by headlining the covers with "A Perry Mason Mystery" or the like. Film, radio, and television have profited by creating series based on characters such as Nick and Nora Charles from single prose works. Of course, plots are important, but the detective character determines the popularity of a story series.

Why, though, do individual mystery fans favor one sleuth over another? Once a favorite is found, how does a *fictional* character furnish ideal images that a *real* reader can incorporate? The answers may be provided by the "object relations" school of psychoanalysis—in combination with ontological precepts on nonexistent objects. It may be best to explore the philosophical matters first as this captures the conscious process of reading, which needs to occur before any unconscious effects can take place.

Ontologist Terence Parsons writes, "We do tend focus on what exists. . . . But we also have a contrary tendency to believe in particular examples of nonexistent objects, such as Pegasus and Sherlock Holmes" (4). Parsons splits the process of thinking about fictional objects into extranuclear and nuclear predications, and his examples are appropriate to detective fiction. Extranuclear predications of Sherlock Holmes, for instance, involve statements about the object that are true in relation to the external context of the text: "He's a fictional detective" or "He is admired by many real detectives." Nuclear predications involve statements about the object that are true within the text itself: "He's a detective" or "He lived at 221B Baker Street." While Sherlock Holmes does not truly exist, "nonexistence does not preclude the having of properties" (52-54), and the nuclear properties of a detective character are what interest most readers while engaged in the act of reading.

Conventionally, reading fiction involves entering the text's nuclear realm through suspending disbelief and ignoring the extranuclear realities of the author's fabrication. This may be especially the case with detective fiction, since so many of its readers do not read critically but read for escape. Fictional detectives—described and defined by all of their individual "properties"—may be perceived almost as if they are real. More than that, when we "match wits" with or simply admire the detective hero, we make very real comparisons and contrasts between the properties of the detective and the properties of ourselves.

A notable identifying property of Holmes, for example, is revealed in Arthur Conan Doyle's "A Scandal in Bohemia." Dr. Watson says that Holmes greatly admires Irene Adler, though he could feel no love for her or any other woman. Indeed, Holmes is "the most perfect reasoning and observing machine that the world has seen, but as a lover he would have placed himself in a false position" (161). In essence, Holmes is celibate because of his exorbitant intellect. We can recognize a major concern of our own in this, since an awareness of one's mind and one's body provides a "basic tension between two worlds or dimensions of experience." Moving between and reconciling these two poles— the mental and the material—is a fundamental aspect of daily functioning (Eigen 317). When we compare and contrast ourselves to such properties of (fictional) objects, object-relations psychology then becomes applicable.

Otto Kernberg, a leading proponent of object relations, says that "perception and memory traces help to sort out the origin of stimuli and gradually differentiate self- and object-images" (146). In understanding detective narratives, it is helpful to apply the important clarification Elizabeth Moberly makes to Kernberg's statement. She writes, "Perception and memory traces are important for the reception of stimuli, but it is the *evaluation* of these stimuli that is the crucial factor" (62). When reading fiction, we are stimulated by the images, the background information (serving like memory traces), and the evaluation that an author offers. Since no two readers read exactly alike, each reader's imagination, memories, and interpretations help to make the detective character into an object. This occurs on the extranuclear level.

It is within the nuclear realm, though, that most readers relate to the (fictional) detective. Here, the narrator objectifies the detective with perceptions, background, and evaluation. We already have seen an example of Watson, a first-person narrator, providing background on Holmes's celibacy and evaluation in his comment that Holmes is the world's most perfect reasoning and observing machine. Watson, with a limited perspective even though involved in the stories, similarly objectifies Holmes in the majority of their stories.[2] The "Watson" method of narration and objectification of the detective has been used reliably since Edgar Allan Poe set the mold with C. Auguste Dupin.

Dashiell Hammett's *The Maltese Falcon*, however, is narrated by an omniscient third-person narrator. The opening paragraph provides an example of how objectification still occurs:

Samuel Spade's jaw was long and bony, his chin a jutting v under the more flexible v of his mouth. His nostrils curved back to make another, smaller, v. His yellow-grey eyes were horizontal. The v motif was picked up again by thickish brows rising outward from twin creases above a hooked nose, and his pale brown hair grew down—from high flat temples—in a point on his forehead. He looked rather pleasantly like a blond satan. (295)

The narrator provides perceptions of Spade's facial geometry, remaining impartial until the final sentence. The narrator then appraises those stimuli, working with the reader to form an evaluation of Spade.

Detectives can even be objectified by themselves through their own first-person narration, the standard of the hard-boiled sub-genre. When a detective tells his or her own story, there is essentially one character serving *two* roles: the detective acting in the story *and* the detective narrating those actions. Add the conventional past-tense narration, and these two roles may be more easily understood temporally: the older detective perceives, provides background on, and evaluates the *younger* detective. This method hints at a view of the detective that is shaped by subjectivity (as shown below in a passage narrated by Holmes himself), and readers must do some evaluating and objectifying on their own. The extranuclear author can use virtually any nuclear narrational method to assist the reader in objectifying the detective character, and the reader can identify with that character in highly individual ways and to highly individual degrees.

IDENTIFICATION AND THE
DETECTIVE AS IDEAL IMAGO

Among the rare Sherlock Holmes stories not narrated by Watson are "The Adventure of the Blanched Soldier" and "The Adventure of the Lion's Mane." Holmes himself narrates both of these, and it is in the former that Holmes shares his evaluation of Watson with the reader. This "subjectification" reveals more about the narrator's subjective self than about Watson. Holmes says: "Watson has some remarkable characteristics of his own to which in his modesty he has given small attention amid his exaggerated estimates of my own performances. A confederate who foresees your conclusions and course of action is always dangerous, but one to whom each development comes as a perpetual surprise, and to whom the future is always a closed book, is indeed an ideal helpmate" (1000). Damning him with faint praise, Holmes shows Watson to be ideal because of his limitations. Still, though Watson is excluded from this story, Conan Doyle relies on the properties that differentiate him from Holmes for characterization. The properties are Watson's continual mystification and Holmes's mastery in mystery-solving, which is the very heart of this famous literary relationship.

The power to solve mysteries is, of course, the fundamental—and, quite possibly, the only—property that distinguishes all detectives of conventional mystery fiction. It is this ideal constant that pulls readers to the genre, and it is this property that a reader admires and/or against which a reader "matches wits." The ideal nature of this property enters into the conscious and unconscious creation of the ideal imago. The individual then identifies with this image to function creatively in his or her material reality. Otto Kernberg states that ego identity may be thought of as the supraordinate integration of identifications into a dynamic, unified structure. In the broadest sense of the term, identification refers to a modeling of the self after an object. . . . Crude, dissociated "imitations" of the object may signal the completion of an identification embedded in a primitive ego structure, in contrast to the subtle, discreet modification of the self-concept with few behavioral manifestations characteristic of identification at a stage of greater ego integration. (76-77)

In other words, the reader who quickly dons a pipe and deerstalker cap after identifying with Sherlock Holmes suggests arrested ego-development. A mature reader, though, can quietly use the mental images Conan Doyle has stimulated to restructure his or her ego.

Pederson-Krag opposes the thesis that readers identify with detectives. "Though the detective is a genius and a leader of men, he is often portrayed as addicted to morphine or to drink, excessively fat or thin, foppish or pedantic, or a quaint homespun philosopher." Such peculiarities, she reasons, "should deter the average reader from imagining himself to be such characters" (208). However, only psychologically immature (or, perhaps, arrested) individuals imagine themselves to be the object with which they identify.[3] An infant is unable to differentiate self- and object-images, sensing that its primary caretaker and itself are one being. In fact, this stage leads to the formation of the ego-ideal. Images of ideality emerge from the safety, pleasure, and comfort experienced within the union of infant and caretaker. Such ideality gives the child a pleasurable feeling of omnipotence, an omnipotence that carries into ideal self-representation and ideal object representation as greater differentiation between self and object-images occurs (Tyson and Tyson 83).

The passage into maturity is explored by Arnold Modell, who says that the gradual acceptance of objects as separate from the self accompanies an acceptance of the limitations and reality of other people. Without realistic limitations—something like those Pederson-Krag describes—mature readers would have difficulty perceiving and evaluating detective characters as objects. Modell explains that the process of forming an autonomous identity for oneself

is not to be thought of as final and complete—separateness can never be fully accepted. One may relinquish belief in one's own omnipotence, but belief in an unlimited power may be preserved as an "ego ideal"—something to be achieved in the future. . . . [T]he acceptance of the limitations of parental objects is gradual and painful, but belief that there are some omnipotent objects persists. Religion has heretofore provided the institutional structure for the gratification of this wish. And it may be that the loss of religious belief has placed on contemporary man a special strain on the process of identity, leading to an obsessive preoccupation with the problem of identity. (60)

Religion, under the growing weight of scientific rationality in the nineteenth and twentieth centuries, strains to be the source of answers to the mysteries of life—particularly, those of death. As a likely consequence, religious institutions are less relied upon to provide a code of morality. Fictional detectives, often employing the rationality of our time, can serve these purposes in solving the mysteries of crime—particularly, those of murder—to uphold a moral code. They do this on a far humbler scale than that of religion; however, it is a scale more identifiable to our own realities.

Even that "blond satan" Sam Spade becomes a quasi-religious figure. He explains to Brigid O'Shaughnessy, whom, though he loves her, he will still hand over to the police. There is an institutional code that determines what is good and bad, and it is greater than himself.

When a man's partner is killed he's supposed to do something about it. It doesn't make any difference what you thought of him. . . . Well, when one of your organization gets killed it's bad business to let the killer get away with it. It's bad all around—bad for that one organization, bad for every detective everywhere. Third, I'm a detective and expecting me to run criminals down and then let them go free is like asking a dog to catch a rabbit and let it go. It can be done, all right, and sometimes it is done, but it's not the natural thing. (438)

William David Spencer, who devotes a book to the many fictional members of the clergy who double as amateur-sleuths, sums the point up nicely: "The mystery story . . . in its quest for the criminal and the interdiction of evil and restoration of the good, images the quest through a fallen world for the great good God" (11).

This, then, provides a psychological reason for the fluctuating popularity of detectives, matching that popularity with societal and individual variances in what is considered "ideal." The sexually repressed society of Victorian England may have considered the celibate Sherlock Holmes as ideal, while this "perfect reasoning and observing machine" retains his popularity in a society that embraces computer technology. For the more carnal, more cynical ideology of Prohibition-era America, Sam Spade may have been the ideal for many readers.[4] Of course, the individual search for identity and ideals calls for a preference of one particular detective character over another.

At each mystery's conclusion, the detective is revealed to be the one capable of making sense out of a world of mysteries. Each sleuth rises above his or her own limitations—and far above the limitations of other characters in the story (made especially visible in Holmes's superiority over Lestrade or Spade's triumph over Lieutenant Dundy). The closure of a piece of detective fiction is particularly strong, with all the details of the case accounted for and the criminals sent to their just deserts. On finishing the tale, the reader returns to the extranuclear world and is reminded that such mastery of mystery is not real. The important distinction between the real and ideal/fictional is made in the psychologically sound reader, but the images of what constitutes the ideal is redefined, shaped, enhanced. The reader is better able to manage reality creatively, striving to rise above the norm and deduce solutions to the many mysteries people face.

Aaron H. Esman writes that psychoanalytic criticism "represents only one of the many windows" available to understand the literary experience. Biases are reflected because "each pane in that window itself may yield a different view—one of latent fantasy, or of levels of self-object differentiation, or of experiences of object loss and restitution" (19-20). I have restricted my sights to an object-relations pane to glimpse psychological explanations of the popularity of detective fiction. Such an explanation has been distorted by a pane that too often has depicted all detective fiction readers as bound to infantile conflicts. This explanation, however, ignores the great variety of mature readers and the socialization provided by the ideal-image detective. Unlike most detective fiction, literary criticism and reality offer solutions that are less than absolute.

NOTES

1. Originally published in 1949, Pederson-Krag's "Detective Stories and the Primal Scene" appears to survive as the standard of psychoanalytic thought on the genre. The essay has been reprinted in *Dimensions of Detective Fiction* (edited by Larry N. Landrum, Pat Browne, and Ray B. Browne, Bowling Green, OH: Popular Press, 1976) and *The Poetics of Murder: Detective Fiction and Literary Theory* (edited by Glenn W. Most and William W. Stowe, San Diego, CA: Harcourt Brace Jovanovich, 1983).

2. All four novels are narrated by Watson. Only two of the fifty-four short stories, "His Last Bow" and "Adventure of the Mazarin Stone," are told in third-person narration. Perhaps Watson accounts for these third-person narratives when he comments on still-untold chronicles of Holmes's cases in "The Problem of Thor Bridge": "In some I was myself concerned and can speak as an eye-witness, while in others, I was either not present or played so small a part that they could only be told as by a third person" (Doyle 1099).

3. As suggested by Kernberg, the difference between wishing to be *like* rather than *be* the ideal object indicates psychological maturity. Michael Eigen recounts the progress of a troubled musician who created an ideal imago based on a favorite teacher from the past. The musician attempted to become a teacher himself, failed, but was able to transfer the good feeling associated with the image to his music. "It gradually began to dawn on [the musician] that all of the feeling evoked by his ideal image were his and could be applied to anything he did" (333-34).

4. See Ernest Mandel's book for a comprehensive look at how detective fiction has mirrored changing societal concerns through the nineteenth and twentieth centuries.

REFERENCES

Buxbaum, Edith. "The Role of Detective Stories in a Child Analysis." *Psychoanalytic Quarterly* 10 (1941): 373-81.

Doyle, Sir Arthur Conan. *The Complete Sherlock Holmes*. Garden City, NY: Doubleday, 1930.

Eigen, Michael. "Creativity, Instinctual Fantasy and Ideal Images." *Psychoanalytic Review* 69 (1982): 317-39.

Esman, Aaron H. "Psychoanalysis and Literary Criticism—A Limited Partnership." *Psychoanalysis and Contemporary Thought* 5 (1982): 17-25.

Hammett, Dashiell. *The Maltese Falcon*. In *The Novels of Dashiell Hammett*. New York: Alfred A. Knopf, 1965. First published in 1930.

Hutter, Albert D. "Dreams, Transformations, and Literature: The Implications of Detective Fiction." *Victorian Studies* 14 (1975): 181-209.

Kernberg, Otto F. *Object-Relations Theory and Clinical Psychoanalysis*. New York: Jason Aronson, 1976.

Mandel, Ernest. *Delightful Murder: A Social History of the Crime Story*. Minneapolis: University of Minnesota Press, 1984.

Moberly, Elizabeth. *The Psychology of Self and Other*. London: Tavistock, 1985.

Modell, Arnold H. *Object Love and Reality: An Introduction to a Psychoanalytic Theory of Object Relations*. New York: International Universities Press, 1968.

Parsons, Terence. *Nonexistent Objects*. New Haven, CT: Yale University Press, 1980.

Pederson-Krag, Geraldine. "Detective Stories and the Primal Scene." *Psychoanalytic Quarterly* 18 (1949): 207-14.

Rycroft, Charles. "A Detective Story: Psychoanalytic Observations." *Psychoanalytic Quarterly* 26 (1957): 229-45.

Spencer, William David. *Mysterium and Mystery: The Clerical Crime Novel*. Ann Arbor, MI: UMI Research Press, 1989.

Tyson, Phyllis, and Robert L. Tyson. "Narcissism and Superego Development." *Journal of the American Psychoanalytic Association* 32 (1984): 75-96.

4

The Politics of Secrecy and Publicity: The Functions of Hidden Stories in Some Recent British Mystery Fiction

Peter Hühn

Narrating a story is one of the most fundamental and powerful means man possesses of ordering and interpreting the world. During the eighteenth century, the novel, as William Ray has shown (1-23), came to be considered as a medium that—by its combination of truth and fiction, history and story—both represented and shaped the structure of social reality and in which the act of narration was endowed with the authority of integrating private experience and collective reality. Moreover, the novel foregrounded this narrative act by being self-consciously a story about a story. It can be argued that classic detective fiction, as a late spin-off of the mainstream novel during the nineteenth century, perfected this ordering function of narration and preserved it far into the twentieth century, when the serious novel had long begun to problematize its efficacy. In fact, classic detective fiction is constituted by the very process and problem of storytelling. It foregrounds the centrality of narration by employing the principle of *secrecy* as the motivating force for the construction of its stories, thus emphatically basing the plot development on the *cognitive* dimension and on the power inherent in secrecy and cognition,[1] as this plot is acted out in the contest between detective and criminal for control over narrating or concealing the story of the crime. In this essay, I will, first, sketch an abstract model of the role of story and narration in detective fiction and, second, discuss some interesting modifications of this role in three examples, by Agatha Christie, John Le Carré, and Ruth Rendell, that demonstrate that the function of the secret story remains constitutive even in extreme variations of the classic formula.

WRITING AND READING STORY AND DISCOURSE

Every narrative text is constituted by the dialectical constellation of *story* and *discourse*,[2] which can be considered a special case of the duality of *signified* and *signifier* and which thus shares the dual properties of any sign. The two terms are ultimately interdependent and do not represent a hierarchical order. On the one hand, *discourse*, that is, the narrative text, inherently presupposes a reference to an empirically real story, a chain of events and acts that exists prior to and independent of its verbal representation and possesses an underlying coherent structure defined by causality and human intentionality. On the other hand, this coherent *story* exists only inasmuch as it is being narrated and thereby produced as well as constituted in its structure by *discourse* (in the text).[3]

A detective novel of the classic formula foregrounds the function of narrativity by multiplying the story-discourse constellation through recursive reapplication to itself. On one level, the relation between the genesis of the crime (by necessity concealed) and its subsequent detection can plausibly be described as a duplication of the story-discourse duality.[4] Through his investigations the detective retrieves the hidden *story* of the crime so that he is finally able to mediate it in his detailed *narrative discourse*. On a second level, however, the written text of the novel forms the basis for this constellation to recur twice over, at each of its two poles, the crime and its detection. The *crime story*, in the very course of being perpetrated, leaves traces in the world. It unavoidably inscribes itself in the environment, and the convention requires the author to include these signs in the text of the book, however distortedly, as some form of (as yet obscure) discourse. These traces can be read by the competent detective for what they signify about the events and acts. Analogous to the crime story, furthermore, the reading efforts on the part of the detective in their turn also present a chain of acts that constitute a story in its own right, the *story of crime detection*. The investigation story as such is equally mediated, namely, through the detective's behavior during the protracted middle part of the novel—for example, through his inconclusive remarks and enigmatic activities. Typically, these heterogeneous signs are actually presented as a written text, the chronicle composed by the Dr. Watson figure, who in his narration faithfully but uncomprehendingly registers the observed data, thereby producing another obscure discourse. It is only at the very end that this imperfect and obscure mediation is transformed into a *clear discourse* when the detective himself finally consents to narrate his detection story—together with the reconstrued crime story, both of which are normally quoted verbatim in the coadjutor's chronicle. In a manner of speaking, the investigation story narrates itself through its protagonist.

As for the types of story used, the basic internal tension in a classic-formula novel can be conceptualized as a contest between writing and reading or, more precisely, between *writing* stories and *reading* stories.[5] The criminal devises or *writes* the story of his criminal act, at the same time, however, protecting it against reading, composing it as an unreadable secret story. The detective attempts to decipher its traces and interpret their meaning, and in the end he succeeds in *reading* it. But the *story* of his interpretation and reading process is also hidden from its readers. The first reader is the Dr. Watson figure, who tries to decipher it for his chronicle. The usual setup, the coadjutor's obtuseness, is meant to stimulate the novel's readers to compete with him in trying to read the detection—before the detective himself, voluntarily, writes it out in plain language.

For a complete description of this constellation of stories and discourses it is useful to draw particular attention to the deviser or *author* of the *story* in question and his attempts to control not only its practical enactment but also its semiotic mediation, that is, its *discourse*. Given the retentive medium of the world, enactment necessarily entails mediation, which is as much as to say that discourse can never be completely suppressed. The criminal and the detective both enact, that is, write, a story *and* intend it to remain secret. They both try to control the writing of their respective stories by hiding or confusing their traces so that these become illegible. With regard to the devices for achieving this end, the criminal has essentially two choices.[6] First, he can try to suppress or at least obscure the mediation of his crime so that there seems to be no story at all or only some unexplainable mystery, which, however, has the disadvantage of arousing suspicion. To avoid this, he may, second, manipulate the clues in such a manner that they suggest a *different* coherent story; that is, he may attempt to *rewrite* his crime story.[7] As described in Goffman's terminology of "frame analysis,"[8] the criminal transforms the traces into a different kind of frame, that is, into some other meaningful pattern, and produces a "fabrication," in order to cover up the true (primary) frame and deceive the public. The fabricated frame typically "frames" another person as the author, inducing the reader (police, detective) to attribute the crime story to a false culprit. Moreover, the fundamental possibility of this device is apt to point to the decisive role that attribution, rather than actual causation, ultimately plays in reading and interpreting the crime story, as it generally does in perceiving actions in a social context (Jones et al.).

One specific ploy for masking a story separates the positions of author and, as it were, actual writer or scribe, that is, the executing agent of the crime plot. As far as the criminal is concerned, these two figures tend to be identified in one person who both invents and personally executes the murder story. But if the criminal separates the two positions by transferring the practical perpetration or writing of the murder to someone else, the difficulty of reading the story and attributing it to its real author will be considerably increased.

From the very beginnings of the detective genre, a somewhat analogous device has been employed in the representation of the *detective*. His investigation story remains hidden under his reticence, being only indirectly inscribed in his inconclusive utterances and unintelligible moves, whereas the actual *writing* of it is delegated to another person, the Dr. Watson figure. Only at the end are the positions of author and writer collapsed, when the detective finally breaks his reticence, telling his story himself: This story is then reported in the coadjutor's chronicle, at which level the multiplication of writing and reading stories finally comes to an end. In Dr. Watson the positions of author and writer always coincide, since he never hides anything, immediately imparting whatever he sees and knows to the reader. Then he does not have much to hide anyway.

The two-tier constellation of story and discourse and its internal recursive repetition, as it is constitutive of classic detective fiction, may be summed up as follows:

Tier *1: crime*

crime story (as enacted)—**obscure discourse of crime story**
                                  (traces in the world)
----**detection** produces: **clear discourse of crime story**

Tier *2: detection*

detection story (as enacted)—**obscure discourse of detection story**
                                  (symptoms in detective's behavior,
                                  faithfully chronicled by coadjutor)

----**detective's own narrative** produces: **clear discourse of detection story**
                                  including **clear discourse of crime story**

THE FUNCTION OF SECRECY

The crucial principle that regulates the separation of story and discourse in classic detective novels on all levels is *secrecy* and, as its main device, delusion.[9] Discourse is invariably intended to be incongruous with story. The authors of the different stories try to keep them hidden by exercising control over the discourse media in such a manner that these do not adequately convey the stories but rewrite, that is conceal, distort, or mask, them. The protagonists engaged in writing the *discourse*, on the other hand, always attempt to extract and publicize the secret story. These conflicting intentions produce a pervasive contest between the representatives of the levels of story and discourse, a contest that extends all the way through the novel, providing the dynamic impulse for its progression toward the end. In particular, this conflict produces a latent structural contradiction in the central figure of the *detective* since he strives simultaneously for publicity and secrecy, attempting on the one side to read the crime story and on the other to make his own investigation story unreadable. In other words, he inflicts on his own readers the very secrecy that he denies the criminal.

The constitutive role of secrecy for the narrative organization of detective fiction implies an underlying intellectualist ideology that ascribes decisive importance to *cognition*, to the gaining and withholding of *knowledge* as the prime regulating factors of social life. In other words, secrecy and cognition tend to function as instruments of *power*. This kind of function incidentally presupposes the constitution of a liberal bourgeois society, regulated by the universal public validity of an impartial legal system in which public evidence and rational argument alone guarantee the application of the law and the administering of justice.[10] Furthermore, the centrality of cognition expressly involves the principle of *rationality*, that is, the conscious orientation to clear pragmatic aims and the methodically controlled strategy of achieving them. Moreover, rationality in this sense conventionally guides the devising and enacting of *all* stories in a detective novel, on both the criminal and the investigative levels. In the method of rationality, as well as in the strategic manipulation of cognition and knowledge, the detective is ultimately the analogue of the criminal.[11] The basic energy of detective fiction, therefore, seems to derive less from the concrete fight between the protagonists of law and crime as such than from the competition between the opposed but mutually related principles of secrecy and rational cognition.

The two protagonists' interest in secrecy is, however, motivated differently. Through his story the criminal typically gratifies a vital private desire (such as for wealth, love, revenge, or pleasure), ultimately asserting and fulfilling himself as a more complete individual person. But since this gratification violates the norms of society, the criminal arrogates to himself an illegitimate freedom by writing his crime story, and he employs the policy of secrecy to enable this individualist freedom and protect it from the established restrictions of the collective public order (Moretti 134-39). In order to succeed, he has to contrive to close his story definitively after having committed the crime and secured its benefits for himself. By contrast, the detective's primary aim is to penetrate the criminal's protective secrecy and subject it to the restrictions of the public order system, thereby depriving him of his wrongful individual freedom. He achieves this not only by publicly narrating the secret crime story but also by adding another—a socially more conforming—closure to it. Often the final conclusion, as brought about by the detective's publication of the criminal story, consists in some kind of repetition of its beginning,[12] which—reapplied to the perpetrator—is ideally tantamount to its cancellation: The murder is "repeated" in the murderer's (capital) punishment. More specifically, in Christie's *The Murder of Roger Ackroyd* (1926), for instance, the murderer is forced to imitate in his final suicide by poison the death he caused in the beginning. The detective's motivation for secrecy, on the other hand, has professional and literary reasons, the greatest possible prolongation of suspense and thrill for the sake of exemplifying the great detective's unique stature, as well as enhancing the readers' pleasure. In the final analysis, this is not so much, of course, in the personal interest of the detective as in that of the author of the book, who hereby asserts and realizes himself in his reputation as a good mystery novelist preventing the premature disclosure of the solution.

Against the background of this abstract structure of the classic detective formula, as it underlies, for example, many of Agatha Christie's novels, it is interesting to note the narrative significance of some plot variations by three very different crime writers. The novels chosen do not all belong to the same genre: Strictly speaking, the first is a classic whodunit, the second a spy novel, and the third a crime thriller. What they have in common is the elaborate handling of the relationship between story and discourse and the increasing difficulty of controlling story through narration.

THE CRIMINAL SECRECY OF THE CLASSICAL DETECTIVE: CHRISTIE'S LAST CASE

Agatha Christie's last published novel is an example of an extreme variation of the formula. In *Curtain: Poirot's Last Case*,[13] Poirot (together with Hastings) returns to Styles Court, the scene of *The Mysterious Affair at Styles* (1920), his first classic case, where he had been able to extract the criminal story and—by publicizing it—reestablish the old order of the community. The fundamental setup underlying *Curtain* seems still to be the conventional one: the English country-house setting with a closed circle of upper-middle-class characters, one of whom turns out to be the culprit. But the crime story has been perfected to such a degree that its secrecy has become impenetrable and "unpublishable." The technique consists in radically separating author from executing agent. Exploiting the innate aggressiveness to which everyone is prone and manipulating the situation accordingly, the criminal (Norton) activates the inborn killing drive within his victims and insidiously induces them to commit the murders, forcing them to become his vicarious agents. The criminal merely acts as a catalyst, thereby rendering it impossible for the detective to connect him with the criminal deeds, especially in view of the apparent absence of a personal motive. This is one of the versions of the perfect murder. The separation between author and protagonist is so complete that no one suspects the connection, as is highlighted by the newspaper reports on the various cases, which are so heterogeneous that there does not seem to be a common story behind them. Only Poirot, still retaining his genius in spite of physical decline, is able to read this connection and to foresee the next murders. Nevertheless, he, too, fails to prevent them and to prove Norton's responsibility for the former ones.

The impossibility of extracting the crime story and attributing it to its author is not due to social or political reasons (as in the hard-boiled novel) but to psychological ones. The criminal is no longer a singularly diseased or evil individual; crime is proven to be universally human. Although Norton is the actual criminal, there exists a kind of unrecognized, preestablished collusion between him as the instigator and corresponding dispositions and desires in most people. Basically, the murderer is outside the control of the law because what he plans is potentially part of everyone's nature. The seriousness of the situation arising from the inaccessibility of the criminal's secrets is exacerbated by the fact that the crime story is not yet closed. Norton's secret motive for the constant repetition of his crimes lies in his traumatic childhood experiences. Since the crime story and its indefinite continuation compensate for the lack of closure of another story, Norton's incomplete socialization, the criminal presents a continuous (but secret) threat to society.

The intensification of secrecy goes for both stories, the genesis of the crimes as well as the detective's investigations, and the impenetrability of the first is the reason for that of the second. Because of the separation between author and agent, the crime story can no longer be ascribed to the criminal and the detective's cognitive ability to narrate the secret crime story is to no avail. Therefore, the detective has to resort to other means of ending it: to destroying the criminal and becoming a criminal in his own "right." In fact, Poirot writes a secret crime story himself: killing Norton but framing it as suicide. The perfection of the secret crime necessitates the recursive reapplication of its own principles to the investigation—unlawful violence and secrecy. The criminal's perfect fabrication is matched as well as cancelled by an equally impenetrable fabrication on the detective's part. Instead of resolving the crime story through publicity, the detective has to end it under cover of permanent secrecy, like the crime story itself. Although he thus manages to preserve his good *public* reputation, his ethical principles oblige him to kill himself: Secret crime stories have to end with the criminal's elimination, which now applies to his own person. He fulfills this obligation, once again in the form of a secret story: His suicide is disguised as a heart attack. In this extreme case, the politics of secrecy and publicity, the struggle between concealment and exposure cannot be continued. The detective, whose secretive behavior had always resembled that of the criminal, now definitely colludes with him, turning criminal himself and completely hiding his own secrets together with those of the culprit.

As neither Poirot's chronicler nor the reader is able to decipher the clues of either story, the novel almost ends with all the secrets definitively concealed. It is only by way of a postscript, a letter from Poirot received months after his death, that the secrets are finally—but in secret—revealed to Hastings, which highlights the extremely precarious nature of narration. Although the secret crime story can no longer be narrated and subjected to public control, the reader at least is finally acquainted with the true solution. Nevertheless, in *Curtain* Agatha Christie comes very close to dissolving the basic premises of the classic formula, the existence and accessibility of the absolute and unambiguous truth.

THE SECRECY OF THE SECRET AGENT:
LE CARRÉ'S FIRST (REAL) SPY

In *The Spy Who Came in from the Cold*, John Le Carré raises the method of secret story writing and the politics of secrecy to a new level of sophistication. In concrete terms, the novel presents a plot on the part of the British Secret Service to frame, discredit, and thereby eliminate Mundt, the head of East German counterespionage. For this purpose Leamas, the former head of British operations in the GDR, pretends to defect to East Germany and suggest through information provided by him that Mundt is a British spy. Structurally, this setup amounts to an inversion of the classic formula, with the focus on what in detective fiction would be the writing of the hidden crime story. The essential difference is, however, that here the authors of the secret story do not attempt to hide a crime but deliberately set about writing a story for the other side (the equivalent of the detective) to *read*. According to the allegedly open story told by Leamas to his communist interrogators, he defected to East Germany because of grievances against his institution in London. The secret story intentionally hidden behind it is to suggest inadvertently, through the secrets he betrays, that Mundt is a British secret agent. The ingenious strategy employed permits his interrogators to deduce such a reading from certain clues contained in his reports while explicitly and credibly denying it. Initially this secret story works well because by it Fiedler, Mundt's right-hand man, feels confirmed in his suspicions of Mundt, so that he in fact uses the narrated story to attack him. But the first secret story hides a second one. The head of British Intelligence (Control) signals through certain suggestive clues that Leamas's story of defection is a put-up job to discredit Mundt. This revelation can be used by Mundt to discredit Fiedler's accusations and in turn eliminate him, which has been the purpose behind this second secret story all along, namely, to save Mundt, who in fact *is* a British spy.

In several respects, this writing of the hidden story is considerably more sophisticated than in normal detective fiction. Not only does the secret story now hide another, which the protagonist, Leamas, knows nothing about and can thus enact the more truthfully, but, in addition, the second hidden story is a repetition of the first or, rather, a framing of it. If the first story is the inadvertent betrayal of Mundt's role as a secret agent, the second story is the insinuated foregrounding of the first, where the fact of the framing intention is meant to suggest that its content is merely simulated. Using Niklas Luhmann's distinction between communication and information (193ff), one can say that the first story conveys the *information* of Mundt's treachery, which, as deduced information, suggests disinterestedness and therefore truthfulness, whereas the second story contains the *communication* of Mundt's treachery, which is apt to discredit its information content because of the visible intention behind conveying it. The second story is particularly successful because the fact of its framing as communication has to be drawn out by cunning and therefore is not recognizable as another frame. The truth is manipulated so as to imply that it cannot be the truth; that is, every clue of the correct situation (Mundt is a British spy) is easily discredited as a planted clue, since it was first introduced as part of a fabrication that is now exposed *as* a fabrication. The intended reading of the secret story (and the protection of the real secret) stabilizes itself, since the exposure of the fabrication is not suspected as yet another fabrication. The story hides itself through its foregrounded repetition. This presupposes a complete separation between author (Control) and actual scribe (Leamas). Paradoxically, the secret story protects itself against publication by publishing the secret and discrediting this very fact as a fabricated frame.

The whole setup, once seen through, proves deeply disturbing for the agent since it reveals to him that he was just a tool, steered in all his acts by remote control. The individual has been deprived of the control over his story by the institution, the anonymous apparatus. And the final awareness of this loss deprives him of the energy to live on (the novel ends with Leamas's death). On the other hand, the relevance of storytelling as such is heightened enormously. The conflict between nations or even power blocs is fought with stories as the prime weapons. The power and the resources of elaborate apparatuses are used to write stories, control them in every tiny detail, and manipulate their reading in advance. As this story is never uncovered and publicized by detection, writing has ultimately won over reading. It is true that the agent does detect the real secret story in the end, but he lacks the power and the will to do anything with it.

SECRECY WITHOUT AN AUTHOR: RUTH RENDELL'S PSYCHOPATHS

Whereas in the Christie and Le Carré novels secrecy is employed as a conscious strategy on the part of the individual story writers, Ruth Rendell, in her crime thriller *A Judgement in Stone*, situates the secrets at a deeper level, within the mind of the protagonists, and explores the consequences for the concept of narrativity. The novel focuses on the genesis of a crime story, the events leading to the massacre of the Coverdale family by their housekeeper Eunice Parchment and her friend Joan Smith. But this story has no author who designs or writes it. Instead, it is produced by the chance interactions of the individual story lines, the impetus for which is provided by different forms of secrecy in the minds of the various protagonists—secretiveness, self-intransparency, and ignorance. Parchment's story line is crucially motivated by secrecy: her psychopathic dread of revealing her illiteracy, which she obsessively considers a blemish to be concealed at all costs. Ironically, a number of coincidences as well as the well-meaning attempts of her employers to make life more pleasant for her inadvertently lead to the disclosure of her morbidly guarded secret, and her close association with Joan Smith, another psychopath, finally triggers the shooting of the Coverdales.

A similar chain of coincidences characterizes the detection story that starts close to the end of the novel, when the criminal herself calls the police and cunningly creates a cover story, a frame for herself to hide her involvement. The only relevant clues (the marginal notes in a *TV Times* and a tape) are concealed by the criminals, as well as discovered by the police through mere chance. There is no systematic investigation, but in the end the criminal is in fact identified and arrested.

Although the classic formula constellation of crime and detection stories is structurally still recognizable, their presentation emphasizes the radical modification of the concept of the story. The narration starts with a mention of the disastrous end and then traces the way in which coincidences and the interaction of the separate story lines propel the development to its conclusion, the killings and their subsequent detection, shifting the perspective among all persons involved: first between the criminals and the victims and then between the detective and the suspects. The effect is that it is only at the *discourse* level that the coherence and directedness of the stories become constituted. The principal criminal does not pursue a clear course of action, much less a criminal one: Eunice Parchment merely reacts to circumstances as they occur in order to protect her secret deficiency. She is essentially a lethargic person who can only insufficiently understand her own motives. Her associate Joan Smith is even more intransparent to herself. Nor does the detective ever get to understand the full extent of, and the motivating coincidences behind, the crime story. So both the crime and the detection stories lack authorial consciousness. Inside the novel no one controls the stories. This is foregrounded by the narrative discourse, which continuously emphasizes the ignorance of all characters about their interactions and about the consequences of their acts and which at every juncture points to the possible alternative routes not taken. The narration thus creates a strong sense of the tragic inexorableness of the catastrophe and of the irony in the crime and detection stories—a narrative development showing obvious affinities with the structure of classical Greek tragedy. Irony, which stresses the uncontrollableness of action, is pervasive: The Coverdales unwittingly promote their own death through acts of kindness; illiterate Eunice is finally betrayed by marginal notes in a program and inadvertently most painfully punished by the public revelation of her illiteracy. Somewhat like those of Le Carré, the characters are all helplessly caught in their stories. But there is no human mastermind behind them, and they can no longer be completely narrated in the public world of the novel. Only the reader—with a painful sense of powerlessness—can see everything coming.

In contrast to the other two novels, which demonstrate how secrets are strategically employed to enable the writing of private stories and secure personal benefits, *A Judgement in Stone* primarily emphasizes the reverse: Secrets tend to produce stories on their own and deprive the protagonists of control over their own stories. The control over the story is now completely and exclusively transferred to the author of the book. The narrator's consciousness as manifest in the discourse of the novel is the only position from which the coherence of the story and its orderly progress from beginning to end can be defined as well as recognized. Indeed, this order is imposed on the story by the discourse, and it is clearly the order of fictional and literary convention (for example, that of ancient tragedy). The crime story is constructed from the end, which is mentioned at the very beginning of the novel and toward which the events are shown to progress inexorably and fatally. This is paradoxical because the foregrounded literary order and control are meant to pinpoint the *lack* of purpose and order on the level of character and action. Whereas Christie and Le Carré still used characters *in* the novel who were able to write and read and thus control secret stories, in spite of the increased difficulty of the policy of publicity, Rendell radically undermines the possibility of an orderly policy of secrecy and publicity in the novel while emphatically retaining it on the level of discourse.

NOTES

1. For a basic model describing the cognitive dimension, see Greimas and Courtès (433-47).
2. See especially the Genette and Chatman books.
3. See Culler particularly.
4. See, for example, Todorov.
5. See, for example, the articles by Stowe and Hühn.
6. The most effective method of protecting a secret is, of course, to hide also the fact that one has a secret, to make the secret itself a secret, that is, to reapply secrecy recursively to itself. See Sievers (26ff).
7. Greimas and Courtès term this activity "persuasive doing" and set it against "interpretive doing" (440-41), the form of activity typical of the reading detective, thereby emphasizing the interrelationship between these two activities.
8. See especially Chapter 4 ("Designs and Fabrications") and Chapter 6 ("Structural Issues in Fabrications").
9. For a general discussion of the nature and function of secrecy, see Bok.
10. The ideological bias of the classic-formula novel has frequently been defined as bourgeois, mostly with an emphasis on the repressive and manipulative tendencies inherent in the underlying ideology. See, for example, the books by Knight, Palmer, and Porter.
11. There are, of course, exceptions, like Poe's "The Murders in the Rue Morgue," where the commission of the crime story is the result of coincidence and chance, not of purposeful rational planning.
12. For a general discussion of the relation between beginning and end as governed by the figure of repetition, see Ricoeur, 130-56, especially 134-39.
13. Probably written in the late 1940s, this final book featuring Poirot was held back by the author almost until the end of her life.

REFERENCES

Bok, Sissela. *Secrets: On the Ethics of Concealment and Revelation*. New York: Pantheon, 1982.

Chatman, Seymour. *Story and Discourse: Narrative Structure in Fiction and Film*. Ithaca: Cornell University Press, 1978.

Christie, Agatha. *Curtain: Poirot's Last Case*. London: Collins, 1975.

Culler, Jonathan. "Story and Discourse in the Analysis of Narrative." In *The Pursuit of Signs: Semiotics, Literature, Deconstruction*, 169-87. London: Routledge and Kegan Paul, 1981.

Genette, Gérard. *Narrative Discourse: An Essay in Method*. Ithaca, NY: Cornell University Press, 1980.

Goffman, Erving. *Frame Analysis: An Essay on the Organization of Experience*. New York: Harper and Row, 1974.

Greimas, A.-J., and J. Courtès. "The Cognitive Dimension of Narrative Discourse." *New Literary History* 7 (1976): 433-47.

Hühn, Peter. "The Detective as Reader: Narrativity and Reading Concepts in Detective Fiction." *Modern Fiction Studies* 33 (1987): 451-66.

Jones, Edward, et al. *Attribution: Perceiving the Causes of Behavior*. Morristown, NJ: General Learning Press, 1971.

Knight, Stephen. *Form and Ideology in Crime Fiction*. London: Macmillan, 1980.

Le Carré, John. *The Spy Who Came in from the Cold*. London: Victor Gollancz, 1963.

Luhmann, Niklas. *Soziale Systeme: Grundiss einer allgemeinen Theorie*. Frankfurt/Main: Suhrkamp, 1984.

Moretti, Franco. "Clues." In *Signs Taken for Wonders: Essays in the Sociology of Literary Forms*, 130-56. London: Verso, 1988.

Palmer, Jerry. *Thrillers: Genesis and Structure of a Popular Genre*. London: Edward Arnold, 1978.

Porter, Dennis. *The Pursuit of Crime: Art and Ideology in Detective Fiction*. New Haven, CT: Yale University Press, 1981.

Ray, William. *Story and History: Narrative Authority and Social Identity in the Eighteenth-Century French and English Novel*. Oxford: Blackwell, 1990.

Rendell, Ruth. *Judgement in Stone*. London: Hutchinson, 1977.

Ricoeur, Paul. "Narrative Time." In *On Narrative*, edited by W.T.J. Mitchell, 165-86. Chicago: University of Chicago Press, 1981.

Sievers, Burkhard. *Geheimnis und Geheimhaltung in sozialen Systemen*. Opladen: Westdeutscher Verlag, 1974.

Stowe, William. "From Semiotics to Hermeneutics: Modes of Detection in Doyle and Chandler." In *The Poetics of Murder: Detective Fiction and Literary Theory*, edited by Glenn Most and William Stowe, 366-83. San Diego, CA: Harcourt, 1983.

Todorov, Tzvetan. "The Typology of Detective Fiction." In *The Poetics of Prose*, 42-52. Ithaca, NY: Cornell University Press, 1977.

5

Not So Much "Whodunnit" as "Whoizzit": Margaret Millar's Command of a Metonymic Sub-Genre

Ann Thompson and John O. Thompson

The concept of metonymy can be especially useful as an analytical tool with which to examine one of the most important ways in which the detective genre has been able to deepen and complicate itself. Almost everybody who tries to use *metonymy* for *any* critical purpose does so inspired by Roman Jakobson's deployment of the metaphor/metonymy opposition in his classic essay "Two Aspects of Language and Two Types of Aphasic Disturbances." The fundamental argument of that essay depends on a dichotomy that long predates Jakobson, being at the center of "associationist" psychological speculations at least since John Locke. This is the dichotomy between *resemblance* and *contiguity* as motivating links between one mental operation and the next. Basically, Jakobson lines up a wide variety of formal aspects of verbal art as involving resemblance (or contrast, as antiresemblance) and counterposes to these an equally wide variety of ways in which contiguity is the principle at work in the text. The classical rhetorical figures that Jakobson brings in to head these two columns, so to speak, are metaphor and metonymy respectively.

"[I]t is the predominance of metonymy which underlies and actually predetermines the so-called realistic trend," wrote Jakobson; "following the path of contiguous relationships, the realistic author metonymically digresses from the plot to the atmosphere and from the characters to the setting in space and time" (78). Jakobson did not himself ask whether the contiguity principle might be generically super-exploitable *within* certain types of plot construction, or whether the roll call of the characters might itself be something that a systematic play with aspects of contiguity within a fiction might pleasurably and instructively "make strange." Our contention is that crime fiction in general, but especially in the hands of its most talented exponents (such as Agatha Christie and Margaret Millar), is a realm in which the contiguous comes into its own in just these ways.

Contiguity itself is not so everyday a term as *similarity* is. Contiguity is next-to-ness, and one has but to think about this for a moment to see how central contiguity is to crime narratives of any sort. Whose hand is next to the wallet as it is removed from the pocket *of* (next to, spatially and in terms of possession) the rightful owner? Whose finger was *on* (next to, pressing down on) the trigger? Whose hand *held* the knife? The genre has popularly been christened the "whodunnit." The "it" of "whodunnit" is the crime, typically murder; the "who" is a character, identity enigmatic; the "dun" involves that character having been in hurtful, criminal contiguity with another character, typically with fatal results.

What makes the "whodunnit" an investigative genre, involving a detective (professional or amateur), is that the *connection* between criminal and crime has to be established through the reading of clues. A clue is anything *left behind* by the criminal, contiguous to the criminal once, the erstwhile contiguity of which can be "read" and then demonstrated. Much narrative pleasure within the genre depends on making the linkage a puzzle, but at the denouement the puzzle's solution is given, and a complete *picture* (who was where when, doing what, why) is delivered to the reader. The presentation of this picture by the detective to the assembled group of characters concerned (many of them suspects) in a final chapter has been a well-loved, much parodied, generic convention.

But what if there is something about the field of suspects itself that involves an enigma that goes beyond establishing the identity of the person whose finger was on the trigger, whose hand held the knife? What if identities within the field have themselves been doubled? What if, in elaborating the "whodunnit" aspect of the fiction, the author has found herself moving across into what we might call the "whoizzit" mode?

The simplest version of the "whoizzit," easily compatible with the assembling-of-the-suspects denouement, would involve the investigator unmasking a suspect who had disguised himself or herself in order to get away with the crime under investigation. The detective discovers and reveals the fact that X is actually Y; Y has pretended to be X so that the criminal contiguity cannot be traced to Y, but finally the pretense breaks down.

An example of this is Agatha Christie's *Sad Cypress*, a novel in which Christie has moved the center of interest in the direction of the romantic-fiction genre, leaving the investigatory narrative on the straightforward, slightly perfunctory side. In this novel the heroine, Elinor Carlisle, is accused of murdering a younger woman, Mary Gerrard, partly out of jealousy for the romantic interest taken in Mary by her fiancé and partly out of a desire to inherit the entire fortune of an aunt who had expressed a desire to make a will in Mary's favor. Elinor is later also accused of having previously murdered the aunt. It seems that no one else has a motive for either of the crimes. But through the investigations of Hercule Poirot, it is revealed that (1) Mary was, in fact, the illegitimate daughter of the aunt, and (2) the only person to know this, "Nurse Hopkins" (who was attending the old lady), is also, and really,

Mary Riley, the distant relative supposed to be in New Zealand to whom Mary Gerrard, in turn, had bequeathed all her possessions. The courtroom revelation of the double identity of "Nurse Hopkins" solves the puzzles of the case in one stroke.

The mode of narrative construction on which we want to focus, however, is one in which the "whoizzit" question arises in a different way. What if the feigning of an identity has been motivated, at least initially, by factors independent of the crime itself? Here is a familiar example: In Hitchcock's *Psycho*, Marion and Arbogast seem to be killed by "Mother," who turns out to be Norman. But Norman's dressing up as his mother is not some ingenious transvestite disguise to elude capture. The Mother-is-Norman identity enigma is the product of a *previous* crime not under current investigation: Norman's matricide.

A striking example of this narrative mode within the Christie oeuvre occurs in *By the Pricking of My Thumbs*. The investigator, Tuppence Beresford, becomes involved in the stories of two women, Mrs. Lancaster and Julia Starke. Mrs. Lancaster is encountered as an old lady in a nursing home who refers mysteriously to a dead child behind a fireplace. Subsequently, she disappears, removed by "relatives" who are impossible to trace; and Tuppence, assuming that the old lady possesses potentially dangerous knowledge of criminal activity and fearing for her safety, tries to find her. Her only lead is a picture formerly belonging to Mrs. Lancaster of a house by a canal. Julia Starke emerges only gradually in the course of the investigation as (1) the supposedly dead wife of Sir Philip Starke, landowner in the area of Sutton Chancellor where the Canal House turns out to be located; (2) a former dancer famous in the role of "Waterlily"; and (3) "Killer Kate," who killed her own illegitimate baby and subsequently "sacrificed" other local children. It is ultimately revealed that Mrs. Lancaster and Julia Starke are the same person, who is also responsible for some apparently arbitrary deaths in the nursing home. In a climactic scene, which takes place *after* a conventional but inconclusive assembly of suspects at the vicarage, Tuppence meets Mrs. Lancaster at Canal House, learns of her double identity, and is nearly killed by her. As in *Psycho*, the disguise relates to a much earlier crime (infanticide) and is not merely one adopted pragmatically, but is symptomatic of a deeper crisis of identity amounting to insanity.

The work of Margaret Millar, a successor novelist to Agatha Christie, exploits to the full the possibilities of the "whoizzit." Though some will be well acquainted with Millar's work, in the world at large she seems still a figure not generally celebrated, which reflects the usual thoughtless way in which genre fiction gets marginalized. One of the better reasons for developing accounts of this body of work using a linguistic/rhetorical/philosophical base is to demonstrate forcefully just how intricate and how moving Millar's novels are.

Millar's *How Like an Angel*, first published in 1962, presents a dizzying array of identity-shift issues, with virtually every character the locus of some form of doubt about his or her real self or intentions; but the novel's central enigma is of primary concern. Patrick O'Gorman is missing, presumed dead; he was a payroll clerk, a husband, a father, and an inhabitant of the town of Chicote and so on. Brother Tongue of Prophets is an inhabitant of a small religious community living in the mountains of southern California, known as the Tower (synecdochically, from the community's one expensive building); he is virtually mute, has a shaven head, is dependent upon Sister Blessing for attention, is very fond of a pet bird in a wooden cage, and so on. The answer to the mystery of O'Gorman's fate turns out to lie in Brother Tongue's identity, for Brother Tongue is revealed (though not *definitely* revealed until the novel's final two lines) to be Patrick O'Gorman.

In theory, and if Millar were not writing and we were not reading "in genre," so to speak, the events of the story, which are many, could be told without the O'Gorman-Tongue identity being concealed. The introduction of Brother Tongue could be handled in some such way as this:

Through a chink between the half-logs Brother Tongue of Prophets saw the stranger coming and began making small animal noises of distress. "Now what are you making a fuss about?" Sister Blessing said briskly (6-7). [And Millar could have continued.] How was she to know that Brother Tongue had very good reasons for being nervous when any stranger came to the Tower—that his real name was Patrick O'Gorman, and that in the outside world he was missing, presumed dead, having faked his own death as part of a conspiracy with a woman called Alberta Haywood?

And so on. For the narration to "spill the beans" at this point would have been virtually inevitable before well-known nineteenth-century developments in narrative technique allowed the author to keep what is stated at a given moment within the range of what is known by the focal character; here that character is Sister Blessing, and what she doesn't know needn't be revealed. Brother Tongue *could* himself have been made focal, but he needn't be: He is just one more member of the community and may be unfocal because he seems to be minor. (In fact, at the end of this little scene, Millar does make Brother Tongue focal for a moment, teasingly, by implying that if there were a fire, he would keep quiet about it and would be concerned only about saving his parakeet [8]. This seems simply like minor-character vividness, and only in the light of the subsequent narrative does it emerge as appropriately an O'Gorman, as well as a Brother Tongue, thought).

The major focal consciousness within investigative-genre work is usually that of the investigator (though, of course, keeping the reader out of Sherlock Holmes's or Hercule Poirot's mind until the time is ripe is of the utmost importance to one branch of the genre). In *How Like an Angel* the investigator is, in fact, the stranger whom Brother Tongue sees approaching, a down-on-his-luck private investigator called Joe Quinn. Sister Blessing will give Quinn the O'Gorman name and nothing else to investigate. (*Why* she should do so is made one of the narrative enigmas; it will turn out, very late [257], that Brother

Tongue has so repeated the name in his sleep that she thinks his conscience may have been bothering him, since the information brought back to her by Quinn is that O'Gorman is dead, and misidentifies Brother Tongue's crime as O'Gorman's murder). The task allows Quinn to open up two investigative *locales*: Chicote, the small oil town in which O'Gorman had lived, and the Tower community itself, inherently enigmatic as the site of a cult, the locus of the enigma of the task itself, and finally the site of the only two real deaths the narrative contains. Chicote, in turn, develops into two investigative *spaces*, as Quinn finds himself investigating not only the O'Gorman "murder" but also the town's other mystery, the embezzlement by Alberta Haywood of a large sum of money, still unrecovered, from the bank where she had worked as a teller.

What constitutes the identity of a character in verbal fiction? Quinn works within the various investigative spaces to put together a picture of the "dead" O'Gorman, to put together an account of the crime that has removed him from the scene (and other crimes that subsequently unfold), and to bring into relation characters and events *across* the separated spaces. (Within constructions such as Millar's, it is unlikely that Criminal Scene X will turn out to have nothing more to do with Criminal Scene Y than that both came into the investigator's life at around the same time; contrast this with police-procedural narratives, where a different pleasure is produced through providing a one-thing-after-another sheer variety of incident). O'Gorman, as an identity, *is* the picture-built-up, the acts-assembled, the connections-with-other-characters-made.

Narrative skill within the "whoizzit" genre will thus consist in building up two identities in which:

(1) Identity A and Identity B are represented as *looking* different. In contiguity terms: The assemblage of physical traits characterizing the two identities are not such that it is immediately apparent to the investigator that the two are one and the same.

(2) Non-obvious, but cogent, similarities between Identity A personality traits and Identity B personality traits are provided for the reader. In contiguity terms: Personality traits may be considered to be parts of, in the sense of aspects of, individuals.

(3) Clue-like objects belonging to Identity A turn out to fall into place as relatable equally to Identity B, or vice versa. In contiguity terms: Significant objects are those that have been "next to" characters in ways that serve to identify those characters and/or to make clear what they have done.

(4) The actions of Identity A and Identity B, apparently ascribable to two identities and as such (as well as for other reasons) enigmatic, are eventually revealed to be the actions of a single agent and are shown to "hang together" understandably as such. In contiguity terms: Actions, especially insofar as our grammatical system tends to reify them (*What* did he commit? A *crime*), are felt to exist "next to" those responsible for them (metonymy) or to constitute parts of the whole, which is the totality of a character's being-and-doing over time (synecdoche).

(5)   The contrasting settings in which Identity A and Identity B have unfolded are brought into even more piquant contrast by turning out to have mirrored (via the mechanisms of the "agent-scene ratio" analyzed by Kenneth Burke) only a single identity. In contiguity terms: Settings are, straightforwardly enough, what characters are next to, as their surroundings.

In the case of *How Like an Angel*, the O'Gorman/Brother Tongue separation and revelatory identification can be easily mapped onto these categories.

(1)   *Physical appearance*. The shaven head and institutionalized garb of Brother Tongue de-individualize him. This is remarked upon where Quinn says, "When a group of people all wear the same shapeless gray robes it's hard to differentiate them" (73). (Quinn then thinks contrariwise about the actual individualities of those he has met at the Tower and is led to characterize Brother Tongue in a manner that keeps him far from the O'Gorman identity, accurate though it is: "Brother Tongue, mute, with only a little bird for his voice"). O'Gorman, as "dead," has to be visualized through photographs. These themselves are described in a way suggesting that O'Gorman has some sort of figure-ground contiguity problem:

In every case O'Gorman looked like a part of the background, and it was the dog and cat, the children, Martha, the bicycle, which seemed the real subjects of the pictures. Only the formal photograph showed O'Gorman's face clearly. He'd been a handsome young man with curly black hair and large gentle eyes with a faint expression of bafflement in them, as though he found life puzzling and not quite what he'd been led to expect (56).

The two appearances are reconciled close to the end of the novel:

For too long he had been out of contact with human beings. . . . [T]he young ones he hurried past, expecting them to jeer at his robe and shaved head and bare feet. Then he caught sight of himself in the window of a little neighborhood grocery store, and he realized they would have no reasons to jeer at him now. He looked like any ordinary man. During his weeks in the forest his hair had grown in, curly and black with touches of gray. (271)

(2)   *Personality traits*. To cite two key examples:
O'Gorman's love of animals is briefly mentioned when Martha remarks on her son's preference for a well-done barbecue: "Richard's like his father, he has to have all meat burned so it's less likely to remind him of—well, the source of it. He loves animals, as Patrick did" (157). Brother Tongue's fondness for his little bird is a key characterizing detail. O'Gorman's pattern of dependency on Martha (whom he then cruelly deceives) corresponds to Brother Tongue's dependency on Sister Blessing (whom he then cruelly murders).

(3)   *Objects/Clues*. Notable in this category are the *letter* "confessing" to O'Gorman's "murder," written by Tongue and precipitating both of the novel's real deaths; the *clothes* worn by O'Gorman after his disappearance, given him

by his co-conspirator Alberta, which belonged to her brother George who eventually becomes Brother Tongue's first victim; and the *typewriter* that was in the car when the disappearance was staged, which O'Gorman took with him into the woods while hiding out, hearing which led Karma (child of a Tower community member) to find him in the woods (thus introducing him to the community), which Karma got Brother Tongue to give her at the point when the community disperses in flight, and which he murderously endeavors to recover from her in the novel's denouement.

(4) *Actions*. Both O'Gorman and Brother Tongue are presented as men with a severely restricted ability to act: The latter as an eccentric religious cult-member with some sort of speech handicap, the former as a weak man, dependent upon Martha and unable to make a success of anything. The novel, once it does make the O'Gorman/Tongue consciousness focal (without yet quite naming it as such) in the crucial Chapter 23, presents a radically different picture in which O'Gorman's agency, while still most unlucky, emerges as effective—indeed, murderously so.

(5) *Settings*. The otherness of the Tower community is eventually shown to be very much joined to O'Gorman's other space, Chicote, just as more generally its otherness crumbles as the narrative unfolds. Yet Chicote and the more narratively mysterious (in the sense of not apparently functional) space of San Felice so memorably and metaphorically evoked on the novel's opening page ("the tree-lined streets of San Felice, with the ocean glittering in the distance like a jewel not to be touched or sold") are brought out in their own individuality with great skill. And the denouement involves a further space—urban Los Angeles—that is both neutral with respect to all the other spaces in the novel (which are revealed as rural or *small*-city spaces) and is also thereby more *truly* other and alienating than they; appropriately, walking through this space, this most banal of spaces, O'Gorman/Tongue accomplishes his final descent into madness.

The preceding details give some sense of the microlevel contiguity relationships that such an elaborately constructed "whoizzit" as *How Like an Angel* puts into play. Standing back from that, though, two questions might be raised in conclusion. Why should this *kind* of text constitute a deepening of the investigative genre? How might *this* novel in particular—of which this account is only the beginning of a single narrative strand—strike the contiguity-conscious reader as particularly masterly?

The great advantage of the complex "whoizzit," in which there is some reason over and above immediate disguise for there to be feigned identity, is that the narrative material around that reason can afford to be more diverse than that which sustains basic "whodunnit" plotting. Insofar as the feigned identify material is centered on non–death-focused material or on non–death-*puzzle*-focused material, the generic limits on a "whodunnit" can be broadened, and other kinds of stories can be embedded to the point of constituting the narrative's truth within a broadly investigative framework. Edmund Wilson's

"Who Cares Who Killed Roger Ackroyd" query can thus be defused; behind the narrowly generic array of murder/suspects/motives/clues can lie any number of unfortunate linkages that characters have covered over and that—for the investigator *and* for the reader—need uncovering.

How Like an Angel brings this out with an extra turn of the screw in its problematization of the classic murder-motif itself. The murder that comes under investigation (O'Gorman's murder) is no murder. The motivation for disguise lying behind this (the O'Gorman/Alberta Haywood love affair and conspiracy) involves fraud but not homicide. Only when Quinn starts the investigation are the events unleashed that lead to the novel's real deaths. Yet—to move in conclusion to a few words about *How Like an Angel* as a whole—the ultimate effect of Margaret Millar's bravura construction is to emphasize not so much the real deaths as the infernal machine that has generated them: the mystery of the Patrick-Alberta *folie à deux* in the context of both characters' otherwise blocked lives. Though setting all this up as something that the reader comes to as the solution of a puzzle, Millar opens up to that reader the possibility of pondering the situation once the puzzle fades and learning from it in the classical instruction-through-pleasure mode.

This, however, does not quite give an account of how the novel's climax works. Brother Tongue/O'Gorman moves toward Karma through suburban Los Angeles, knife in pocket, but psychically disintegrating. Quinn, the investigator, now in love with and loved by Martha, finds himself (on her insistence) accompanied by her in giving backup support for Karma. (Not having the benefit of Chapter 23, Quinn has less-than-perfect evidence at this point for O'Gorman's aliveness, which must excuse his being prepared to let Martha in for the final shock.) O'Gorman arrives at the door, is parried by Karma until the police arrive, but is then recognized by Martha:

[T]he woman with him [with Quinn—i.e., Martha] began to scream, "Patrick, Patrick! Oh, my God, Patrick!" [Patrick] stared at her wondering why she looked so familiar to him and who Omigod Patrick was. (278)

Against the most poignant of reconnectednesses, the back-from-the-dead recognition of him by his wife, Patrick presents the most poignant of nonrecognitions, of next-to-ness gone blank: nonrecognition of Martha, nonrecognition of his own name.

REFERENCES

Burke, Kenneth. *A Grammar of Motives*. New York: Prentice-Hall, 1945.
Christie, Agatha. *By the Pricking of My Thumbs*. 1968. Reprint. London: Fontana, 1989.
Christie, Agatha. *Sad Cypress*. 1940. Reprint. London: Fontana, 1989.
Jakobson, Roman. "Two Aspects of Language and Two Types of Aphasic Disturbances."
    In *Fundamentals of Languages*, 55-82. 'S-Gravenhage: Mouton, 1956.

Millar, Margaret. *How Like an Angel*. 1962. Reprint. New York: International
    Polygonics, 1982.

6

Parody and Detective Fiction

Janice MacDonald

The three most popular stances to take regarding detective fiction have been labeled as the psychological approach, the sociocultural approach, and the historical method. Of course, most of these methods are interested in detective fiction primarily as artifact rather than art, for as we've all been told by Edmund Wilson and others, detective fiction is, at best, sub-literary.

The psychological approach attempts to answer the question of why people read detective fiction. So does the sociocultural approach, but it also addresses the questions of why the formula is so massively popular and why literature of this sort came to be written. The historical survey, of course, tells what has been written where and when. The question still to be asked is "how": How does the genre generate new material within each sub-genre, how do these sub-genres evolve, and how does the formula plot stay true without becoming tiresome? John G. Cawelti sees these changes occurring in response to changes in the cultural climate (51), but this explanation cannot be the complete answer. There must also be an internal dynamic within the genre that aids in its propagation and flexibility, and parody can be considered a key dynamic element in the development of the popular formulaic genre known as detective fiction.

As yet there has been no consensus on a concise definition of parody. The *Oxford English Dictionary* definition is

A composition in prose or verse in which the characteristic turns of thought and phrase in an author or class of authors are imitated in such a way as to make them appear ridiculous, especially by applying them to ludicrously inappropriate subjects; an imitation of a work more or less closely modeled on the original, but so turned as to produce a ridiculous effect. (489)

This definition has often been called into question, because it is based on only one of the two meanings of the etymological root of *parody*. J. Hillis Miller explains the ambiguity of the word (from the Greek "parodia") by defining "para" as a

double antithetical prefix signifying at once proximity and distance, similarity and difference, interiority and exteriority, something inside . . . and at the same time outside, . . . something simultaneously this side of a boundary line, threshold or margin, and also beyond it. (cited in Conlon 221-22)

As Linda Hutcheon suggests, this double meaning allows parody to cut both ways; it can either refer to "counter" (as in against) or it can mean "beside" (as in parallel) and therefore provide "a suggestion of an accord or intimacy instead of a contrast" (32). In light of this expanded etymology, parody can be freed from the constant need to ridicule.

There are critics who have recognized the importance of parody and have made an attempt to define it as a positive force. The Russian Formalists in general and Jurij Tynjanov in particular view parody as "a lever of literary change" (Erlich 165) and a "sign of emancipation, indeed an act of literary 'warfare'" (Erlich 225). While many critics and theorists will grant to parody an element of literary criticism, J. Gerald Kennedy comes closest to the Russian Formalists when he labels parody "exorcism":

Precisely because great writing weighs upon subsequent writers, exacting the tribute of con-scious or unconscious emulation, any author who wishes to establish his own voice must come to terms with the "enemy"—the genius of his predecessors. (166-67)

Formalist criticism takes this individual exorcism one step further: The presence of parody indicates another step in the evolution of literature as a whole. As Victor Erlich explains, to the Formalist critic, parody is:

how literary change comes about. The old is presented, as it were, in a new key. The obsolete device is not thrown overboard, but repeated in a new, incongruous context, and thus either rendered absurd through the agency of mechanization or made "perceptible" again. In other words, a new art is not an antithesis of the preceding one, but its reorganization, a "regrouping of the old elements." (226)

More recently, Linda Hutcheon has devoted herself to the discovery of a positive definition of the term and has winnowed through the various explanations of parody to synthesize them into a useful working definition:

parody is repetition, but repetition that includes difference; it is limitation with critical ironic distance, whose irony can cut both ways. Ironic versions of "trans-contextualization" and inversion are its major formal operatives, and the range of pragmatic ethos is from scornful ridicule to reverential homage. (37)

Considering these definitions one can see parody as a positive influence on literature. At the same time that it acknowledges its predecessors, a parodic work carves out its own territory by means of a delicate critical distancing. Through self-consciousness and self-reflexiveness, a parodic work repeats "in a new, incongrous context" (Erlich 226) and thus acknowledges a debt at the same time that it "exorcises" what has gone before. Irony is also a major component of a parodic work. As Hutcheon argues, because of the structural similarities between parody and irony, "parody can use irony easily and naturally as a preferred, even privileged, rhetorical mechanism" (54). While there has been much thought devoted to parody, most critics discuss the term as a genre rather than a literary device. Margaret Rose, however, is an exception to this tendency. In *Parody/Metafiction*, her study of intertextuality in a range of postmodernist works, she has shown that a parodic (according to my definition above) device can be an important element in texts that are not primarily parodies.

I wish to follow Rose's lead to examine how parodic elements work within detective fiction and how certain features of parody affect and structure this literary genre. There are reasons to believe that parody is at work within the genre of detective fiction. The first indication is that detective fiction creates the context necessary for audience recognition of parody. Readers of detective fiction often read widely within the genre, and "addicted" readers are likely to have read (and recognize allusions to) the original of any given parody. This preknowledge is necessary to the appreciation of parody. As J. G. Riewald says, since "the recognition of the original is a primary condition of the integral enjoyment of parody, it must be granted that the reader who is ignorant of the original is severely handicapped" (128).

Furthermore, because of the imitative nature of parody, it is especially interesting to study its effects and uses in an inherently formulaic genre. There are striking similarities between Cawelti's definition of a successful formulaic work, as "in addition to the pleasure inherent in the conventional structure, it brings a new element into the formula, or embodies the personal vision of the creator" (12), and Linda Hutcheon's definition of parody as "repetition that includes difference" (37). This is not to say that all formulaic fiction is parodic in nature, but it does lend credence to the study of parody within a formulaic genre.

There is parody at work within the specific formula of a detective narrative as well as within the larger aspect of the genre as a whole. As Lacan has stated, the basic formula of a detective novel is one in which the detective's actions parody those of the murderer (21-54). In his ability to deduce the criminal's actions or "reconstruct the scene of the crime," the detective effects a repetition that includes difference. The ironic and incongrous effect is that the character who embodies ultimate good (the detective) is the only character who can understand ultimate evil.

Also central to the formula are "red herrings," which are parodies of clues. These ultimately unimportant details must be enough like real clues to confuse the reader, but they must also contain enough of a difference from real clues to keep the reader from claiming foul play on the part of the author. Red herrings emphasize the importance placed on reading correctly and also ironically delineate the fine line betwen appearance and reality that is the essence of both parody and detection.

Another parodic element often found within the formula is the slow-witted partner of the Great Detective. There is, of course, a sense in which the Watson character is merely a foil. As Julian Symons says: "[Poe] established the convention by which the brilliant intelligence of the detective is made to shine more brightly through the comparative obtuseness of his friend who tells the story" (38). As well as serving this function, however, the secondary character so often found in detective fiction fulfills another, parodic, function. He situates the reader in terms of the text by portraying a parodic example of a naive reader. As Margaret Rose writes:

the parodist creates a situation whereby the reader must also relate to himself as an object of the author's discourse if he is to understand the status of other objects represented in the fiction. He must, that is, see his own world through the image of himself, the reader, in the text before him, as a part of a fiction which, as he himself, has taken on a different form than in the world of objects. (65)

As indicated, there are various ways in which parody functions within the genre of detective fiction. A study of selected works by Edgar Allan Poe, Wilkie Collins, Fergus Hume, and Sir Arthur Conan Doyle will delineate the function of parody in two ways: first, as the catalyst (by way of mocking both the novel of manners and the gothic) that creates a new genre and, second, as the means of establishing one's unique authority within the limitations of a prescribed form.

In "From Poe to Valery" (1948), T. S. Eliot remarked that, "as far as detective fiction is concerned, nearly everything can be traced to two authors: Poe and Wilkie Collins" (208). The genre now known as detective fiction came about partially because of a perceived need for rational and logical solutions within the sensational and gothic horror novels popular in the late eighteenth and early nineteenth centuries. The patterns developed by Poe, Collins, and, to a lesser extent, Charles Dickens almost immmedately became formulaic.

While the four "tales of ratiocination" ("The Murders in the Rue Morgue," "The Purloined Letter," "The Gold Bug," and "The Mystery of Marie Roget") are Poe's only detective stories, one must note his stance as a critic as well as an author to determine how instrumental parody was in the birth of detective fiction. Many scholars, including W. H. Auden, saw Poe as a self-appointed guardian of good taste and clear writing. Robert Daniel, in "Poe's Detective God," connects Poe's critical stance to his literary work: "There are several ways in which the detective stories appear to be extensions of Poe's criticism. As a reviewer, he is very much the sleuthhound; he ferrets out plagiarism, and hunts down writers guilty of bad taste, confused thinking, or the murder of the language. Contrariwise, the detective stories may be regarded as essays in criticism" (105). Daniel's reading of the tales of ratiocination as literary criticism equates with the Russian Formalist definition of parody as literary criticism, in which "the obsolete device is not thrown overboard, but repeated in a new, incongruous context, and thus either rendered absurd through the agency of mechanization or made 'perceptible' again" (Erlich 226). In order, however, to accept Daniel's statement one must examine Poe's focus as a literary critic and whether Poe used the tool of parody as the Russian Formalists have defined and prescribed.

The crux of Poe's critical stance is that he unites the two opposing forces of rationalism and imagination. David Ketterer explains this undercurrent present in Poe's tales of ratiocination. Poe distrusted reason because he considered "imagination [to be] the only avenue to a perception of ideality and reason being largely responsible for man's state of deception" (238). Privileging the imagination did not mean, however, that reason had no place in the work of an artist. Poe waged war on artists who he believed used "slovenly diction" (Auden 1950, xiii) or suffered from "confused thinking" (Daniel 105). Poe developed a theory of artistic synthesis between the two states. Both the declaration and the demonstration of this position are to be found in the tales of ratiocination. It is Dupin's companion, the narrator, who says it most succinctly, in the opening of "The Murders in the Rue Morgue": "It will be found, in fact, that the ingenious are always fanciful, and the *truly* imaginative never otherwise than analytic" (179).

By examining the synthesis of reason and imagination in his tales of ratiocination, Poe accomplished two things. He imposed standards of quality onto tales of gothic and sensational horror. No longer could writers indulge in horrific sequences for sensation's sake alone. By sticking Mademoiselle L'Espanaye in the chimney upside down in "The Murders in the Rue Morgue," Poe had outdone any horror imaginable. By deducing a logical reason for this terrifying action, he challenged writers to be responsible for their creative powers. He had proved that a reasonable explanation could be just as terrifying and far more believable than an unexplained phenomenon. It is important to note that Poe did not dismiss elements of the sensational; by using horror and intrigue to tell a story of rationality, he made it impossible for readers to be satisfied with the old formula. As Erlich describes parody according to the Russian Formalists, Poe created a new formula that was "not an antithesis of the preceding one, but its reorganization, a 'regrouping of the old elements'" (226).

In addition to imposing standards on gothic thrillers, Poe developed the prototype for all detective fiction that was to follow. "The Murders in the Rue Morgue" is the first locked-room mystery, a style John Dickson Carr later personalized with his detective, Dr. Gideon Fell. "The Murder of Marie Roget" is the first example of the armchair detective. Baroness Orczy's Old Man in the Corner is the most famous descendant of this line, though Agatha Christie's Miss Marple might be said to indulge in this sport from time to time. One of the basic rules of detective fiction is that the most unlikely answer will be the correct answer, and the acknowledged prototype for this is Poe's "The Purloined Letter." "The Gold Bug," which involves M. Legrand rather than the amazing Dupin, is based on Poe's love of cryptography; without it, Dorothy L. Sayers's *Have His Carcase* might not have been written.

If Edgar Allan Poe is the father of the detective story, then Wilkie Collins is the father of the detective novel. His two best-known works, *The Woman in White* (1860) and *The Moonstone* (1868), are the prototypes for the mystery thriller and the detective novel, respectively. Collins takes the basic recipe for the sensational gothic thriller and, like Poe, uses the ingredients to devise a new and far more satisfying concoction.

The Woman in White contains various essential elements from the standard sensational novel of the time (43-49). These include a case of switched and mistaken identity, kidnapping, drugs, true love, and a dusty and unused wing of a manor house. There is even an insane asylum thrown in for good measure. Two additions to this list are what signaled Collins as an innovator: Count Fosco, an evil mastermind the likes of whom literature had never seen, and the fact that, for all the mysterious and horrific events that occur throughout the novel, the seeds of plausibility and rationality are sown from the beginning. In this latter respect, Collins differed from Poe in the degree of his consistency; while Poe privileged rationality, there have been countless articles proving that Dupin could not have seen the address on the purloined letter, that the Rue Morgue orangutan could not have reached the shutter from the drainpipe, and that Mary Rogers likely took her own life. Collins, on the other hand, does not suffer from similar attacks. Every clue is planted from the beginning, and no loose ends are left trailing.

Collins had trained in law; this discipline is perhaps what persuaded him to use the technique of switching narrators throughout the novel. Each narrator speaks of only what he could have known at the time; although the narrating characters know the ultimate truth as they relate the story, they are honor-bound not to reveal the conclusion until the reader is apprised of all the facts in the case. In the preface to *The Woman in White*, Collins writes: "the story here presented will be told by more than one pen, as the story of an offense against the laws is told in Court by more than one witness—with the same object, in both cases, to present the truth always in its most direct and most intelligible aspect" (1). Multiple narrators create a built-in self-consciousness in the text that, paradoxically, enforces the plausibility of the situation.

Collins often pushed this self-consciousness to the extreme. A case in point is the first narrator of *The Moonstone*, Gabriel Betteredge. Betteredge himself believes in the power and veracity of literature. He shows that a novel can be as powerful as scripture by discovering truths in rereadings and consultations with his well-worn copy of *Robinson Crusoe*.

I have tried that book for years—generally in combination with a pipe of tobacco—and have found it my friend in need in all the necessities of this mortal life. When my spirits are bad—*Robinson Crusoe*. When I want advice—*Robinson Crusoe*. In past times, when my wife plagued me; in present times, when I have had a drop too much—*Robinson Crusoe*. I have worn out six stout *Robinson Crusoes* with hard work in my service. On my lady's last birthday she gave me a seventh. I took a drop too much on the strength of it; and *Robinson Crusoe* put me right again. (34-35)

In the fifth chapter of his narrative, Betteredge makes a highly self-conscious statement to the reader:

Here follows the substance of what I said, written out entirely for your benefit. Pay attention to it, or you will be all abroad, when we get deeper into the story. Clear your mind of the children, or the dinner, or the new bonnet, or what not. Try if you can't forget politics, horses, prices in the City, and grievances at the club. I hope you won't take this freedom on my part amiss; it's the only way I have of appealing to the gentle reader. Lord! haven't I seen you with the greatest authors in your hands, and don't I know how ready your attention is to wander when it's a book that asks for it, instead of a person? (54)

This passage is remarkably similar to the opening paragraph of Italo Calvino's postmodernist novel, *If on a Winter's Night a Traveler*:

You are about to begin reading Italo Calvino's new novel, *If on a Winter's Night a Traveler*. Relax. Concentrate. Dispel every other thought. Let the world around you fade. Best to close the door; the TV is always on in the next room. Tell the others right away, "No, I don't want to watch TV!" Raise your voice—they won't hear you otherwise—"I'm reading! I don't want to be disturbed!" (3)

The difference between these two passages, both parodies of the standard evocation to the gentle reader, is that Calvino's opening automatically creates a barrier between the text and the reader who wishes merely to sink into a fiction. It challenges the reader to participate rather than merely read. This postmodernist barrier is created by means of the voice Calvino uses, the voice of the implied author, but Collins is doing something different. True, he is parodying the Richardsonian style of appealing to the reader to demonstrate the truth of what is written, but at the same time, he is creating a convincing portrait of someone who has been asked to relate the truth as he witnessed it. By using multiple narrators rather than an omniscient, unseen storyteller, Collins has already created an atmosphere of veracity; once he has established this reality for his readers, he can parody the wooden stylistic devices of others with impunity. By inserting his authorial address to the reader, Calvino raises the question of his narrative's plausibility. Collins is self-conscious about the form of his narrative, but only in order to prove that the substance of his narrative is true.

Poe played with the possibilities of detective fiction, but quickly tired of the genre. Collins likewise ventured into new areas (without as much success) after *The Moonstone*. Gavin Lambert says of Collins, "he was the first to grasp [the mystery novel's] expressive possibilities. The genre became personal with *The Woman in White* and mechanical soon afterwards" (ix). Perhaps it was this fear of the mechanical that kept these innovators from continuing to write in the genre they had helped to forge. Needless to say, many writers were willing to jump into the breach. Detective fiction became and has remained one of the most popular genres of formulaic fiction. Parody and self-consciousness, tools that helped to create the genre, continued as elements of the genre. Indeed, parody quickly became an element of the formula itself: an element designed both to foster credibility and to generate new material within the highly mechanical formula.

The history of detective fiction is studded with successful practitioners of the craft who denigrated both the genre and their own fame within it. This seeming distaste occurred very early but made no difference to the proliferation of the genre or, indeed, the productivity of the particular authors. Although the name Fergus W. Hume does not evoke the same recognition as that of his contemporary Sir Arthur Conan Doyle, at one time his *The Mystery of a Hansom Cab* (1886) outsold the Sherlock Holmes stories. Hailed as the best-selling mystery novel of the nineteenth century, Hume's first foray into detective fiction was written not for any special love of the form but to make his name known in order to advance his career as a budding playwright. In a preface written in 1896 (ten years after *Cab* was first published), Hume describes the manner in which he came to write the book:

I enquired of a leading Melbourne bookseller what style of book he sold most of. He replied that the detective stories of Gaboriau had a large sale; and as, at this time I had never heard of this author, I bought all his works . . . and read them carefully. The style of these stories attracted me, and I determined to write a book of the same class; containing a mystery, a murder, and a description of low life in Melbourne. This was the origin of the "*Cab*." (8)

Hume never became a playwright. He wrote over a hundred more thrillers and, though none of them reached the popularity of the *Cab*, he made a comfortable living.

The Mystery of a Hansom Cab is indeed a respectable mystery novel, but it is the manner by which Hume claimed to have written it that makes it of interest today. One can infer from his explanation that, even as early as 1886, the detective novel had reached such a stage of formula that any reasonably intelligent wordsmith could manufacture one, given an accurate recipe. Almost from its inception, the detective genre was relegated to the readership that Wilkie Collins had once named the "unknown public" (Symons 42). Detective fiction was not serious literature; and no serious writer, no matter how much he might profit from it, could admit to championing it. By denigrating the genre Hume insinuated that he, indeed, was a serious writer who had, to crib from Oliver Goldsmith, "stooped to conquer." The implication was that a detective novel written by an author who realized how inconsequential such novels were could not be of the same low stature as most detective novels. Like many writers who were to come, Hume managed by this subterfuge to claim superior status for his novel, which actually followed the hateful formula stringently.

Self-consciousness, which Wilkie Collins had used to plead the plausibility of his narrative, was now being used to distinguish one's novel from the morass of the formulaic. In the *Cab*, reference is made to other works of detective fiction in a very self-conscious way. One would assume that this reminder to the reader of the existence of the genre would necessarily harm the verisimilitude attempted by the author. In postmodernist fiction, self-consciousness is used deliberately to highlight the fictionality of the work in which it appears. However, in detective fiction, a peculiar double negative effect seems to occur. References to fictional works, and especially those within the same genre, enhance rather than deny the reality of the given novel. In much the same way as the play-within-the play structure gives credence to the outer drama that frames the interior "fiction," references to fiction within detective novels extend the distance between the acknowledged formulaic genre and the particular example at hand. "If this were a detective plot, I should expect so-and-so to be the murderer, but . . ." is a familiar utterance to mystery readers. Statements such as these remind the reader forcefully of the formulaic and predictable nature of the genre, but in addition they imply that the story that houses them is superior to such conventions. The argument is as convincing as it is fallacious: Detective novels follow an obvious and predictable formula; if this were such a novel it would not speak disdainfully of its ilk; therefore, this is not such a novel. Hume is no stranger to this ploy.

"Puts one in mind of *The Leavenworth Case*, and all that sort of thing," said Felix, whose reading was of the lightest description. (48)

"Murdered in a cab," he said, lighting a fresh cigarette, and blowing a cloud of smoke. "A romance in real life, which beats Miss Braddon hollow." (56)

"But do you know anything of the detective business?" someone would ask. "Oh, dear yes," with an airy wave of his hand; "I've read Gaboriau, you know; awfully jolly life, 'tectives.'" (88)

The key to a successful detective novel, which Fergus W. Hume (and countless writers since) discovered, seems to be this: Follow the formula to the letter, and deny doing so at every turn.

While Hume had followed Collins by concentrating on the persona of the law officer or professional as detective, Sir Arthur Conan Doyle turned back to Edgar Allan Poe and Gaboriau for his models. As Ian Ousby states: "Doyle's achievement was to create a stereotype of the private detective as complete and as expressive of its time as the earlier stereotype of the police detective had been" (136). Sherlock Holmes owes much to the Chevalier Auguste Dupin, who dislikes the sun, lives in seclusion, and astounds his companion/narrator with his acts of rational deduction. Holmes, too, is an eccentric: He is a cocaine addict, plays the violin, is insufferably arrogant, demonstrates misogynistic tendencies, and indulges in elaborate disguises. In his memoirs, Conan Doyle acknowledged his debt to Poe, but Holmes himself made clear what he thought of the comparison in *A Study in Scarlet*: "Now, in my opinion, Dupin was a very inferior fellow. That trick of his of breaking in on his friends' thoughts with an apropos remark after a quarter of an hour's silence is really very showy and superficial. He had some analytical genius, no doubt; but he was by no means such a phenomenon as Poe appeared to imagine" (1: 24).

Sherlock Holmes may then be considered a parody of Auguste Dupin, in the sense that Doyle recontextualized many features of Poe's logical hero. He is similar in order to qualify for the position of Great Detective; he is different from his predecessor in order to justify his existence as a separate entity. He is a repetition with a difference (Hutcheon 37); he is a "reorganization" of Dupin, to make him perceptible again (Erlich 226); he is Doyle's way of "coming to terms with the genius of his predecessors" (Kennedy 166). The above passage not only demonstrates the previously discussed disparagement of similar fiction to enhance the position of one's own, it also shows how the great detective often owes his creation to the detectives who go before.

The passage also highlights another feature often found in the makeup of fictional detectives of the "great detective" mold—eccentricity. As Conan Doyle's brother-in-law, E. W. Hornung (creator of Raffles), once humorously penned: "Though he might be more humble, there's no police like Holmes" (Symons 85). Arrogance is not always a synonym for eccentricity, nor is it necessarily a prerequisite for a great detective. However, in the etiquette-filled minefield of Victorian England, where self-congratulations would be considered an exercise in bad taste, arrogance in the demeanor of an otherwise respectable gentleman would be the height of eccentricity. Eccentricity is a necessary element for a great detective. An ordinary individual cannot move freely through all circles of society. Anyone who can (and a detective must) has to be seen to be unlike other people; the greater his skills as a detective, the greater his eccentricities. As a parodic element, eccentricities can be defined as exaggerations of certain features of behavior and therefore as parodies, or verbal caricatures, of the great detective. At the same time that the detective writer had to impress the reader with the plausibility of his fiction, he had to underline the ultimate impossibility of his hero. As readers, to accept a fictional great detective as real, we must be convinced of his "superhumanness" or, indeed, his fictionality. A successful great detective must be a paradox of reality and illusion, a realistically articulated figment.

As shown from Poe's determination for rationality and Collins's insistence on a plausible explanation for the sensational, detective fiction owes its inception to parody, as a "lever of literary change" (Erlich 165). The formula almost immediately absorbed the device of parody, and authors used it to situate their novels self-consciously above those of their predecessors and competitors. Parody also infiltrated the persona of the great detective by molding each new character on those who had gone before and exaggerating his abilities and foibles alike to emphasize his superhumanness. Since that time, parody has also been seen in the works of writers, most notably female, who use detective novel writers as protagonists in the inversion of the formula created by the hard-boiled school; and, working as an agent against the formula, in the works of various postmodernist "antidetectives."

If the detective formula were imagined as some sort of powerful bacterium, able to isolate, overpower, and absorb anything thrown in its way, it would be close to my vision of how detective fiction developed. Every addition automatically becomes part of the formula. Parody, as part of the initial impulse of detective fiction, has remained through the years as an essential element. Whether it consists of a minor tribute to the novel's antecedents or functions through wild bouts of self-reflexiveness, parody makes its presence known.

REFERENCES

Auden, W. H. "The Guilty Vicarage." 1948. In *Detective Fiction: A Collection of Critical Essays*, edited by Robin W. Winks, 15-25. Englewood Cliffs, NJ: Prentice-Hall, 1980.

___. "Introduction." In *Selected Prose, Poetry, and Eureka* by Edgar Allan Poe, v-xvii. New York: Holt, Rinehart and Winston, 1950.

Calvino, Italo. *If on a Winter's Night a Traveler*, translated by William Weaver. San Diego, CA: Harcourt Brace Jovanovich, 1981.

Cawelti, John G. *Adventure, Mystery and Romance: Formula Stories as Art and Popular Culture*. Chicago: University of Chicago Press, 1976.

Collins, Wilkie. *The Moonstone*. 1868. Reprint. New York: Signet, 1984.

___. *The Woman in White*. 1860. Reprint. Toronto: Bantam, 1985.

Conlon, Michael J. "Singing Beside-Against: Parody and the Example of Swift's 'A Description of a City Shower.'" *Genre* 16 (Fall 1983): 219-32.

Daniel, Robert. "Poe's Detective God." In *Twentieth Century Interpretations of Poe's Tales*. Englewood Cliffs, NJ: Prentice-Hall, 1971.

Doyle, Sir Arthur Conan. *The Complete Sherlock Holmes*. 2 vol. Garden City, NY: Doubleday and Co., 1972.

Eliot, T. S. "From Poe to Valery." 1948. In *The Recognition of Edgar Allan Poe*, edited by Eric W. Carlson, 205-19. Ann Arbor: University of Michigan Press, 1966.

Erlich, Victor. *Russian Formalism: History—Doctrine*. 1955. Reprint. New Haven, CT: Yale University Press, 1965.

Fowler, H. W. *A Dictionary of Modern English Usage*. 2d ed. Oxford: Clarendon Press, 1968.

Hume, Fergus. *The Mystery of a Hansom Cab*. 1886. Reprint. New York: Dover, 1982.

Hutcheon, Linda. *A Theory of Parody: The Teachings of Twentieth-Century Art Forms*. New York: Methuen, 1985.

Kennedy, J. Gerald. "Parody as Exorcism: 'The Raven' and 'The Jewbird.'" *Genre* 13 (Summer 1980): 161-69.

Ketterer, David. *The Rationale of Deception in Poe*. Baton Rouge: Louisiana State University Press, 1979.

Knight, Stephen. *Form and Ideology in Crime Fiction*. Bloomington: Indiana University Press, 1980.

Lacan, Jacques. "Seminar on 'The Purloined Letter.'" 1972. Reprint, translated by Jeffrey Mehlman. In *The Poetics of Murder: Detective Fiction and Literary Theory*, edited by Glenn W. Most and William W. Stowe. San Diego, CA: Harcourt Brace Jovanovich, 1983.

Lambert, Gavin. *The Dangerous Edge*. London: Barrie and Jenkins, 1975.

Most, Glenn W., and William W. Stowe, eds. *The Poetics of Murder: Detective Fiction and Literary Theory*. San Diego, CA: Harcourt Brace Jovanovich, 1983.

Ousby, Ian. *Bloodhounds of Heaven: The Detective in English from Godwin to Doyle*. Cambridge, MA: Harvard University Press, 1976.

Oxford English Dictionary. Vol. 7. 1933. Reprint. Oxford: Clarendon Press, 1961.

Poe, Edgar Allan. *Collected Works of Edgar Allan Poe: Tales and Sketches 1831-1842*, edited by Thomas Ollive Mabbott. Cambridge, MA: Harvard University Press, 1978.

Riewald, J. G. "Parody as Criticism." *Neophilologus* 50 (January 1966): 125-48.

Rose, Margaret. *Parody/Metafiction*. London: Croom Helm, 1979.

Symons, Julian. *Bloody Murder: From the Detective Story to the Crime Novel*. London: Faber and Faber, 1972.

Wilson, Edmund. "Who Cares Who Killed Roger Ackroyd?" 1945. Reprints. In *Classics and Commercials: A Literary Chronicle of the Forties*. New York: Vintage Books, 1962.

Winks, Robin W., ed. *Detective Fiction: A Collection of Critical Essays*. Englewood Cliffs, NJ: Prentice-Hall, 1980.

7

"The Game's Afoot": Predecessors and Pursuits of a Postmodern Detective Novel

Kathleen Belin Owen

The detective story today inevitably finds itself judged by the reader's experience of the genre's ancestry and traditions. A postmodern detective story cannot evade the context of the detective fiction genre it is "post" to, but the postmodern detective story seeks not to evade or eliminate echoes of its genre's traditions; rather, it embraces the traditional, then turns it right on its head. We often think of postmodernism as inventing such deconstructive inversion, but these inversions actually find their beginnings within the very tradition of British ratiocinative detective fiction. The dilemma confronting postmodern detective fiction is that the nature—the "formula"—of the detective tradition calls for a grounding in episte-mological inquiry that postmodernism has abandoned to modernism's realm in favor of ontological pursuits (McHale 10). Hence the seeming contradiction of a postmodern detective story, which cannot establish itself epistemologically, but seems to need to do so in order to exist as a detective story at all. Does this mean the death of the detective story, the "doomed detective," in the postmodern age?

The distinctions between epistemological and ontological inquiries do not remain rigidly separate when applied to the detective genre. Certainly the postmodern detective novel inverts form, content, and expectations found in the traditional detective story; however, it need not leave behind epistemological issues while embracing ontological ones. Further, not all postmodern critics discover the postmodern absence of epistemology that others proclaim. Michael Holquist, for example, posits a different view: He maintains that post-modernist writers have used the detective story genre as a means to "experiment with the possibilities, limitations, and the power of conscious perception and the search for knowledge" (173). The result is the "metaphysical" detective story form. Using Holquist's argument, then, there is a thriving, though transformed, postmodern detective rather than a "doomed" one.

A telling example of a detective story that possesses both metaphysical and postmodern natures is Douglas Adams's *Dirk Gently's Holistic Detective Agency*. Using this novel, though also considering more "traditional" detective fiction of the ratiocinative (as opposed to the "hard boiled") variety, substantiates several ideas. First, the traditional detective genre (specifically the works of Arthur Conan Doyle, Dorothy Sayers, and Agatha Christie) possesses several traits that have equipped it with the beginnings of postmodernity, thereby keeping the genre unconventional despite some of its own core rules, achieving freshness and innovation by means of violating the rules. Detective fiction has often been characterized as static, formulaic, and contrived (Tani 5). Not that rules, formulas, and standards do not exist; on the contrary, they flourish. Detective fiction's "game rule" structure provides opportunity for inversion and subversion of those rules because of the heightened consciousness between the author and the innovation-demanding reader who both know the rules exist.[1] These are the seeds in traditional ratiocinative detective fiction for the postmodern "metaphysical" detective novel.

The next governing idea of this study addresses what postmodernism does with detective fiction to change it, and Douglas Adams's novel serves this purpose, not because it is the definitive postmodern detective novel (it would be self-defeating to search for such a novel, for "definitive" and "postmodern" are contradictory terms) but because it most readily presents itself as both postmodern and detective—clearly detective, despite its postmodern permutations. The postmodern detective novel, despite some assertions that it possesses a "lack of center" and a "nonsolution" (Tani 40), does initially ground itself in the typical detective genre declarations of a mystery, a detective, an epistemological search (though the *solution* is ontological, for in postmodernism the "rational" explanations about states of being cannot be assumed), and a goal of resolution. The *nature* of these properties may be vastly different, often parodic of detective fiction ancestors (the ontological solution, for example, becomes the priority, even if other more traditional solutions have not been found), but the postmodern detective story still seeks a solution: "If, in the detective story, death must be solved, in the new metaphysical detective story, it is *life* which must be solved" (Holquist 149).

I have focused upon the British ratiocinative detective school because the puzzle-solving detective of the British "intellectual" school, rather than the "hard-boiled dick" of the American "brawn" school, engages in purely epistemologically based pursuits. This latter point will be important later in determining the role of the nature of investigating—*how* one knows—in the postmodern detective novel. Does the epistemological process of the novel retain the significance of its predecessors? What has been eliminated? Of course, the methods of the post-modern detective differ from those of the earlier sleuths, yet successive detectives in the British tradition also eschewed the methods of their predecessors and formulated new (and, they presumed, better) philosophies of investigation. Douglas Adams's postmodern detective, Dirk Gently, presents a similar epistemological intensity in testing the efficacy of his pet method.

FEATURES OF THE TRADITIONAL DETECTIVE GENRE

In considering three leading British detectives—Sherlock Holmes, Lord Peter Wimsey, and Hercule Poirot—one can extrapolate certain "formulas" and expectations of the traditional detective genre.

Eccentricity is one of the obvious traits these three share. Sherlock Holmes, "the world's first consulting detective," was conveniently rendered inactive between cases, having been equipped by the author with a reclusive personality; he "loathed every form of society with his whole Bohemian soul." His chronicler, Dr. John H. Watson, characterizes Holmes as emotionless, unable to love, possessing a cold and detached mind, a mind that Watson equates with a scientific instrument:

He was, I take it, the most perfect reasoning and observing machine that the world has seen; but, as a lover, he would have placed himself in a false position . . . for the trained reasoner to admit such intrusions into his own delicate and finely adjusted temperament was to introduce a distracting factor which would throw a doubt upon all his mental results. Grit in a sensitive instrument, or a crack in one of his own high-power lenses, would not be more disturbing than a strong emotion in a nature such as his. (Doyle 11)

In addition to behavior, temperament, and appearance (over six feet tall, extremely thin, with sharp, piercing eyes), Holmes's collection of knowledge, too, is eccentric, is some areas highly detailed and in others demonstrating astonishing ignorance and indifference. He possesses comprehensive knowledge of chemistry, poisons, and sensational literature, has a "good working knowledge" of British law, but eschews any nonrelevant areas of scholarship that may clutter his "brain attic." Holmes also evinces odd personal habits: He conducts chemical experiments in his rooms, keeps tobacco in the toe of a Persian slipper, and, during periods of intellectual boredom, uses cocaine.

Hercule Poirot, a creation of Agatha Christie and the only fictional detective to have a *New York Times* obituary printed on page one (Penzler et al. 68), is a decided opposite to the Holmes figure. He possesses his own set of eccentricities, often chronicled by his young companion, Captain John Hastings, or by other characters when Poirot has supposedly "retired." Poirot is Belgian (not French, as he would indignantly point out), fiftyish, short (five feet four inches), with "an egg-shaped head, partially covered with suspiciously black hair, two immense mustaches, and a pair of watchful eyes" (Christie 26). He is vain, emotional, excitable, and tenacious. Unlike Holmes, he appreciates feminine beauty. He calls his work "the study of human nature" and possesses what seems to be the obligatory swaggering confidence of his detective abilities. In

The Murder of Roger Ackroyd, Poirot has retired to raise pumpkins but finds himself bored and easily persuaded to take on a local case.

Dorothy Sayers's detective, Lord Peter Wimsey, possesses eccentric features particular to his aristocratic standing. Detection is only one of his many hobbies: collecting rare books; driving fast, expensive cars; dabbling in music and diplomacy. He wears a monocle and an affected manner of "wimsey," which cloaks a keen and observant mind. He calls his investigations "meddling" and often claims he has tried to cure himself of it.

Lord Peter Wimsey's detective role lacks the rigid delineations of Holmes's or Poirot's roles. In fact, the trilogy of detective novels by Sayers in which Wimsey meets, falls in love with, and marries the mystery writer Harriet Vane features more romance than detection, particularly *Busman's Honeymoon*, the third book of the trilogy. Sayers herself, in the foreword to this novel, comments: "It has been said, by myself and others, that a love-interest is only an intrusion upon a detective story. But to the characters involved, the detective-interest might well seem an irritating intrusion upon their love-story. This book deals with such a situation."

Stefano Tani condemns Sayers's fiction because of this porousness between detection and love story, claiming that it marks the "disintegration" of British detective fiction: "the detective novel becomes a novel of manners, a sentimental portrait of a declining British aristocracy, fiction wherein murder and detection are little more than plot excuses for sociological nostalgia" (18). Michael Holquist labels Sayers's brand of detective story an "impure stream," where "stories of crime . . . depended for their appeal on the devices of mainstream fiction; literature, if you will." Sayers, among other writers like Raymond Chandler and Dashiell Hammett, "sought to write novels, not detective novels as such. The characters were more fully rounded, the settings more ordinary— or at least less formulaic—the plots less implausible. The detective is more human and so are the criminals and victims" (163). In other words, rather than "sociological nostalgia," Sayers's "impure stream" could evince another kind of innovation compounded upon the standard detective expectation of innovation and eccentricity.

Another standard in detective fiction calls for a guiding principle of investigation to which the detective allies himself. Sherlock Holmes provides the prototype for the British ratiocinative detective's approach. His deductive style of reasoning follows the belief that "once you have eliminated the impossible, whatever remains, however improbable, must be true." This philosophy assumes the existence of absolute truth, unlike later postmodern detective fiction: Holmes's inquiry, purely epistemological, bases itself on empirical data, whereas Dirk Gently, the postmodern detective of Adams's novel, has to account for ontological uncertainty (such as ghosts and time travel) and intangible "evidence." Even before the postmodern detective novel's emergence, however, Holmes's philosophy of investigation had been modified or rejected altogether by later heroes of traditional detective fiction. Hercule Poirot, for example, eschews tracking down Holmes's favorite physical clues such as cigarette ashes and footprints in order to obtain the solution. He places faith in his "little gray cells"—his brain—observing people and their reactions, deducing from this psychological data what he needs to know. Wimsey's guiding principle often possesses no more rigidity or structure than "as my Wimsey takes me." Yet, what all of these traditional detectives have in common is a belief that, no matter how bizarre or under what impossible circumstances the crime was committed, one can arrive at the solution by a rational explanation. This idea of "rational" will radically change with the postmodern detective novel.

Another feature these detectives share is the contradiction between each sleuth's outer appearance, demeanor, or method and his inner abilities. "The tendency to disguise the detective has often been great" (Heissenbuttel 89). Bumbling police detectives and arrogant, self-important characters who are complacent in their limited (and often erroneous) knowledge provide an effective foil against which the maligned and misunderstood detective brilliantly reveals his powers. Holmes's theatrical methods and almost catatonic periods of deep thought mislead all but Watson (and Watson's alert and knowing readers). Inspector Jones of Scotland Yard once said condescendingly of Holmes: "He has his own little methods, which are . . . just a little too theoretical and fantastic, but he has the makings of a good detective in him" ("The Red-Headed League" 36).

Hercule Poirot was one fictional detective Heissenbuttel obviously had in mind as a character whose appearance belies his abilities. In *The Murder of Roger Ackroyd*, the first person narrator, a country doctor, meets Poirot as a neighbor—and a very eccentric one, the doctor concludes. In a rage of boredom and frustration over his recent retirement (in which he raises pumpkins), Poirot hurls a vegetable over the wall, narrowly missing the doctor on the other side. The doctor responds to Poirot's apologies: "Before such profuse apologies, my anger was forced to melt. After all, the wretched vegetable hadn't hit me. But I sincerely hoped that throwing large vegetables over walls was not our new friend's hobby. Such a habit could hardly endear him to us as a neighbor" (27). As the scene commences, the doctor, who had been curious about what Poirot's former profession could have been, particularly after Poirot's remark of "my work was interesting work. The most interesting work there is in the world. . . . The study of human nature, monsieur!", concludes to himself: "Clearly a retired hairdresser. Who knows the secrets of human nature better than a hairdresser?" (27).

The character of Lord Peter Wimsey, too, embraces the contradictions between his appearance and his detective work. He is the most self-conscious of the three fictional detectives studied here. *Busman's Honeymoon*, the story of his wedding and honeymoon with Harriet Vane, becomes a murder mystery when they discover a body in the cottage in which they are staying. Wimsey must decide whether or not to "meddle" during his honeymoon and, in one scene, reflects upon his already strange role as detective in the past: "'Murders go to my head like drink. . . . How often am I "called in," I wonder,' he demanded, rather bitterly. 'I call myself in, half the time, out of sheer mischief and inquisitiveness. Lord Peter Wimsey the aristocratic sleuth—my God! The idle rich gentleman who dabbles in detection. That's what they say, isn't it?'" (107). The "reluctant" and self-abnegating detective demonstrates another variation of this "tendency to disguise."

A reliable (often first-person) narrator who will provide all the details as he or she sees them constitutes another important part of the detective story formula. As part of the "game rule" structure, this narrator must in fairness reveal *everything* he knows in order for readers to arrive at a solution on their own; however, the narrator's understanding, hence the reader's, must always be limited to comparison to the detective's. Therefore, from an aficionado's standpoint, a "proper" detective story consists of the detective arriving at the solution before the reader with a greater understanding than the reader could have had. This comprises the function of the detective's chronicler. The Sherlock Holmes stories play a central role in establishing this arrangement as a standard detective fiction formula. Watson as narrator not only provides a reliable though limited view but also reflects the reader's response to the detective's reasoning powers. Watson clearly demonstrates that the difference between befuddlement and understanding depends upon the reticence of the detective, rather than that of the narrator. After an early demonstration of Holmes's powers in "A Scandal in Bohemia," Watson comments: "I could not help laughing at the ease with which he explained his process of deduction. 'When I hear you give your reasons,' I remarked, 'the thing always appears to me to be so ridiculously simple that I could do it myself, though at each successive instance of your reasoning, I am baffled until you explain your process'" (12). When the puzzle goes beyond the mere deductive display detailed above, Holmes does not reveal his analyses *in medias res*. Rather, he keeps Watson and therefore the reader unenlightened until Holmes captures the perpetrator. Meanwhile, Watson and the rest of us do what we are supposed to do: remain confused and in suspense, willing victims of this delaying tactic. Watson describes it as follows: "I was always oppressed with a sense of my own stupidity in my dealings with Sherlock Holmes. Here I had heard what he had heard, I had seen what he had seen, and yet . . . he saw clearly not only what happened, but what was about to happen; while to me, the whole business was still confused and grotesque" ("The Red-Headed League" 35). Here we have a pact with the narrator: We hear "what he had heard" and see "what he had seen," yet we remain in the "confused and grotesque" mode, trying to puzzle it out, trusting in the presence of an absolute truth that is temporarily hidden.

THE READER DEMAND FOR RULE-SUBVERSION

The detective story reader, as aware as the author is of the standard formulas of detective fiction, demands innovation, which ultimately subverts such formulas. Although they still remain within their ontological parameters, these subversions comprise the beginnings of postmodernity and its questioning of both the epistemological and ontological givens in traditional detective fiction. Among these innovations are the private solution, or no solution; the violation of trust by the narrator, who has concealed an important piece of information; and the emotional attachment and regret the detective feels toward the criminal rather than the victim.

The Sherlock Holmes stories provide several examples of subverting the solution. In "A Scandal in Bohemia," Holmes is outwitted by a woman who escapes before Holmes can obtain the object by which his client, the King of Bohemia, had been blackmailed. Watson ends the tale with: "And that was how a great scandal threatened to affect the kingdom of Bohemia and how the best plans of Mr. Sherlock Holmes were beaten by a woman's wit" (25). The solution, then, remained a private, unprosecutable one. Several other Holmes stories also fall into this category. Watson reflects upon his experience with cases of varying degrees of resolution:

Some [cases] have baffled his analytical skill and would be, as narratives, beginnings without an ending, while others have been but partially cleared up, and have their explanations founded rather upon conjecture and surmise than on that absolute logical proof which was so dear to him. There is, however, one of these last which was so remarkable in its details and so startling in its results, that I am tempted to give some account of it, in spite of the fact that there are points in connection with it which never have been, and probably never will be, entirely cleared up. ("The Five Orange Pips" 69)

This "nonsolution" inversion in detective fiction extends the expectation back to the readers to extrapolate the solution and to ally themselves with the detective's unprovable surmises.

A crucial feature that readers of detective fiction have become complacent about has been the narrator as a reliable, though limited, source of information. At least, we *had been* complacent, until Agatha Christie's *The Murder of Roger Ackroyd* startled us—the narrator, we discover at the end of the novel, is the murderer. Readers have argued ever since about whether or not the solution was a fair one. However, the clues are all there for analysis. The narrator, Dr. Sheppard, even boasts of the ingenious way in which he provided the clues without lying to the reader or giving himself away. His final chapter, entitled "Apologia," presents mixed feelings of regret in being discovered by Poirot and triumph in deceiving the reader up to that point:

A strange end to my manuscript. I meant it to be published some day as the history of one of Poirot's failures! Odd, how things pan out. . . . I am rather pleased with myself as a writer. What could be neater, for instance, than the following: "*the letters were brought in at twenty minutes to nine. It was just on ten minutes to nine when I left him, the letter still unread. I hesitated with my hand on the door handle, looking back and wondering if there was anything I had left undone.*"

All true, you see. But suppose I had put a row of stars after the first sentence! Would somebody then have wondered what exactly happened in that blank ten minutes? (253-54)

Yet the narrator, even as the murderer, does not understand the reason for everything that happens: His perception still has its limits. In his "apologia," the murderer says: "all through the case there have been things that puzzled me hopelessly. Every one seems to have taken a hand" (255). This statement echoes Dr. Watson's and the reader's confusion during a criminal investigation, though ironically coming from an individual who should know the most.

Another observation that has been made about the traditional, formulaic detective points to his emotional disengagement from the case and the restriction of his role, namely, that he merely solves puzzles and does not take part in or have an interest in what becomes of the culprit after his capture. Such has been the standard for the ratiocinative detective, yet this rule, too, has been broken. Lord Peter Wimsey, for example, though claiming: "'When I'm investigating a murder, I hate to have too much sympathy with the corpse. Personal feelings cramp the style'" (Sayers 107), neglects to mention his feelings of guilt over discovering the murderer and seeing him sentenced to death. At the end of *Busman's Honeymoon*, Wimsey suffers along with the condemned prisoner; this novel does not end with the mere presentation of the solution. The final scene of the novel details the vigil Wimsey keeps with his wife (and co-sleuth), Harriet Vane, the night before the criminal's execution. Near the end of their vigil: "The light grew stronger as they waited. Quite suddenly, he said, 'Oh damn!' and began to cry—in an awkward, unpracticed way at first, then more easily. So she held him, crouched at her knees, against her breast, huddling his head in her arms that he might not hear eight o'clock strike" (318).

THE POSTMODERN DETECTIVE NOVEL AS SUBVERTER OF "REALITY"

Innovations in detective fiction rely upon the standard rules of the "game" for their effectiveness. The postmodern detective novel goes beyond subverting the traditions of detective fiction, since these formulas are not enough to determine ontological answers (or, simply put, "reality") in a more complex age. However, a postmodern detective novel such as Douglas Adams's *Dirk Gently's Holistic Detective Agency* relies upon the presence of these traditional features in his detective story in order to make us aware, once again, of the "rules" and the consequent reader expectations. These expectations can then be twisted, inverted, and parodied so that when we laugh at our assumptions two inquiries are emphasized: one, the ontological, investigating the nature of the external reality of the story, and two, the epistemological, the "how" of what we have come to accept as the standard means by which we discover answers.

The very title, *Dirk Gently's Holistic Detective Agency*, declares a centrality that is a mirage. Though the novel contains a detective and a central theory, their ontological natures break down any formulaic "system" or "unity" inherent in knowing something in traditional ways. The increasingly meaningless jargon word "holistic" in the title also indicates a parodic, mocking disregard for the empirical style of detection and gives the detective's pursuits a disreputable, "con-artist" air. Dirk Gently proclaims that he does not concern himself with traditional physical clues—"pocket fluff" and "inane footprints," as he calls them. Specifically, Dirk Gently states his guiding principle of investigation as follows:

The term 'holistic' refers to my conviction that what we are concerned with here is the fundamental interconnectedness of all things. I do not concern myself with . . . fingerprint powder, telltale pieces of pocket fluff and inane footprints. I see the solution to each problem as being detectable in the pattern and web of the whole. The connections between causes and effects are often much more subtle and complex than we . . . might naturally suppose. (115)

Among the comic undertones of this passage is the fact that the client to whom he explains his philosophy, a woman with a missing cat, can only base the detective's progress and his rate of payment upon her perception of reality that looks to external manifestations as reference points: the very footprints and "pocket fluff" eschewed by Gently—after all, it worked for Sherlock Holmes, didn't it? Dirk Gently, however, like other detectives before him, will find the nature of the solution determined by the nature of his inquiry: Here, metaphysical answers will stem from a "holistic" search.

Dirk Gently as detective hero shares that traditional trait of eccentricity with his ratiocinative predecessors; even his names are strange, and he changes them from time to time. His real name, by which he was known in his college days, Svlad Cjelli, makes "Dirk Gently" seem less of an assumed name by contrast. We get the impression that the name and the outward appearance are removable, yet somehow "interconnected" (a Dirk Gently word) with the substance of the detective, whose inner identity eludes us. Indeed, in the postmodern detective realm, we cannot be certain if inner substance exists, for surface is all we get: "Svlad Cjelli. Popularly known as Dirk, though, again, 'popular' was hardly right. Notorious, certainly; sought after, endlessly speculated about, those too were true. But popular? Only in the sense that a serious accident on the motorway might be popular—everyone slows down to have a good look, but no one will get too close to the flames" (38). Dirk's unsavory nature points to a motiveless, self-conscious eccentricity, one very different from the eccentricities of modernism's detective heroes.

Postmodernism also transforms the detection process of the story, a process by which the detective novel traditionally had entangled the reader in the confusion of determining the solution, had exhibited the detective's prowess as he begins to make his discoveries, and promised the satisfaction of the solution finally revealed, with its consequent restoration of world order. Specifically, in Adams's novel, the ontological nature of both the puzzles and their solution (for there is *one* "interconnected" solution) transcends the traditional formulaic, rational standard, for the puzzles and solution are metaphysical, supernatural. The means to a solution here require the reader to accept such outrageous elements as a ghost (the murder victim), an alien from another planet who came to our world when humans were still "slimy things with legs" walking out of the sea, a time machine run by the chief representative of absent-minded professors, and a short-circuiting "Electric Monk" and his horse, who came from the aforementioned alien culture, where the inhabitants created electronic devices to "believe" in things for them to save them the trouble. What kind of "rational" philosophy of detection can embrace such elements? Only a guiding principle that contorts the clues of the physical world to account for the metaphysical one. Dirk Gently explains: "'the only thing which prevented me from seeing the solution was the trifling fact that it was *completely impossible*. Sherlock Holmes observed that once you have eliminated the impossible, then whatever remains, however improbable, must be the answer. I, however, do not like to eliminate the impossible'" (181). Again, we have the nature of the detective's pursuit as the factor in determining the nature of the solution, here the postmodern detective's unusual perspective results in an ontological solution. Note, too, the specific inversion of the Holmesian principle, with which the majority of readers would be familiar.

As in other features of this novel, the traditional becomes easily absorbed into the postmodern by either inversion or subversion of its nature. The most traditional mystery of the novel, for example, consists of a good old-fashioned murder. However, the solution to this mystery is revealed to the reader at the time it occurs, though for the detective and the rest of the novel's characters, the murder remains without solution. Why is solving a murder, the central event of countless other detective novels, so unimportant in this one? By way of an answer, let us examine several "rules" that have been violated in the murder; first, we know who commits the murder; second, the detective who is expected to bring the culprit to justice digresses in his pursuit and, instead, follows what at first seem trivial puzzles; and third, the murderer, the "Electric Monk," is a machine and unprosecutable, having committed the crime not out of malice but because of circuitry error. The omniscient narrator reports the Electric Monk's confusion after having committed the deed:

In his [the Monk's] own world when people were shot at like that they came back next week for another episode. . . . He hadn't felt at all comfortable about the way the person he had shot at had just lain there. . . . There was definitely an expression on the person's face which seemed to suggest that something was up, that this didn't fit in with the scheme of things. The Monk worried that he might have badly spoiled his evening. (129)

Lastly, another broken rule lies in the fact that the victim's consciousness continues after his murder, in ghost form, trying to interact with the living world and aid the detective in finding the solution, not of his murder, but of a larger puzzle, the threat of human extinction. This certainly contradicts the static function of the victim traditional to detective fiction: "As a reconstructed character, the corpse has the very least valuable personal position at the end of the exemplum" (Heissenbuttel 84). In the novel, the murder carries significance only because of its "interconnectedness" to the greater threat of human extinction by a hostile alien, an understanding Dirk Gently stumbles onto because of his "holistic" method of detection, tracking down the minor puzzles that indicate the greater mystery. He must search for the correct mystery first before he searches for the solution.

What is purely postmodern about this novel and unborrowed from traditional detective fiction is its narrative style, which is humorous, mocking, and self-conscious. The style enhances our ability to recognize our traditional expectations of the detective and the mystery, laugh at ourselves, and revel in our confusion and this new suspension of expectation. The novel pokes fun at narrative suspense and its traditional overuse. For example, in one gripping scene, the dramatic moment is marked by the following: "Outside, the wind ceased. Owls halted in mid-flight. Well, maybe they did, maybe they didn't, certainly the central heating chose that moment to shut down, unable perhaps to cope with the supernatural chill that suddenly whipped through the room" (91). The novel is replete with such awarenesses—the "it was a dark and stormy night" of parodic undertone: "There was a rumble of thunder, and the onset of that interminable light drizzle . . . by which so many of the world's most momentous events seem to be accompanied" (185). The novel's parodic style also serves to integrate within the reader's awareness of foiled expectations and rules all of its other detective subversions. It also makes us wonder, What game is "afoot" now?

This study grounds itself in certain premises that distinguish postmodernity from modernity, a distinction that not all contemporary critics would support. One can go back and forth about the similar innovations, subversions, and radicalisms the two modes embrace, and the "if only" elusive traits that would make postmodernism consistently definable. The strong presence of narrative humor and a metaphysical solution within the Dirk Gently novel make it "postmodern" rather than "modern."

Even though he may have to pit his abilities against supernatural conditions and more-than-human adversaries, the detective is alive and well in the postmodern age and has so far survived the hybrid of postmodernism and detection. Like that of his predecessors, his epistemological inquiry determines the ontological solution he pursues. The traditional detective novel can subvert expectations and "dupe" the reader within the parameters of its "reality," whereas the postmodern novel turns the rules inside out; readers become aware of their assumptions of reality and laugh at them. From this perspective, not only can the impossible be the answer, but also the nature of knowledge can encompass a broader ontological range of solutions by suspending the limits of what the mind has been taught.

NOTE

1. I have discovered a similar opinion regarding the greater possibility of low fiction's rule subversion in Dennis Porter's *The Pursuit of Crime: Art and Ideology in Detective Fiction*. His chapter entitled "Detection and Digression" argues that the characteristics of Barthes's *texte de plaisir* exist in the detective story's digressions and their delaying effects. Porter says: "In the language of the Formalists, one important source of literary pleasure is in the artful deviation from the norm. In this respect, therefore, a detective novel is not less literary than a major work of the highbrow culture but more so. No other genre is more conscious of the models from which it borrows and from which it knowingly departs" (54).

REFERENCES

Adams, Douglas. *Dirk Gently's Holistic Detective Agency*. New York: Simon and Schuster, 1987.

Christie, Agatha. *The Murder of Roger Ackroyd*. New York: Dodd, Mead and Co., 1926.

Doyle, Arthur Conan. "A Scandal in Bohemia," "The Five Orange Pips," and "The Red-Headed League." In *The Original Illustrated Sherlock Holmes*. Secaucus, NJ: Castle Books, 1981.

Heissenbuttel, Helmut. "Rules of the Game of the Crime Novel." In *The Poetics of Murder: Detective Fiction and Literary Theory*, edited by Glenn W. Most and William W. Stowe. San Diego, CA: Harcourt Brace Jovanovich, 1983.

Holquist, Michael. "Whodunit and Other Questions: Metaphysical Detective Stories in Postwar Fiction." In *The Poetics of Murder: Detective Fiction and Literary Theory*, edited by Glenn W. Most and Willam W. Stowe. San Diego, CA: Harcourt Brace Jovanovich, 1983.

McHale, Brian. *Postmodernist Fiction*. New York: Methuen, 1987.

Penzler, Otto, et al., eds. *Detectionary: A Biographical Dictionary of Leading Characters in Detective and Mystery Fiction*. New York: Overlook Press, 1977.

Porter, Dennis. *The Pursuit of Crime: Art and Ideology in Detective Fiction*. New Haven, CT: Yale University Press, 1981.

Sayers, Dorothy L. *Busman's Honeymoon*. New York: Avon Books, 1937.

Tani, Stefano. *The Doomed Detective: The Contribution of the Detective Novel to Postmodern American and Italian Fiction*. Carbondale: Southern Illinois University Press, 1984.

II

Agatha Christie and British Detective Fiction

For the better part of the twentieth century, Agatha Christie has been perhaps the most popular, and certainly the best-selling, mystery writer in the world. Until the past ten years, little critical attention has been paid to what exactly constitutes her appeal, the nature of her art, and the relationship between the author, her readers, and her literary heirs. In the essays that follow, contemporary critics approach Christie from a variety of perspectives and shed new light on what now we may regard as a complex relationship between the author and her world. Further, this section seeks to explore the contemporary British detective fiction that shares the "classic" structure Christie (and *her* progenitors) developed. It considers too other modern writers who employ techniques and venues similar to Christie's but depart radically from her emphasis on puzzles and solutions in order to explore the insoluble mysteries of the human psyche that earlier detective fiction only faintly implied.

Robert Merrill's detailed, intriguing study of Christie's "games" and "plots" seeks to answer the basic question commonly raised about Christie: whether her work does warrant serious critical attention. Robin Woods's essay examines the fate of Christie's famous detective, Hercule Poirot, in her last novel, *Curtain*, and indicates how the author's resolution of the plot and her detective's fate points to a new kind of crime genre of the mid 1970s—the true-crime novel, featuring motiveless murder with psychopathic villains. In a different vein, Ina Rae Hark suggests that Christie's texts are far more sophisticated than readers have generally perceived them, that, indeed, there were always present the deeper psychological strata so pervasive in detective fiction today. For Christie, Hark indicates, no such creature as a person incapable of murder exists, a pervasive theme, as she points out, in the films of Alfred Hitchcock. In a historical-cultural approach to Christie's popularity, Mary Anne Ackershoek explores the social change in England after World War I, particularly as it affected women's lives. She finds in Christie's novels an example of the shift from a male-author-dominated genre to one where women writers expressed new attitudes toward British society, and particularly toward the role of traditional authority figures. Rather than viewing Christie as upholding British upper-class attitudes, Ackershoek sees in her novels the country manors collapsing and concludes that the theme that resonates through her novels is that of the rotting society.

Moving from Christie to her most prominent successor, P. D. James, Carolyn F. Scott finds in John Webster's play, *The Duchess of Malfi*, essential elements in the plot of James's *The Skull beneath the Skin* as well as contributions to the framework of that narrative. Further, she concludes, the Webster play achieves a new resolution itself in the conclusion of James's work. Marnie Jones and Barbara Barker offer a detailed commentary on the world and work of James's prime detective, Adam Dalgleish, who is caught up in the "filthy trade" of crime detection, a profession they believe James suggests is not suitable for anyone.

James's most popular contemporary mystery writer, Ruth Rendell, uses the crime, or the mystery, as an excuse to probe the deepest and darkest secrets hidden in the twisted psyches of her protagonists. Martha Stoddard Holmes focuses on an approach to Rendell through gender, analyzing Rendell's Inspector Wexford novels, which feature as objects of investigation a "host of terrifying women." His investigations of their relations to crimes reveal his own attitudes toward gender as well as his notions about his own masculinity.

In another contemporary critical approach to British detective fiction, Iska S. Alter probes the intersections of presumably fixed categories of class, gender, and sexuality that provoke the very crimes that those fixed categories would seem to preclude. Her subject is Anne Perry's Victorian world, and she offers insight not only into Perry's fictions but also into the buried, suppressed life hidden by an ironic world of masks.

Jasmine Y. Hall offers a key to the two unrelated conclusions of one of the most revered British detective novels, Dorothy Sayers's *Gaudy Nights*, in an illuminating discussion of the ideology underlying the vocation of the detective, Lord Peter Wimsey. In her discussion, she demonstrates that Sayers grafts the genre of the heart (the love story) onto the genre of the mind (the detective story). In the final essay in this section, we move from genre and genre approaches to a cultural-historical study of the middle class of detective fiction: James E. Bartell's thesis is that the hero of detective fiction is an "idealized bureaucrat who speaks directly and deeply to the needs of readers who themselves function as bureaucrats in their jobs or some other aspect of their lives." He goes on to define bureaucracy and its relation to the values of British detective fiction. Bartell's paper takes a wide-ranging view of detective fiction (including Christie's) and its relation to the development of Western bureaucracy as expressed in novels dating from Defoe. Thus, this section concludes by placing in the broadest possible framework the popular phenomenon we have embraced as British detective fiction.

8

Christie's Narrative Games

Robert Merrill

Agatha Christie continues to appeal to us because she devised intellectual challenges or games of unusual, even unparalled ingenuity. This remark may seem a virtual commonplace, but it often seems contradicted by critical writing on detective fiction in general and on Christie in particular. General studies tend to emphasize the ideological element in crime fiction (as in books by Dennis Porter and Stephen Knight) or its sociological insights (as in John Cawelti's discussion of classic detective fiction). Book-length studies of Christie acknowledge her skill as a maker of puzzles but spend very few pages on the subject, preferring instead to stress Christie's characterizations: Maida and Spornick devote seventeen pages to what they call "The Puzzle-Game" (68-84) eighty-five pages to Christie's various detectives (85-170); Bargainnier's chapter on Christie's plots covers twenty-three pages (144-66), whereas his chapter on her characters runs to 106 pages (38-143); and even Gillian Gill, who offers the best commentary on Christie's narrative strategies, intersperses her remarks on plot throughout a narrative largely devoted to biographical matters. Thus, we have what seems to me the central irony about Christie's reputation: Everyone knows that her distinction lies in her clever plots, but no one bothers to say much about them. To explain a Christie plot is apparently equivalent to explaining a joke—not so hard to do, perhaps, but somewhat in poor taste.[1]

My own view is that no other approach will tell us much about Christie's distinction as a detective writer. Our supreme puzzlemaker, Christie succeeds as a maker of engaging plots or does not succeed at all. I adopt the plural form in "games" and "plots" because I think Christie excels in offering successful variations on the classic formula defined by Cawelti and others. Like her peers, Christie introduces her detective, provides a crime and clues, details an investigation, permits her detective to announce his or her solution and to explain how it was arrived at, and concludes with a denouement consistent with the comic structure and assumptions of her chosen form.[2] Within this extremely conventional pattern, however, Christie manages to play any number of fascinating narrative games, as I hope to illustrate by discussing several of Christie's more representative plots. This analysis should allow me to distinguish between the narrative patterns that inform the Hercule Poirot and Miss Marple novels, respectively. And it should allow me to conclude by reviewing one of the oldest and perhaps most basic questions about Christie: whether her work really warrants serious critical attention.

REPRESENTATIVE PLOTS

My first examples, *Death on the Nile* (1937) and *Evil under the Sun* (1941), might seem to illustrate Christie's *lack* of originality, for these two Hercule Poirot novels share what appears to be a very similar, if not identical, plot.[3] In each case the murder victim is a wealthy woman who appears to have taken a handsome young man from his fiancée or wife, though in reality the supposedly estranged couple are plotting this woman's death for financial reasons. In each novel we first observe the couple's efforts to convince the vacationing Poirot that they're indeed estranged. After this fairly elaborate introduction (elaborate by Christie's standards), each novel proceeds to describe a murder for which the estranged couple have what appear to be perfect alibis. At this point in each book Poirot begins to investigate the crime, for which something like a dozen suspects seem plausible solutions. In each case the interrogation turns on opportunity even more than on motive, for it is Poirot's task to explain when and how each murder was committed, as well as by whom and why. In each case, of course, Poirot discovers that the estranged couple are not estranged at all and that the crime was fiendishly premeditated (as Poirot's rather dull companions, Hastings and Race, might put it). In each book Poirot punctures the couple's imperfect alibis and effectively exonerates the other suspects.

Those who have not read these two books but have seen the lavish films based on them (*Death on the Nile*, 1978; *Evil under the Sun*, 1982) will be especially struck by their similarities, for the two films share a plot structure extremely popular with television productions such as *Murder, She Wrote*, innumerable detective novelists throughout the century, and the Christie of such books as *Evil under the Sun*. In this structure nearly every character introduced is a plausible suspect with an equally reasonable motive and opportunity to commit the crime. There are twelve such characters in *Evil under the Sun*, conveniently grouped as the "cast of characters" at the beginning of the book. (I might add that Christie favors this number of suspects—large enough for the desired complexity, not too large to be recalled by an alert reader.) Most of the suspects get about equal attention and space, thus reinforcing the notion that they are equally likely to be guilty. Unlike her film adapters, Christie does not provide a plausible motive for *every* character, but she does develop a good many such motives and makes sure that Poirot gives them roughly equal consideration. In books of this kind Poirot becomes an equal opportunity detective who really believes that *anyone* might commit murder, the jaundiced view of human nature he shares with Jane Marple. The solution to such mysteries often seems somewhat arbitrary, for any number of alternative solutions might have been substituted without changing the work's essential structure.

The narrative game just described has advantages and disadvantages that are closely related. Each character is of interest to us, for each is a genuine suspect. No one can be very fully developed, however, for the very nature of the game requires that Christie spread her attention about equally among her relatively large cast. The ultimate solution is almost always surprising, but it also seems to arise from only a few of the details generated by the detective's investigation. Indeed, most of what we learn in the course of this investigation concerns the now discarded alternative solutions, or red herrings. The resulting sense of superficiality is almost a narrative necessity in a book like *Evil under the Sun*, for the murderers' ploy is not sufficiently clever to withstand much narrative attention. If we were encouraged to review the actions of Patrick and Christine Redfern more closely than those of the other suspects, we would be all too likely to guess how Patrick might have killed his wealthy lover *after* he supposedly found her dead body—and once this idea occurs to us, the game is over. So, Christie provides very few details about the Redferns even though they are two-thirds of the love triangle apparently at the heart of the novel's primary action, and she is especially careful to give no hint as to *why* the Redferns might profit from Arlena Marshall's death. Such tactics of concealment permit a certain kind of narrative game to continue until the novel's final pages, where we learn almost everything of relevance about our killers as well as about the crime Poirot has undertaken to solve. For some readers, the element of surprise is sufficient to carry the day; for others, the arbitrariness of the solution will seem a relatively unsatisfactory climax.

Critics of detective fiction often discuss their subject as if the pattern just described were inevitable—recall Auden's famous essay, "The Guilty Vicarage," or Frye's memorable description of the finger of guilt moving from suspect to suspect until it falls on the true culprit. Many of Christie's best novels employ very different patterns, however, even if these books seem extremely similar otherwise. *Death on the Nile* is an excellent example. Though this famous whodunit develops the same dramatic situation Christie would later employ in *Evil under the Sun*, Christie's game here is radically different from that played in the later book.

Death on the Nile belies the claim advanced by Cawelti and others that Christie favors the so-called least likely person in resolving her mysteries. This claim does not fit works such as *Evil under the Sun*, either, for the Redferns are not obscure figures but simply undistinguished from the other characters. In *Death on the Nile*, however, Cawelti's claim is all but refuted, for the estranged couple—Jacqueline de Bellefort and Simon Doyle—are the most likely suspects, the ones with the most to gain. Moreover, Christie handles the situation so as to all but assure the experienced reader of detective fiction that Jackie and Simon are not only the most likely suspects but also the actual killers. Her game here is one in which the reader is led to anticipate the final solution but still cannot figure out how the "obvious" murderers managed to achieve their unsavory end. Christie wins this game by allowing us to see very early that Jackie and Simon are the all but certain answers to whodunit, for this accentuates our frustration (and surprise) at being unable to figure out just *how* they did it.

Christie is fond of implicating the most likely suspect, in fact, as she acknowledges in her autobiography.[4] She takes great delight in seeming to exonerate the "obvious" candidate by means of an apparently unshakable alibi, then revealing this person to be the guilty party after all. (Often, of course, the "person" is actually a couple, always a man and a woman. By Bargainnier's count, Christie develops this dramatic situation no fewer than nineteen times in her novels [Bargainnier 122]). A good example of the most-likely-suspect ploy is one of her most famous novels, *Ten Little Indians* (1939) (also known as *And Then There Were None*). Here, ten people are enticed to a remote island in order to be executed for crimes they committed in the past without punishment. It soon becomes apparent that one of the ten is the executioner, and for most of the novel the reader surely suspects the retired judge, Justice Wargrave, who is known to have been a hanging judge and who seems the one person on the island of sufficient intelligence to plan the very complicated series of executions. But then Wargrave himself is apparently killed, and so the reader must look elsewhere for a solution that does not seem possible. Christie lifts the reader's all but certain confusion, even bewilderment, only with the final chapter, in which she prints Wargrave's confession. Christie's victory, if I may call it that, comes in forcing us to entertain unlikely solutions we cannot dismiss even though we cannot believe in them. After all, we know by the rules of the game that *someone* must be guilty. Near the end of this novel, however, all ten suspects seem to be exonerated by nothing less than death itself.

In *Death on the Nile*, by contrast, the likely suspects are never really exonerated. Jackie and Simon are far too prominent throughout to be ignored at the end (for contrary to Cawelti's casual remarks, Christie seldom takes her primary murderer from the dramatic periphery); and when they turn up with wonderful alibis in the middle of the book, Christie is all but announcing they will ultimately be exposed as the murderers. Indeed, Christie's focus on this couple, especially Jackie de Bellefort, is nearly unprecedented among the Poirot novels. The jilted lover of Simon Doyle and the betrayed best friend of Linnet Ridgeway Doyle, Jackie is one of Christie's most fully developed and sympathetic characters. Christie repeatedly brings her together with Poirot, who cautions her not to open her heart to evil[5] and observes her apparent despair with the greatest concern (110-11). The all but complete narrative focus on this love triangle for 120 pages, one of the longest buildups to murder in all of

Christie, virtually assures us that Jackie and Simon will eventually prove to be central to the final solution. When Linnet is murdered precisely as Jackie imagined killing her (64, 128), we should take the event as a virtual confession.

In fact, however, we have 150 pages to go—an elaborate investigation in almost any form of detective fiction. As I have suggested, Christie's game here is directed at the experienced reader, who can hardly doubt that Jackie and Simon are guilty. I remember all too well reading and rereading the relevant scene in which, somehow, the lovers manage to murder Linnet (116-27), and I especially recall my annoyance at being unable to penetrate the "obvious" deception and guess the method they employed. I also remember my embarrassment at being given another 120 pages to review the evidence and failing to know anything more at the end than I knew at midpoint. Christie seems to pursue this embarrassment with some zeal for she has Poirot repeatedly summarize the evidence in order to highlight the relevant clues, all of which *must* somehow point back to Jackie and Simon but don't seem to do so (see especially 216, 242-43). Indeed, Christie plays with us throughout, as when she allows Colonel Race to offer a list of no fewer than fourteen suspects—none of whom is Jackie or Simon (177)—or when she develops the other suspects so carelessly or perfunctorily no serious reader can entertain them for a moment (one so-called suspect, a man named Fleetwood, enters the book at page 149, while more plausible candidates such as Pennington are effectively exposed well before the murder is even committed). Further, she allows her murderers practically to announce their conspiracy by having the rather dull Simon employ Jackie's metaphor of the sun eclipsing the moon to describe what Linnet has done to Jackie—a figure he obviously got from Jackie herself, despite their supposed estrangement (61-62, 67). This whole structure depends, of course, on the unusual ingenuity of the crime, which must withstand 150 pages of scrutiny. This structure permits Christie to have her cake and eat it too, for she works out her remarkably deceptive puzzle while continuing to focus on the most important characters of the novel's early chapters. This attention to Jackie and Simon allows Christie's conclusion to seem dramatically as well as intellectually satisfying, for the resolution involves characters and dramatic situations we have followed from the novel's first pages. *Death on the Nile* has many weaknesses, but it is perhaps Christie's finest example of a novel that combines the essential features of drama with those of a narrative puzzle. The narrative game played here seems to me one of Christie's most sophisticated gambits, ultimately nothing like the game she plays in *Evil under the Sun*.

Evil under the Sun, *Death on the Nile*, and *Ten Little Indians* offer specific examples of Christie's versatility as a puzzlemaker. I believe that another ten to fifteen works can be adduced as successful variations on the conventional formula with which Christie is identified. These books fall along a narrative spectrum largely determined by the likeliness of the novel's murderer. At one end of the spectrum are those books in which the murderer is indeed the least likely suspect, not because he or she is an unnoticed servant or a distant relative but because he or she appears to be the intended victim or is a member of the investigating team. At midpoint on this spectrum are books such as *Evil under the Sun*, in which most of the characters are at least plausible solutions to the puzzle. At the other end of the spectrum is *Death on the Nile*, the most extreme instance of a book in which Christie focuses on and finally incriminates the most likely suspect(s). Books such as *Ten Little Indians* fall between *Evil under the Sun* and *Death on the Nile*, though closer to the latter than to the former. To place Christie's works along this spectrum allows us to identify the more crucial details of her plots and to highlight the strategies that inform her more interesting books.

Critics as diverse as Dennis Porter, George Grella, and Dorothy Sayers agree that "the Least Likely Person ploy," as Maida and Spornick call it (Maida and Spornick 40), is the standard device in classic detective fiction (Porter 137; Grella 86; Sayers 82). Indeed, Sayers refers to this ploy as already old hat in 1928, at least in the form in which the guilty party is simply ignored until the conclusion (Sayers 106). Christie herself has her fictional counterpart, Ariadne Oliver, exclaim, "It's always the least likely person who did it" (*Cards on the Table* 145), and Christie's critics have tended to see her use of this tactic as "notorious" (Bargainnier 123) and as nothing less than her "trademark" (Maida and Spornick 40). In truth, however, Christie almost never employs this device unless the killer appears to be the intended victim (as in *Peril at End House* [1932], *An Overdose of Death* [1936], *A Murder Is Announced* [1950], and *The Mirror Crack'd* [1962]) or figures among the investigators (as in *The Murder of Roger Ackroyd* [1926], *The ABC Murders* [1936], and *Hercule Poirot's Christmas* [1938]). In these rather special cases, the murderer is not so much the least likely suspect as never suspected at all,[6] so it is misleading to say, with Cawelti, that in such books "the guilt [is] finally projected onto someone on the edge or outside the magic circle" (Cawelti 77), someone who is "marginal" to the book and its central society (Cawelti 93). For such formulations imply that Christie typically settles for a peripheral, "marginal" figure whose guilt conveniently allows the main characters and their comfortable social order to emerge unscathed and, if anything, reaffirmed. Gillian Gill rightly objects that Christie "never keeps her readers in suspense for 200 pages only to cop out at the end by pinning the crime on a person whose motivation has been wholly obscure" (Gill 136), though novels like *Peril at End House* do fight very hard to keep us from looking at the murderer as a *suspect* and thus as someone whose motivation is as dark as it is more or less available. One should never say never, however, and the occasional novel in which Christie does settle for the marginal outsider whose motivation is obscure is the exception that proves the rule. In *Dead Man's Mirror* (1936), for example, Miss Lingard is the most inconspicuous and least likely suspect among the eight people interviewed by Poirot, and her uncovering is one of Christie's least effective conclusions.[7] Novels like *The Murder of Roger Ackroyd* and *Peril at End House* are of course much more famous and more satisfying, but I think it is fair to note the element of the arbitrary that clings to these unusual and far from "typical" Christie texts.

Far more common are the books that lodge near the center of Christie's spectrum, books in which the murderer is but one (or two) of many plausible suspects. For this kind of book Gill's comment is altogether just, for Christie virtually never forbids us access to the motive and clues by which her detective (usually Poirot) discovers the guilty party among ten or so genuinely possible solutions. Well over half of Christie's detective novels fall close to the center of her spectrum, but it is worth remarking that, so far as I can tell, only one book falls absolutely at dead center. Only once, in *Cards on the Table* (1936), does Christie play a version of her game in which all the suspects are equally plausible. In books like *Evil under the Sun* it is all but inevitable that some suspects are slightly more likely than others, either because of their closer connections to the victim, the nature of their motive or opportunity to commit the crime, or the narrative attention devoted to them either before the murder or during the investigation. In *Cards on the Table* all suspects get virtually equal treatment in what Christie notes in her introduction is a narrative experiment. Surely, it is no accident that the book has only four suspects (the lowest number in any Christie novel), for perfectly equal treatment for a dozen suspects would give Christie's novels an absolute symmetry and totally artificial character only someone like Poirot could appreciate.

As Christie noted, her fondness for whodunits in which "somebody obvious" is finally proven guilty (after apparently being exonerated) (*Autobiography* 242), it should not surprise us that a number of her best novels fall at the "most obvious" end of her narrative spectrum. If *Ten Little Indians* and *Death on the Nile* are famous examples, *Lord Edgware Dies* (1934) and *The Hollow* (1946) are additional instances drawn from the Poirot canon. (Indeed, *The Hollow* is one of Christie's most interesting books, as I shall briefly argue in my conclusion). Among the Miss Marple novels almost any book might be cited, as Bargainnier notes (Bargainnier 74), but *The Murder at the Vicarage* (1930), *The Body in the Library* (1942), and *The Mirror Crack'd* amply confirm Miss Marple's own opinion that "it is always the *obvious* person who has done the crime" (*The Mirror Crack'd* 179). In all these novels, but especially *Death on the Nile* and *The Hollow*, Christie must practice a conspicuous art to achieve a surprising effect when her culprit is "the obvious answer," as Poirot remarks of *The Hollow's* Gerda Christow a full hundred pages before he reveals that she is, indeed, guilty (*The Hollow* 153). The key is to exonerate the murderer convincingly (as in *Ten Little Indians*) to merge the most likely suspect with others almost as plausible (as in *The Body in the Library*), or to all but flaunt the most likely solution while continuing to mystify us as to the means by which the crime was committed (as in *Death on the Nile*). More extended study of Christie's games might well focus on this end of her narrative spectrum, for no one has written this kind of detective novel quite so well.

HERCULE POIROT AND MISS MARPLE

A complete analysis of Christie's narrative games would proceed to place all her detective novels along the spectrum I have posited. I would like to pursue a more realistic goal, that of summarizing two broad narrative patterns typical of the thirty-three Poirot novels and the twelve Miss Marple novels, respectively. The games played in the two series are as different as the two detectives themselves, and even a brief review should point up the attractive diversity of Christie's narratives.

The Poirot novels range from 1920 to 1975, but the many texts invariably share a number of features designed to set off their little Belgian detective. Poirot is almost always introduced early, usually with the task of solving a murder committed within the first one hundred pages. (In this respect *Death on the Nile* is atypical, for the first murder occurs after more than 120 pages of preparation. Though it follows much the same pattern, *Evil under the Sun* provides fewer details and arrives at the murder after sixty-five pages. Indeed, the one hundred pages typically employed allow for great variation, from novels in which Poirot is summoned to a body almost at once to novels in which there is "a considerable lead-up to the murder," as Robert Barnard puts it [Barnard, 101]). Poirot's subsequent investigation takes up most of the novel. With the aid of his Watson-like companion (often Hastings, but sometimes a policeman), Poirot investigates the many suspects, discusses the more important clues, ponders alternative scenarios, and in general uncovers and then analyzes the relevant information. Though he never provides a *complete* analysis (until the end, of course), Poirot does identify and sift through virtually all relevant clues. The supreme rationalist (even more so than Holmes), Poirot pursues his solution relentlessly, and the same can be said of the novels in which he appears. Poirot's problem is always complicated, what with his need to assimilate a dozen suspects and the numerous clues they generate into his resolution of the affair. The narrative game is one in which we are invited to follow Poirot through each step of this process. Lest we overlook significant clues, Christie offers Poirot's periodical recapitulations of the more important details to be brought together in the solution. This game stresses ingenuity, for everything is on the table, so to speak, and must therefore be sufficiently complex to defy the clever reader's best efforts to anticipate Poirot's analysis.

Christie's critics have tended to dismiss the idea that her readers actually try to best Poirot at his own game,[8] but the format of the Poirot novels all but requires us to play the same game as Poirot, even if we almost never "win." Indeed, to win would be to lose, for to unravel the crime before Poirot would expose the plot's inadequate ingenuity. Nonetheless, the reader must make such an effort simply to follow the narrative thread, which traces Poirot's efforts to put the case together from the right angle; inevitably, then, the reader ends up playing Poirot's game. Christie acknowledges the pattern to which I point when she says that she "ruined" *The Hollow* by introducing Poirot (*Autobiography*

458). *The Hollow* includes psychological studies that are independent of and perhaps in competition with the problem-solving spirit of the Poirot game, as we might call it. Excellent as it is, *The Hollow* fails to develop fully its psychological insights because it must also attend to Poirot's investigation, and the latter is less fully developed than in many other Poirot novels because the focus is not exclusively on Poirot's evolving theories concerning the murder. Unlike *The Hollow*, then, most of the Poirot novels highlight Poirot's step-by-step analysis of the investigation. I would add that the Poirot novels require that Christie play as fair as possible with the clues; after all, the informing pattern emphasizes the availability of all relevant data. This is why readers of *Death on the Nile* rightly moan when Poirot first mentions the incriminating contents of Linnet Doyle's nail polish and the discovery of a third bullet during his final explanation of the crime (259-60, 266). These late additions to the evidence are not in the essential spirit of the game played whenever Poirot is our detective.

The Jane Marple novels develop a very different kind of game. Unlike Poirot, Miss Marple is almost never the primary investigator. The most extreme example is *The Moving Finger* (1942), in which Miss Marple does not appear until page 142 of a 198-page novel and then figures in only eleven pages before the ten-page conclusion in which she explains her solution. Elsewhere, as in *The Murder at the Vicarage*, *The Mirror Crack'd*, and *At Bertram's Hotel* (1965), Miss Marple is introduced early but then appears intermittently through the rest of the book as we primarily follow the stages of the police investigation. In books like *A Murder Is Announced* and *A Pocket Full of Rye* (1953), Miss Marple first appears after some eighty pages devoted to the murder and the principal suspects. In the rather typical case of *A Pocket Full of Rye*, this means that Miss Marple arrives on the scene fully halfway through the book. As the murder occurs almost on the first page, Miss Marple also arrives halfway through the official investigation, conducted here by Inspector Neele. In the novel's later sections, we are privy to a few of Miss Marple's conversations with the other characters, but her inquiries are often summarized, and the dramatized conversations hardly seem like interrogations. The official investigation is more thorough, or apparently so, and does produce information useful to us and, later, to Miss Marple herself. We know, however, that the inspector's inferences are almost certain to be imperfect, and we do not know what line of approach Miss Marple is pursuing in her apparently random fashion. The game is therefore very un-Poirotish. The relevant clues are only sometimes before us, the alternative scenarios are produced only at the end, when Inspector Neele and Miss Marple finally exchange views, and the lines of inquiry actively pursued by the police can be assumed to be inaccurate. (Thus, Neele's suspicions about Mary Dove virtually assure us that she is not the murderer, and Neele's preference for Percival as opposed to Lance Fortescue points to Lance as the more likely suspect). The trick is to figure out, or intuit, the direction in which Miss Marple is headed. There are fewer suspects and clues, as indeed there must be, given our distance from the crucial evidence, but arriving at Miss Marple's solutions is still much more difficult than arriving at Poirot's.

The Miss Marple books are, in fact, almost impossible to "solve," for the game played stresses mystification rather than deduction. Caroline Sheppard, Miss Marple's prototype, is said to solve her problems by "inspired guesswork" (*The Murder of Roger Ackroyd* 15), and the same might be said of Miss Marple. The most extreme instance is *What Mrs. McGillicuddy Saw!* (1957), in which, as Barnard points out, "Miss Marple apparently solves the crime by divine guidance, for there is very little in the way of clues or logical deduction" (Barnard 193). In truth, however, the Miss Marple novels never emulate the pattern of the Poirot novels, a pattern Barnard deftly defines as "progressive mystification and progressive enlightenment" (Barnard 115), for there is little "enlightenment" to balance the rather dense "mystification" until the end, where we usually are reminded "how much Miss Marple knew all along and never told anyone" (Hart 78). At the end, of course, the mysterious Miss Marple clarifies everything in the manner of a spinsterish Sherlock Holmes and by means almost as unfair to the attentive reader as Doyle's.

These last remarks will seem very harsh to those who love Miss Marple and the novels in which she appears. For many readers, the Miss Marple novels are Christie's best, focusing as they do on a smaller, more fully developed cast of characters and relying on fewer plot turns of an ingenious but improbable nature. For such readers, it is to Christie's credit that she does not have Miss Marple constantly recapitulate the crucial clues and possible solutions; when she does resort to this tactic (briefly, in *A Murder Is Announced* 227), the echo of the Poirot novels may simply seem intrusive. Readers who prefer Miss Marple to Poirot are perhaps a bit like Caroline Sheppard, who wants to know many things about Poirot: "where he comes from, what he does, whether he is married, what his wife was, or is, like, whether he has children, what his mother's maiden name was—and so on" (*The Murder of Roger Ackroyd* 25). The Poirot novels are structured to frustrate Caroline's desires, of course; and while we also learn little about Miss Marple's history, we come to *know* her tastes and character in ways that satisfy this most basic readerly instinct. The Miss Marple novels are punctuated with fine moments in which the heroine's endearing character is crucial to our experience of the book if not to the solution to the crime. My own favorite comes on the last page of *A Pocket Full of Rye*. Here Miss Marple's hypothesis concerning Lance Fortescue's deception of Gladys Martin is confirmed by a photograph Gladys sends Miss Marple through the mail. Miss Marple first feels pity for Gladys and then anger at Lance's heartlessness; then, "displacing both these emotions, there came a surge of triumph—the triumph some specialist might feel who has successfully reconstructed an extinct animal from a fragment of jawbone and a couple of teeth" (*A Pocket Full of Rye* 186). This wonderful moment captures Miss Marple's essential pride and toughness, even as it testifies to the range of human responses we find in her and not in Poirot. Readers alert to such moments will perhaps not care so much that the narrative games played in the Miss Marple novels are less interesting than those in the best of the Poirot novels; indeed, they may feel that my judgment simply expresses one reader's (one gamesplayer's) taste for a certain kind of intellectual competition.[9] In any case, the differences between the Poirot and the Miss Marple novels confirm Christie's ability to fashion complex and markedly different variations within the classic detective novel.

CHRISTIE AS A WRITER

Ironically enough, no one has spoken more eloquently about the limitations of detective fiction than Dorothy Sayers, one of the form's ablest practitioners. Throughout her omnibus review of detective fiction, Sayers notes the inherent restrictions imposed by the form and concludes that no "serious" work can be done within its boundaries: "For, make no mistake about it, the detective story is part of the literature of escape, and not of expression" (Sayers 109). Like the form's most vehement advocates and detractors, Sayers believes that in detective fiction "the primary interest is in the process of solution" (Bargainnier 8)—and how can we take seriously a form that resolutely pursues the ends of a cross-word puzzle?

Insofar as this question is asked of fiction like Christie's (as opposed to Chandler's, say, or Le Carré's), it is perhaps unanswerable. Indeed, we do *not* take it seriously, or very few of us do. The number of readers who stand Christie next to their favorite "serious" authors must be a tiny fraction of her legendary readership. Christie offers a complicated but extremely artificial form of diversion (thus my notion of an intellectual challenge or game). Some people like bridge, and some do not. It is hardly a matter of being right or wrong; either one plays the game and enjoys it or one does not. As someone who both chooses to play and enjoys Christie's game(s), I think it is useful to understand why we are taken with fictions like Christie's. Christie's claims on us are not those of a major novelist, but this does not alter the fact that she did what she did as well as anyone has ever done.

We might conclude by asking why Christie is superior to her classic competitors. Gill amusingly cites the explanations of others: that Christie is "not too intellectual, not too biased, not too complicated, not too descriptive, not too long, not too ambitious, not too theoretical, not too feminine, not too topical, etc." (Gill 227). I think that Gill dismisses these "explanations" a bit abruptly, for there is *some* truth to the claim that Christie does not make uncomfortable demands on us and so keeps us coming back for book after book in her particular vein. But, of course, there must also be some positive reason for Christie's phenomenal success. In my own discussion I have tried to substantiate the obvious: Christie's uncanny grasp of the plot variations available within the conventional detective format. I would add that at her best Christie manages to include serious fictional *elements* within her artificial constructs. Though several of Christie's better-known works are famous (or infamous) for their bizarre conclusions (in particular, *The Murder of Roger Ackroyd* and *Murder on the Orient Express* [1934]), Christie's better works often depend on relatively serious literary techniques for their unique effects.

Here I can only point to several major examples. I have already noted that in *Death on the Nile* it is essential to Christie's narrative strategy that she develop Jackie de Bellefort as an interesting, sympathetic character (and killer). In *Evil under the Sun*, on the other hand, Christie has Christine Redfern play much the same role as inconspicuously as possible, for she cannot afford to give either Patrick or Christine Redfern much "exposure" within the game she plays in this novel. *Death on the Nile* is a happy example of a book in which Christie does much more with her murderer than detective novelists typically manage to do, in large part because the narrative structure itself requires that we come to care a good deal (if not deeply) for the murderer.

The Hollow and *Ten Little Indians* also illustrate Christie's use of techniques we usually identify with serious fiction. In each case, Christie again devises a detective plot in which she is required to do interesting things with character or (in *Ten Little Indians*) the image of human nature projected by the novel as a whole. As I remarked earlier, *The Hollow* is one of Christie's most interesting books from a psychological point of view, including as it does a number of character studies far more extensive and compelling than we usually find in classic detective fiction. One such study is the murderer herself, Gerda Christow. We do not come to know Gerda as intimately as we come to know her husband, John Christow, or John's mistress, Henrietta Savernake, for the Poirot game cannot be stretched so far as to permit access to the murderer's thoughts after she commits the crime. We do enter Gerda's mind early in the book, however, and with striking effects. For example, Gerda's much-remarked stupidity is apparently confirmed in the early sections narrated from her point of view (*The Hollow* 31-33, 41-44, 49, 61-62, 67), and Gerda's obviously sincere adulation for her husband cleverly diverts suspicion when she is later discovered standing over John's dead body. Gerda's sections fit naturally into a book in which much of the narrative is told not from Poirot's perspective but from the points of view of the suspects. These early sections help Christie flesh out a very interesting whodunit in which the killer is a relatively average, uncalculating woman, not the obsessive mastermind whose convoluted plans dominate most such works. Read in retrospect, these sections also confirm Gerda's own later opinion about herself ("I'm not quite so stupid as everyone thinks" [*The Hollow* 243]), thus permitting Christie to reverse the logic by which Gerda, "the obvious answer," is dismissed as a suspect because she is too dense to contrive a murder scheme.

In *Ten Little Indians* Christie also tells her story from the points of view of the ten suspects, for there is no detective throughout the body of the book. Here we learn relatively little about each character, and no one is developed as thoroughly as, say, Henrietta Savernake. What we do learn is extremely relevant to the detective puzzle, however, as well as to the vision of life embodied in the book. In his confession, Justice Wargrave notes that he alone among the ten people brought to Indian Island is not guilty of an earlier murder for which he was not punished (*Ten Little Indians*, 182). This perceptive comment points back to one of the most interesting discoveries we make in reading the several sections narrated by the suspects: Each of them *is* guilty of some form of murder. This discovery makes us suspicious of each character in turn, but Wargrave is right to suggest that it should in fact clear the character in question in the present crisis. This striking revelation about each suspect also contributes to the book's extremely unsentimental character. Here, for once, Christie deals with an unpleasant bunch of people who do not turn out to be anything but the hypocrites and actual killers Wargrave takes them to be. (I refer to Christie's novel, of course, not the dramatic and film versions. Alas, Christie herself revised the stage version to exonerate two of the ten characters, conveniently enough a young man and a young woman who could then participate in a kind of happy ending. It should surprise no one that all three film versions have retained the revised and not the original plot.) *Ten Little Indians* is thus one of Christie's coldest, most precise studies in human venality, unredeemed by the detective's saving competence (indeed, the crime would never have been solved if Wargrave's pride had not driven him to write up an explanation of how he fooled everyone). Among classic detective novels, this book seems to me to stand as one study in scarlet that serious readers and not just detective addicts can reread with pleasure.

I am tempted to end by noting that a final reason to study Christie is to appreciate the ways in which her successors—Chandler and Le Carré, but also Hammett, Macdonald, and many contemporary novelists—adapt the form she perfected to more serious literary uses. Such study is certain to be rewarding, for the writers in question do not so much transcend as revise the conventions we associate with Agatha Christie. I am reluctant to end by deflecting interest from Christie to those who followed her, however, for I continue to think that Christie's work is rich enough to reward even more detailed critical analysis than the one offered here. To engage in such study is to risk being called an addict or fan, but I suspect that Christie's academic readers are more than willing to live with such labels.

NOTES

My thanks to Randall Reid, Susan Baker, and Dotty Merrill for reading versions of this paper.

1. The major exception to my generalization is Robert Barnard, whose *A Talent to Deceive: An Appreciation of Agatha Christie* (1980) is littered with shrewd comments about Christie's strategies.

2. I am summarizing Cawelti's presentation of the classic formula; see Cawelti, 82.

3. This resemblance is noted by others, especially Barnard, who refers to their "virtually identical plots" (Barnard 67).

4. Christie's actual words are as follows: "The whole point of a *good* detective story was that it must be somebody obvious but at the same time, for some reason, you would then find that it was *not* obvious, that he could not possibly have done it. Though really, of course, he *had* done it" (*Autobiography* 242).

5. See *Death on the Nile* 63. Unless otherwise noted, future page references are to this edition.

6. Barnard astutely remarks that "the ones never suspected" is a better formulation than "the least likely suspect[s]" in describing Christie's practice (Barnard 39). He would apply this phrase to books in which the culprits are first suspected, then exonerated, and finally uncovered, however, so "*never* suspected" doesn't seem quite right, either.

7. Charles Osborne notes that Miss Lingard is indeed the "most unlikely" suspect (Osborne 104).

8. Grossvogel, for example, says that "one must assume that only an infinitesimally small number of Agatha Christie's half-billion readers ever undertook or expected to solve her stories in advance of Jane Marple or Hercule Poirot" (Grossvogel 254); and Grella stresses the "display" of a mastermind's work, as opposed to any serious effort to get us to compete with the detective: "These novels do not so much challenge human ingenuity as display it to its furthest limits" (Grella 86).

9. Barnard explicitly shares my own preference for the Poirot novels as intellectual puzzles, for almost all his favorite Christies are Poirots; see his "Annotated List," 187-206. I would think this view is a common one among mystery fans.

REFERENCES

Bargainnier, Earl F. *The Gentle Art of Murder: The Detective Fiction of Agatha Christie.* Bowling Green, OH: Bowling Green University Popular Press, 1980.

Barnard, Robert. *A Talent to Deceive: An Appreciation of Agatha Christie.* New York: Mysterious Press, 1980.

Cawelti, John G. *Adventure, Mystery, and Romance.* Chicago: University of Chicago Press, 1976.

Christie, Agatha. *The ABC Murders.* 1936. Reprint. New York: Pocket Books, 1941.

____. *Agatha Christie: An Autobiography.* 1977. Reprint. New York: Berkley Books, 1941.

____. *At Bertram's Hotel.* 1965. Reprint. New York: Pocket Books, 1967.

____. *The Body in the Library.* 1942. Reprint. New York: Pocket Books, 1965.

____. *Cards on the Table.* 1936. Reprint. New York: Dell, 1980.

____. *Dead Man's Mirror.* 1936. Reprint. New York: Dell, 1978.

____. *Death on the Nile.* 1937. Reprint. New York: Bantam Books, 1978.

____. *Evil under the Sun.* 1941. Reprint. New York: Pocket Books, 1945.

____. *Hercule Poirot's Christmas.* 1938. Reprint. New York: Bantam, 1962 (here entitled *A Holiday for Christmas*).

____. *The Hollow.* 1946. Reprint. New York: Dell, 1976 (here entitled *Murder after Hours*).

____. *Lord Edgware Dies.* 1934. Reprint. New York: Berkley Books, 1984 (here entitled *Thirteen at Dinner*).

____. *The Mirror Crack'd.* 1962. Reprint. New York: Pocket Books, 1964.

____. *The Moving Finger.* 1942. Reprint. New York: Berkley Books, 1984.

____. *The Murder at the Vicarage.* 1930. Reprint. New York: Dell, 1979.

____. *A Murder Is Announced.* 1950. Reprint. New York: Pocket Books, 1951.

____. *Murder on the Orient Express.* 1934. Reprint. New York: Pocket Books, 1987.

____. *The Murder of Roger Ackroyd.* 1926. Reprint. New York: Pocket Books, 1939.

____. *An Overdose of Death.* 1941. Reprint. New York: Berkley Books, 1984 (here entitled *The Patriotic Murders*).

____. *Peril at End House.* 1932. Reprint. New York: Pocket Books, 1942.

____. *A Pocket Full of Rye.* 1953. Reprint. New York: Pocket Books, 1955.

____. *Ten Little Indians.* 1939. Reprint. New York: Dodd, Mead and Co., 1940 (here entitled *And Then There Were None*).

____. *What Mrs. McGillicuddy Saw!* 1957. Reprint. New York: Pocket Books, 1958.

Gill, Gillian. *Agatha Christie: The Woman and Her Mysteries.* New York: Free Press, 1990.

Grella, George. "The Formal Detective Novel." In *Detective Fiction: A Collection of Critical Essays*, edited by Robin W. Winks, 84-102. Woodstock, VT: Foul Play Press, 1988.

Grossvogel, David I. "Agatha Christie: Containment of the Unknown." In *The Poetics of Murder*, edited by Glenn W. Most and William W. Stowe, 252-65. San Diego, CA: Harcourt Brace Jovanovich, 1983.

Hart, Anne. *The Life and Times of Jane Marple.* 1985. Reprint. New York: Berkley Books, 1987.

Knight, Stephen. *Form and Ideology in Crime Fiction.* Bloomington: Indiana University Press, 1980.

Maida, Patricia D., and Nicholas B. Spornick. *Murder She Wrote: A Study of Agatha Christie's Detective Fiction.* Bowling Green, OH: Bowling Green State University Popular Press, 1982.

Osborne, Charles. *The Life and Crimes of Agatha Christie.* New York: Holt, Rinehart and Winston, 1982.

Porter, Dennis. *The Pursuit of Crime: Art and Ideology in Detective Fiction.* New Haven, CT: Yale University Press, 1981.

Sayers, Dorothy L. "The Omnibus of Crime." In *The Art of the Mystery Story*, edited by Howard Haycraft, 71-109. New York: Carroll and Graf, 1974.

9

"It Was the Mark of Cain": Agatha Christie and the Murder of the Mystery

Robin Woods

When Agatha Christie killed Hercule Poirot, both she and the detective novel were in their prime. But even in the 1940s, when she wrote *Curtain*, Christie portrayed, and in a sense foresaw, a new kind of crime that would lie beyond the detective's control. That new crime was motiveless murder. By the mid-1970s, when *Curtain* was finally published (along with Miss Marple's less sensational last case, *Sleeping Murder*), motiveless murder was fast becoming a new and intense focus of the public's fear of crime. And a new genre had appeared: the true-crime novel, which was largely concerned with random murder and replaced the detective novel on the cutting edge of popular crime literature. *Curtain* looks ahead to this genre by presenting as its villain a psychopath who kills without any apparent reason. Poirot defeats this killer and restores order, as he does in so many detective stories. But he does so only at the cost of his own life and that of the detective figure himself, thus changing the terms of the murder mystery and leaving the field to a new kind of crime fighter and crime writer.

In order to understand the importance of *Curtain* and the bridge it builds to the new nonfiction genre, we must first place the detective story in context not only with the true-crime story that follows it but also with the early criminal biography that precedes it. The criminal biography—comprised largely of gallows broadsheets, *The Newgate Calendar*, and Newgate novels—flourished in the eighteenth and nineteenth centuries, when crime and punishment were particularly vexed subjects and the public spectacle of execution demonstrated England's deterrent approach to law enforcement. As has been often noted, the biography presented crime in an ambiguous and discomforting manner. First, it often showed criminal life as romantic (especially when it concerned such crowd-pleasers as Jack Sheppard or Dick Turpin—the latter most lately seen in a Disney film of the 1960s). Second, and more dangerously, it posited an unpleasant correspondence between the criminal's nature and society at large. As Lincoln B. Faller has noted, "It was not [the criminal's] essential difference from the law-abiding majority that tended to be emphasized but his essential similarity. The root cause of crime, one reads again and again, is human depravity" (54).[1] Finally, there is the problem that texts that display criminals, particularly at their moment of execution, run the risk of engaging the reader's sympathy for the wrongdoers. Sympathy for the devil very easily leads to identification with the devil, and when such identification complements the prompting of our own worst selves, then crime comes to appear contagious: You can catch it from sympathizing with a criminal, or associating with unsavory characters, or even, as many believed, by reading about criminals.[2]

But the task of the crime story, even in the genre's earliest forms, is to separate the innocent from the guilty. However imperfectly, the biography combats the dangers inherent within it by imposing a fictional and interpretive structure upon the criminal's life and words. Such structures might explicitly forbid compassion—for example, murderer Francois Benjamin Courvoisier, in the "Affecting Copy of Verses" attributed to him, warns his readers that sympathy "from step to step . . . will delude/ And lead you to dismay" (Hindley 193). Often, they depict a repentant criminal declaring that "I am justly sentenced" (Hindley 189). Or, again as in Courvoisier's case, they interpret the public's response to the criminal as negative: "Great as must have been their abhorrence of his atrocious crime, [they] remained silent spectators."

This solution, as I have said, is not a perfect one. As long as criminals are on display and in communication with their spectators, there is always a good chance that those spectators will perversely insist on sympathizing with the person on the scaffold. In order to guard the community against the contagion of criminality, the criminal must somehow be held in isolation—and at the same time be accessible to the community as a moral lesson and, for the sake of titillation, as a danger.

The classic mystery story solves this problem by presenting a fictional detective who absorbs the attention previously accorded to the criminal. The detective, invented by Poe and enthusiastically adopted by British writers such as Wilkie Collins and Conan Doyle, protected society from crime by standing between community and criminal, providing a kind of moral buffer between the two. The very narrative structure of the detective novel abets the detective by silencing criminals, never allowing them to speak in their own criminal voices. When the time comes for confession in these stories, it is spoken not by the villain but by the detective, who will himself—or herself—tell the story of the crime and leave the criminal only to confirm or deny it. Thus the dangerous criminal voice is silenced, and the dangerous criminal icon is covered by the figure of the detective.

Agatha Christie is perhaps the most successful perpetrator of the detective novel form. Following closely the formula of Conan Doyle, Christie creates a detective—Hercule Poirot and, later, Miss Marple and a host of others—who almost always succeeds in standing between the lawbreaking and the law-abiding world. Indeed, in many ways *The Mysterious Affair at Styles*, Poirot's first case, is a recasting of Doyle's *A Study in Scarlet*. Like Dr. Watson, who has been in Afghanistan, Poirot's sidekick, Captain Hastings, is "invalided home from the Front" (1). Friendless and aimless, he eventually runs across an old acquaintance, John Cavendish, who introduces him to a famous detective and his own destiny as detective's dogsbody.

Most important, Christie exceeds even Doyle in presenting a world of intense normality that is disturbingly, inexplicably, invaded by criminality. But as David Grossvogel points out, in his article "Agatha Christie: Containment of the Unknown," Styles Court represents not normality as the reader knows it but "the bucolic dream of England" (256). Hastings has returned not from trouble in England's possessions but from a world war, with ramifications and consequences reaching far beyond England and India. Styles is not only a "fine old place"; it is also a fortress against the foreign engagements that the war represents and, more important, against the advancing forces of time. The threat to its peace and its way of life is the more dangerous because it is a last bastion of old-style—or old-Styles—harmony.

However, we find that as a fortress Styles Court is hardly secure. The primary threat to order is the murder victim herself, Mrs. Inglethorp, formerly Mrs. Cavendish. Mrs. Inglethorp embodies the disruption of tradition and rightful heritage. She is stepmother, not mother, to John and Lawrence Cavendish; and because of what Hastings calls her "ascendancy" over her husband (2), the late Mr. Cavendish has willed her, rather than his sons, the use of Styles Court and his money for her lifetime. Thus, though John Cavendish gives up his legal practice to live the "congenial life of a country squire" (2), he lacks the money to carry off the role, and both his heritage and he himself are controlled by his mother.[3]

As Grossvogel further notes, it is, in fact, best for everyone in the novel when Mrs. Inglethorp is poisoned—which of course gives them all motives for the murder. Their position as red herrings is more than a legal irritant, however; it means that every character potentially sympathizes with the killer, that every character could in fact *be* the killer. Once Alfred Inglethorp is (temporarily) exonerated, the denizens at Styles begin suspecting their loved ones: Lawrence suspects Cynthia, Hastings suspects Mary Cavendish, and even Edie pretends to suspect John. Often, these suspicions lead them to obstruct justice and place themselves on the side of the killers, against the law.

But they are restored to the right side by the presence of a character who resembles the killer far more closely than they themselves. Hercule Poirot, like all detectives, has devoted himself to a life of crime—or, as Philip Marlowe will later say, trouble is his business. This business requires him to understand criminals, to follow them and think their thoughts. These are, as we know, habits that law-abiding citizens are emphatically required *not* to cultivate; the less they understand about criminals the better. This means that Poirot, like other Golden Age detectives, must remain isolated from the society he serves. Critics are fond of noting such isolation and of pointing out various reasons for it: for example, that the detective's life of danger is incompatible with close personal ties or that the detective's position apart from society enables him or her to see it more clearly. But a more significant reason is that the detective is too close to the criminal ever to become part of society. Otherwise Poirot might transmit criminality back to the communities he is trying to protect, much as the popular criminal biographies ended up placing their readers into closer contact with crime.

Christie isolates Poirot by making him appear ridiculous and even, at times, inconsequential. He is physically odd: short, with an egg-shaped head and a mustache. He is compulsive and excessively vain and utters absurd encomiums to his little gray cells. Most important, he is a foreigner, one who never gives up his Continental habits and indeed stubbornly clings to his eccentricities. Even Hastings, who dogs him through so many novels, never understands him, never notices how Poirot's mind works or what part he himself plays in their investigations. Indeed, whenever Poirot's methods leave Hastings in the dark, he unfailingly confides to the reader or his friends that Poirot's mind must be going at last. Such misconceptions allow Poirot to work unimpeded and prevent others from following him in his exploration of the criminal mind.

Poirot's task is complete when he tells the story of the crime. Though he takes the Styles community through the crime and its cover-up, they—and we— are never exposed to either of the criminals in their roles as criminals. Poirot takes upon himself the role of speaker, and Alfred Inglethorp is left to confirm it with the customary, "You devil!" (169).

Christie's selection of Alfred Inglethorp as the villain assures her story of the happiest possible ending. Alfred Inglethorp is, after all, everyone's criminal of choice: the bearded adventurer of doubtful antecedents. Even if innocent, Inglethorp could not remain at Styles. After the alibi is produced, John Cavendish complains to Hastings that "we were in the wrong, and now there's a beastly feeling that one ought to make amends; which is difficult, when one doesn't like the fellow a bit better than one did before" (105). Inglethorp's guilt spares John the necessity of making amends or even being polite. Edie Howard is a greater loss; but she, too, is different from the rest of the community, unrelated by blood (except to the killer) and set apart from them by her masculine demeanor. No one seems to regret her loss as she drops out of the march toward general felicity.

Poirot successfully conceals the criminal from view almost throughout his career. Even that most anomalous and controversial of detective novels, *The Murder of Roger Ackroyd*, manages an impressive disappearing act. Despite public indignation over Christie's failure to "play fair" with the reader by making her first-person narrator the murderer, she in fact does, as Ackroyd's killer Dr. Sheppard points out, play fair. She—or he—never lies to the reader and only elides certain crucial details that are ultimately unnecessary for solving the case.

Indeed, Christie's great betrayal here is not that she withholds information from her reader but that she allows her killer to get too close to a possibly sympathetic audience. Like the broadsheet villains who spoke directly to an audience, Sheppard addresses his readers in his own voice. By the time we discover his guilt he is a familiar, even intimate, figure, a stand-in for our old friend Hastings. In these circumstances we can hardly fail to sympathize with him. Such intimacy even affects Poirot himself, as we find when he allows the narrator to avoid scandal by committing suicide. "For the sake of your good sister, I am willing to give you the chance of another way out," he tells Sheppard (218). Other criminals in other novels have had sisters, but Poirot has not spared *them*. Caroline Sheppard represents her brother's ties to the community and parallels the link the narrative has established between that brother and ourselves.

Even so, it is Poirot who tells the story at the end; Sheppard himself is left only to confirm Poirot's words, as so many killers do before and after him. Indeed, nowhere in the book does he actually say that he has killed Roger Ackroyd. The closest he comes is to say, "I suppose I meant to murder him all along" (219)—hardly more of a confession than Christie's red herrings often utter. Though shaky, the barricade between criminal and community remains erect.

It is not *The Murder of Roger Ackroyd* but *Curtain* that breaks the Golden Age mystery pattern. In this story, Poirot fails to protect his society from criminal contagion or from the dangers of the criminal voice. This is partly because his adversary, the nondescript Norton, breaks the classic mystery pattern by failing to act on one of the accepted motives of the canon—set out in various places but generally boiling down to money, sex, or revenge. Motive is, after all, part of what separates criminal from community and establishes the murder mystery as a rational and therefore soluble puzzle. But Norton kills more or less at random, for the sheer fun of it. Moreover, and more crucially, he himself never lifts a hand against anyone, but instead convinces others—others in the normally law-abiding community—to kill. This combination of motiveless murder and murder by proxy points to crime that has gotten out of control and has broken through the boundaries erected by the detective. In this aspect *Curtain* prefigures the true-crime novel that takes as its subject the domestic murderer and the serial killer.

Curtain self-consciously recalls the original Poirot story, and at every turn it tells us that the bucolic dream of *The Mysterious Affair at Styles* is now lost. The Cavendish family is dispersed; and Styles Court, that fine old house, is now converted into a guest house: Traditional hospitality has given way to economic necessity. Like the pillars of society, the traditional pillars of the detective story are also undermined. There will be no such clues as fingerprints or incriminating letters. Law-abiding citizens will attempt murder. There will be no police officer waiting to take the murderer away—though there will be, as in *Ackroyd*, a convenient suicide. Rather than concealing the criminal, the detective will become the criminal and tell of the crime in his own voice.

It is, indeed, the abnormality of the crimes that leads Poirot to the killer. He first begins to suspect a pattern among five apparently unconnected murders precisely and perversely because no such pattern exists. The only connection among them is Norton, who was in the vicinity for all the murders but cannot have committed them. Poirot, however, refuses to accept Norton's presence as coincidence, and on this evidence alone—the rejection of the concept of accident—Poirot bases his conviction that Norton is responsible for all these deaths. Either Norton is the murderer or his presence has no meaning. But this meaning is purchased at a heavy price—the general innocence of the community. As a murder "catalyst," Norton makes the people around him tools in a guilty cause—makes them, in fact, killers.

The test case here is Hastings himself. Norton convinces Hastings, obliquely of course, that if the libertine Allerton lives, he will ruin Hastings's daughter Judith. Hastings lays a trap for Allerton, which is fortunately sprung by Poirot.

Hastings is far more important a figure than the killer of Roger Ackroyd. He has guided the reader on several Poirot manhunts, and we have complete trust in his rectitude, if not in his intelligence. Most important, he is, as Watson famously is, the reader's double in the novel. He is ourselves as we stumble along with good intentions, trying to keep up with Poirot. By attempting murder, Hastings betrays himself and us. "*You* are not a murderer, Hastings!" (267) Poirot proclaims in the teeth of the evidence. But the solution to this conundrum is hardly comforting. Poirot writes, "Everyone is a potential murderer—in everything there arises from time to time the *wish* to kill—though not the *will* to kill" (254-55). Norton kills by dissolving that membrane of will—of motive, we might say—that prevents us from following our deep desires and instincts. Hastings may be innocent, but his innocence cannot absolve us, because he is only innocent by virtue of a universal guilt.

The crucial question is one of original sin: What motivates Norton? Poirot tells us that "Norton . . . was a secret sadist. He was an addict of pain, of mental torture" (258). All this tells us, of course, is that Norton is evil because he takes pleasure in evil (an analysis that sociologist Jack Katz will later endorse in his 1988 study *Seductions of Crime*). There is, nominally, a place for such urges in the mystery canon. His vice seems to come under the rubric of what Miss Marple, in her first adventure, calls "queerness." But the detective novel rarely shows anyone killing out of queerness alone. Poirot, naturally, seeks a cause behind the queerness itself and decides that Norton's taste for murder results from his domineering mother and his own deficient personality. It is also, if obscurely, attributable to the modern age: Poirot says that "There has been an epidemic of [sadism] in the world of late years" (258). If crime seems bizarre and infinitely dangerous, it can still be explained away.

But that explanation is not, in this novel, enough to keep the community apart from the criminal. Because the contagion of Norton's criminality has already spread throughout the community, on the level of both the narrator and the reader, Poirot cannot simply isolate and remove it. The law cannot punish universal guilt; it can only (wrongly) punish its manifestations, not the demon who stirs them up.

In this novel, as in the others, it is Poirot who tells the story of the crime. Norton has long since been silenced. But by the time Poirot speaks, he has become the criminal, and his voice is now the criminal voice. Despairing of ever bringing the criminal to justice, Poirot murders Norton and then executes himself for the murder, by putting his heart medicine out of reach. If the revelation of Hastings as a potential killer was shocking, this act is more so, for Poirot does not simply represent the reader. He represents the principle of justice that keeps crime apart from the reader. Once justice executes itself there is no longer any barrier between the community and crime. We are all susceptible, all criminal. The criminal voice again breaks through the criminal text. Norton has corrupted Hastings and Poirot, and through them he corrupts the reader.

In one of the earliest detective stories, "The Purloined Letter," Edgar Allen Poe notes that one prototype for the Golden Age detective story is the *Oresteia*, the story of kin murder and retributive violence, which is finally interrupted by the intervention of Athena and the establishment of a court system. Hastings, at the end of *Curtain*, proposes an alternate myth: "The mark on Norton's forehead—it was like the brand of Cain" (280). This is the mark that sets Cain aside as *homo sacer*, a creature not to be touched and specifically not to be punished by other human beings. In this sense Cain is, like the criminal, like the detective, a creature outside of society. But like the *Oresteia*, the Cain story is a story of kin murder, of familiar murder. It is also an originating myth, an early chapter in the story of our genesis. Though Cain is separated from us, his meaning can never entirely be separate. Moreover, the mark that Hastings identifies as the brand of Cain is explicitly identified with Poirot: Its symmetry makes it, in both Hastings's and Poirot's own views, Poirot's mark—his signature. In this final episode, crime defeats the detective by upsetting the delicate balance of law and lawlessness that he embodies. And after that, it is free to sweep through the community. The Golden Age of detective stories continued after World War II, and classic detective stories are still written today. But *Curtain* shows that new exigencies were arising in the world that the detective novel could no longer completely contain or account for. And it was not long after this that new crime genres began springing up in response. By the time Agatha Christie wrote *Curtain*, the hard-boiled crime novel had already appeared. Such novels feature a detective who, though "not himself mean," as Raymond Chandler maintains (237), lives in a world almost completely corrupted by vice and crime and cannot protect the few innocent people he meets.

But as I have already suggested, *Curtain* really prefigures the modern true-crime novel. Mean as the streets might be in Chandler's Los Angeles or Hammett's San Francisco, the villains there still act out of rational self-interest. And tainted with crime as Spade or Marlowe may be, they are still heroic figures. But in *Curtain*, as in Truman Capote's *In Cold Blood*, Norman Mailer's *The Executioner's Song*, and a multitude of others that followed, the protagonist is not a heroic detective but a criminal, with whom it is, to say the least, dangerous to identify. He is also someone in whose execution we are complicit, since the reading public is also the citizenry that punishes crime. And he is someone whose crimes we cannot fully understand and therefore cannot completely guard against, in our own houses or in our own hearts.

In these respects, *Curtain* also looks back to the criminal biographies. In these works crime is also unexplained or is mostly explained in unconvincing or unsettling ways (the criminal was simply bad, was a "born" criminal, or else "caught" criminality from wicked companions). In these works, too, the criminals take center stage, and the viewers and readers stand next to them on the gallows. No one is ever truly innocent in such a world, either of crime or of punishment. When Agatha Christie killed her Belgian detective, she rang down the curtain not only on Poirot but also on the comfort and safety that the detective story provides.

NOTES

1. See also Michel Foucault, *Discipline and Punish: The Birth of the Prison*, translated by Alan Sheridan (New York: Pantheon Books, 1977).

2. Among these was Hannah More, whose Religious Tract Society sought to replace popular sensational literature with cheap tracts that were morally uplifting.

3. Of course, Styles Court is hardly an ancestral hall, since Mr. Cavendish has purchased rather than inherited it. Thus, even the Cavendishes' ownership of Styles represents a break in tradition.

REFERENCES

Chandler, Raymond. "The Simple Art of Murder." In *Murder for Pleasure*. New York: Carroll and Graf, 1974.

Christie, Agatha. *The Murder of Roger Ackroyd*. 1926. Reprint. Glasgow: William Collins Sons and Co., 1981.

____. *Curtain*. 1975, [and] *The Mysterious Affair at Styles*. 1920. Reprint. New York: Bantam, 1983.

Faller, Lincoln B. *Turned to Account: The Forms and Functions of Criminal Biography in Seventeenth- and Eighteenth-Century England*. Cambridge: Cambridge University Press, 1987.

Grossvogel, David. "Agatha Christie: Containment of the Unknown." In *The Poetics of Murder*, edited by Glenn W. Most and William W. Stowe. New York: Harcourt Brace Jovanovich, 1983.

Hindley, Charles, ed. *Curiosities of Street Literature*. London: Reeves and Turner, 1871.

Katz, Jack. *Seductions of Crime: Moral and Sensual Attractions in Doing Evil*. New York: Basic Books, 1988.

10

Impossible Murderers: Agatha Christie and the Community of Readers

Ina Rae Hark

Peter Hühn in his essay on "The Detective as Reader" notes that "in its elaborately contrived structures, the detective novel . . . presents a number of entangled writing-and-reading contests that ultimately only serve to demonstrate the superior power of *writing* (on the author's part), a power, moreover, that proves itself in two consecutive ways: in first protecting the stories against being read until the very end, and in finally producing a perfect as well as comprehensive reading" (459). In other words, classic detective stories, those whodunits or "clue-puzzles," in Stephen Knight's useful designation, initially offer a poststructuralist's dream of unreadable signification, only in the end to locate indeterminacy beyond the text in the deficient reading competency of all competing readers save that ideal decoder, the detective. As Hühn concludes, "this textual indeterminacy is . . . only a temporary illusion" because the central premise of the genre turns on the existence of determinate meanings (455).

Detective stories are then readerly texts in fancy dress, teasing us into believing ourselves Barthesian producers of textual meaning only to ask us to sit still while the detective's final explanation turns us into the most passive of consumers. Moreover, they are, according to Tzvetan Todorov, just as readerly as a group of texts, belonging to one of the genres of popular literature that, should they once be "properly described," would reveal the best novels as those about which one can find nothing to say (43).

The monumental and apparently undying consumability of Agatha Christie's detective novels has led many commentators to view her as a depressingly successful perfecter of the art of the readerly clue-puzzle. Here we find no characterization, only familiar types to be plugged into the exigencies of the plotting; no potentially destabilizing stylistic flourishes, only flat writing; no awareness of the operations of ideology, only panaceas for what Knight calls the "classic anxious bourgeois class" (133). Apparently substantiating such an assessment are numerous passages from Christie's posthumously published *Auto-biography* that feature such simplistic hierarchical binaries as the following: "We had not then begun to wallow in psychology. I was, like everyone else who wrote books or read them, *against* the criminal and *for* the innocent victim" (424).

Therefore, Christie's clue-puzzles should be the last place in which we should expect to find an indication of the tenuousness of the detective's claim to perceive the truth in matters of guilt or innocence, a recognition of the novel as mere textual battleground between author and reader. I would assert, however, that that is precisely what we do find there, that both intra- and extratextually Agatha Christie mysteries acknowledge themselves as not about crime-solving but about reading. Moreover, they posit the detective's ability to come up with determinate readings as an exception, a product of fantasy, precisely because the texts of guilt and innocence in the real world are so resolutely unreadable. And such unreadability as Christie texts, despite her many pronouncements to the contrary, demonstrate occurs because human guilt and innocence are thoroughly intermixed, rather than being in mutually exclusive binary opposition. If we attempt to read people like books in order to separate the murderous from the nonmurderous, we must fail, because in Christie's view no such creature as a person incapable of murder exists.

The most prominent clue to this unexpectedly sophisticated Christiean textual philosophy reveals itself in the very textual operation Christie is most famous for: The dazzling surprises provoked by the revelation of her murderers' identities. A common thread among the particularly celebrated shockers is that they transgress the conventions for reading detective stories. Structurally, such stories have a tripartite division of characters: the investigators of a crime or crimes; the victims or intended victims; and everybody else, who thereby become the suspects, from which group the investigators eventually identify one or more criminals. Investigators and readers compete to reconcile readings of the circumstances of the crimes with readings of the behavior of the characters in order to effect the solution that matches suspect to guilt. Christie, however, consistently manipulates these categories so that the murderer emerges from the first or second group or has otherwise been exempted from membership in the group of suspects. The result, as Robert Barnard shrewdly observes, is not that Christie murderers are the least likely suspects but that they are among "the ones never suspected" (46).

We thus see crimes committed by the policemen investigating them (*Hercule Poirot's Christmas*, *Three Blind Mice*) or by amateur sleuths helping out the primary detective (*The Murder of Roger Ackroyd*, *The Seven Dials Mystery*). Also linking the murderer to the investigating group is the frequently used device delineated by Gillian Gill: "The prime suspect—the person who stands to gain the most—has an apparently iron-clad alibi for a murder he or she in fact committed" (137). By accepting their alibis or otherwise vouching for them initially, Christie investigators habitually transform most likely suspects into nonsuspects in the reader's mind. A staple ploy since her very first novel, *The Mysterious Affair at Styles*, this premature exoneration via legal system fiat, a kind of innocence by association, arguably has its most dazzling moment in *Witness for the Prosecution*, when the client the barrister protagonist has labored triumphantly to have acquitted, by discrediting the apparently vengeful spouse who testifies against him, turns out to be just as guilty as the prosecution has portrayed him. The wife, who had surmised his guilt and realized that a false alibi from a loving helpmeet would not be believed, had devised the whole complicated scheme in order to exonerate her faithless husband.

Christie's killers also frequently disguise themselves as victims, either reporting a near-miss in an attempt on their lives or convincing everyone that a murder victim has been mistakenly killed in their place. This strategy appeals particularly to her women murderers. In *Peril at End House*, for example, "Nick" Buckley must eliminate her cousin Maggie before it becomes known that it was to her cousin and not to herself that the deceased aviator Michael Seton was engaged and left an enormous fortune. She therefore arranges a series of apparent near-misses on her life and then kills Maggie in a way that suggests the bullet was intended for her. In *The Mirror Crack'd* Marina Gregg realizes at a cocktail party that Heather Badcock, a woman to whom she has been chatting, infected her years before with the German measles that caused her to bear a retarded child. She drops a fatal dose of tranquilizers into her own glass, arranges an exchange with Mrs. Badcock, and passes off the death as a bungled attempt on her own life.

In fact, Christie murderers are astoundingly proficient, no matter how byzantine their Rube Goldberg lethal schemes sometimes appear, and any claim that a bullet or poisoned drink "must have been meant for me" should immediately put readers on their guard. In the *tour de force* novel version of *And Then There Were None*, all the suspects—including the murderer—are also victims. The police arrive to find a house full of corpses, the vigilante jurist having faked his own murder, dispatched the remaining guests, and then committed suicide in a manner that duplicates the circumstances of his first "death."

Christie's transformation of all the suspects into victims in this novel is complemented by her delineation of all the suspects as murderers in *Murder on the Orient Express*. Both novels depend for their shock value on structuralist reader assumptions about the makeup of the pool of suspects. Even that master reader Poirot reports resisting his growing awareness of the extent of the conspiracy in *Orient Express*: "I said to myself: This is extraordinary—they cannot all be in it" (192).

The novel that made her reputation, *The Murder of Roger Ackroyd*, played not only on having the killer in the Dr. Watson role but also on reader assumptions that a first-person narrator could not turn out to be the culprit. The outcry concerning unfairness when the book first appeared in 1926 showed that the reading conventions for consumers of detective fiction excluded the unreliable narrator, who was becoming quite conventional himself in the "high" literature of the time.

When we read Christie at her most distinctive, then, she confronts us with impossible murderers. They are impossible not because of their social class, race or gender, individual psychology, professed ideology, or prominence or peripheralness to the narration but because the ideal reader produced by the conventions of the genre is incapable of considering them as suspects at all. The solutions to her mysteries inevitably require the reader to employ Alexander's sword slash rather than patiently to unravel the Gordian knot of suspects, motives, and clues. The well-trained Christie reader comes to know that there is no such thing as an impossible murderer. Poirot cannot rule out anyone, and, as *Curtain* demonstrates, the reader cannot even rule out Poirot.

Curtain, in which Poirot closes his last case by murdering the murderer, holds a special position in Christie's ongoing dialogue with her community of readers and, perhaps because of this, provides the clearest exposition of her ideology and methodology. Written during World War II as an insurance policy for her family in case she were killed in the blitz, it remained in a safe, awaiting publication after her death. In the upshot, it was published in 1975, a year before her physical demise but as a consequence of the agreement between Christie's daughter Rosalind and her publisher Collins. It was clear after the disappointing 1972 *Postern of Fate* that Christie's days as a writer were over. The author is therefore both absent and present to her readers; the book is Poirot's last case to be published but his twelfth from last to be written. While the text when written could interact only with those produced prior to it, on its first availability to readers it already had an intertextual relationship with a number of books written subsequently that they were likely to have read previously.

Because of *Curtain's* dual temporal standing, Christie also had to criminalize and execute Poirot in a way that would not be inconsistent with his previous behavior or circumscribe any investigations she might pen while it remained "in the bank." And to maintain Poirot's popularity after both their deaths, Christie had to make this most impossible of her murderers at least as forgivable as the *Orient Express* passengers for whom he endorsed an alternative, exonerating clue-puzzle text that the authorities could substitute for his decoding of the actual conspiracy. To that end, Poirot kills only to stop a killer beyond the reach of the law, a procedure Christie tacitly approves not only in *Orient Express* but in *And Then There Were None* and *Cards on the Table*. She also has him stress the benefits of his crime to vulnerable innocents and, to cover all moral bases, put his heart medication out of reach so that God can render justice upon him for violating his lifelong "disapproval" of murder. Christie insists on the need for murderers to be arrested, in the sense of stopped, but cares little for having them arrested by law enforcement officials and paraded through public rituals of punishment.

Like Poirot and her other murderers who leave written confessions as suicide notes, Dr. Sheppard in *Roger Ackroyd* and the Judge in *And Then There Were*

None, the possibility of speaking from the grave seems to have made Christie especially forthcoming about her methods. *Curtain* reveals Christie's clear admission that her books are about texts, not crimes, and that her rationale for choosing murderers who affront readers' preconceptions is about reading mysteries, not about identifying criminals.

Gillian Gill astutely notes that "Whereas material clues tend very often to be red herrings in Agatha Christie's work, the textual clues are almost always important. . . . Textual clues . . . written words on paper, invoke the Great Detective's skill not as an orientalist or organic chemist or bibliophile, but *as a reader*, and the very nature of the genre allows the novel reader to compete" (49). In *Curtain* Poirot recognizes a serial killer behind a series of apparently unrelated murder trials that he has read about in the newspapers. The killer, when unmasked, proves to be quite beyond legal punishment because his murders are themselves textual. Conforming to a literary model, as a latter-day Iago, he reads his targets sufficiently well to manipulate them into committing the murder that, Poirot calmly asserts in his confession, incubates within us all: "Everyone is a potential murderer—in everyone there arises from time to time the *wish* to kill—though not the will to kill . . . X knew the exact word, the exact phrase, the intonation even to suggest and to bring cumulative pressure on a weak spot!" (216-17).

To stop X from writing any further murderous texts upon his random acquaintances, Poirot presents the case to Hastings in much the same way that author Christie offers her mysteries to readers. Having already identified the killer and, it turns out, the means by which he is to be stopped (just as Christie always wrote her unravel-the-plot solutions first), Poirot presents his friend with a written précis of each of the killer's past crimes, then sends him out to mingle with the suspects and observe them for signs of guilt. When Hastings has failed to identify the killer before Poirot's semisuicide, the detective leaves him two further textual clues, copies of *Othello* and St. John Ervine's *Clutie John*, both of which portray murderers who work in the same way that X does. Rightly suspecting that Hastings will still be in the dark without the typical Poirot exegesis, the detective has further arranged for a written solution of all the aspects of the case to be forwarded by his solicitors to his friend four months after his passing.

The novel Poirot writes for Hastings and that Hastings recopies for us is a semi-puzzling, fair-play, not very Christie-like text. Stephen Norton, revealed as the Iago, is not a particularly obvious suspect, but he isn't one of the trademark "never suspected" either. Hastings in fact considers him as "perhaps less unlikely than anyone else" because he is so inconspicuous. The identity of the person Norton succeeds in turning murderous, after false starts with Colonel Lutrell and Hastings himself, is slightly more surprising in that happenstance finally makes a Christie murderer administer poison to someone other than the intended victim—with the mistakenly killed individual being none other than the aspiring killer herself. Barbara Franklin, wanting to rid herself of her scientist-husband, poisons his coffee in a way that will make it look as if his experimentation with alkaloids has proven fatal. Because Hastings revolves the bookcase upon which the couple's cups are placed, however, Barbara unwittingly drinks and dies from the poison she had meant for Dr. Franklin.

At the same time, however, Poirot is planting oblique clues for both Hastings and the reader as to the fact that a simultaneous and archetypal Poirot-Christie plot is unfolding. When Poirot announces to Hastings at the beginning of the novel his certainty that a murder will occur, he is speaking of his own scheme to execute Norton, the only way he can fulfill "my work in life to save the innocent" in the case of a catalytic killer immune to either remorse or legal punishment. While, on the one hand, veteran Christie readers might easily surmise that Poirot is the ultimate impossible murderer and that, should he kill, it would be under just such a set of circumstances, they would also quite likely attribute all the deaths and near-misses in *Curtain* to the mysterious X and overlook as completely as does Hastings the status of one victim as Poirot's target instead.[1]

Aware that reflexive structures for reading Christie might simply supplant those for reading mystery novels in general that her impossible murderers are meant to dislodge, the author here and elsewhere brazenly trots them into plain view, confident that she can misdirect us as handily as the purloiner of Poe's famous letter did the Paris police. (Perhaps her most daring act of nosethumbing was to create another first-person–narrating killer in *Endless Night* despite her notoriety for using the device in *Roger Ackroyd*.) Conversely, the insisted-upon *déjà vu* of *Curtain*, as Hastings and Poirot return to Styles, the location of their first case—"I have done this before," Hastings muses—with Poirot limping from age as he had previously limped from a Great War injury, begs us to look for intertextual clues derived from *The Mysterious Affair at Styles*. However, the crimes and criminals in the two novels are, in fact, totally unrelated. The rhyming of the limp occurs rather because Poirot's scheme to execute Norton only succeeds because Norton also is lame; and lameness, in the *Curtain* context alone, is the signifier that unites the dispenser of justice and his prey.

Christie is at pains to make us distrust structuralist readings, not because she regards the concept of deep structures as false but because she sees all such structures collapsing into one: Every human text is a potential murder mystery. A truly proficient deep reader could only come to the *Orient Express* conclusion: They're all in it, and I'm one of them. Despite her carefully calculated persona as the shy, inarticulate Devonshire housewife, a pietistic Christian who turned out annual sanguinary best-sellers, much in the way her neighbors cultivated prize roses for the yearly garden-club show, Christie had as baleful a view of the potential depravity of Everyman as we find, for instance, in the films of Alfred Hitchcock.

The Hitchcockian idea of transference of guilt may, in fact, help explain two other Christie predilections: her insistence that identifying murderers has value primarily in protecting the innocent and her lack of concern about murderers being brought to justice as long as the first objective has been accomplished. Because we are all potentially murderous and likely to be read as such, it is important to arrest such reading operations through conclusive identifications of those who have actually behaved murderously, not just who might have. At the same time, the metaphysical complicity of all persons in such behavior renders public preening on the disposition of offenders a hollow exercise. Thus, Miss Marple gives her blessing to Jason Rudd's tampering with his tormented, murderous wife Marina's medication in order to put her out of her misery; and Poirot says of Nick Buckley's likely drug overdose-suicide: "It is the best way. Better than the hangman's rope. But pst! we must not say so before M. Vyse who is all law and order" (176).

Christie insists that the failure to arrive at conclusive readings of human behavior (as opposed to human intentionality), all too common in quotidian reality, can cause significant and persistent harm. An impulse to fashion her texts as privileged spaces in which such harm may be corrected informs her retrospective cases like *Five Little Pigs* or *Ordeal by Innocence*, where so much effort goes into revising the misreadings of falsely convicted killers, even though they are long dead. Poirot's identification of Iago-X provides this collateral benefit as well. The much-criticized superficiality of Christie, in fact, merely acknowledges that sorting out the tangle of signifiers produced by an incident is the one reading operation having any pragmatic social utility.

Therefore, only on the behavioral level does Christie endorse structuralist readings, as in Miss Marple's solving crimes by having suspects' actions remind her of analogous ones, demonstrated by village acquaintances in her past. Furthermore, she is quite aware that those without Miss Marple's special talents will misread such recurring structures much more frequently than they will decode them, so that the interpretive strategies of the St. Mary Mead sleuth have little widespread applicability.

The ability of Christie's detective super-readers to sort surface innocence from surface guilt does not then indicate any simpleminded assumption on the author's part that such distinctions will eventually emerge in all the puzzles of life. She offers their solutions as a fantasy consolation to her readers because she knows that they are a fantasy, as she knows the considerable pain that life's generally remaining intractably unreadable causes. After all, for eleven days in December 1926, from the time she abandoned her wrecked car until she was discovered living in a Harrogate spa under the name of her husband's mistress, Agatha Christie participated in events that have resisted conclusive interpretation even by herself, if her claim of amnesia is to be believed. A generator of various textual explanations by tabloid reporters, friends and family, biographers, and Kathleen Tynan in her charming novel *Agatha* (filmed by Michael Apted with Vanessa Redgrave and Dustin Hoffman), the incident is represented only by its absence in the *Autobiography*. And fifteen years after

Christie's death, no letter from anyone's solicitor has arrived to turn that mass of indeterminate signifiers into a comfortably readerly text.

NOTE

1. When, after having read all of Christie's full-length mystery novels, I heard that she had written Poirot's last case and that it was soon to be published, I wagered with some fellow Christie aficionadoes that in it, Poirot would commit murder in order to eliminate someone the law couldn't touch and to protect innocents from coming to any further harm—and that he would then commit suicide. Nevertheless, when I actually read *Curtain*, which followed the pattern I had predicted to the letter, I was sure up to the point that Poirot's missive to Hastings arrived that I had been mistaken.

REFERENCES

Barnard, Robert. *A Talent to Deceive: An Appreciation of Agatha Christie*. London: Collins, 1980.

Christie, Agatha. *An Autobiography*. New York: Dodd, Mead, 1977.

____. *Curtain*. New York: Dodd, Mead, 1975.

____. *Murder on the Orient Express*. 1934. New York: Pocket Books, 1969. Reprint.

____. *Peril at End House*. 1932. New York: Pocket Books, 1971. Reprint.

Gill, Gillian. *Agatha Christie: The Woman and Her Mysteries*. New York: Macmillan, 1990.

Hühn, Peter. "The Detective as Reader: Narrativity and Reading Concepts in Detective Fiction." *Modern Fiction Studies* 33 (1987).

Knight, Stephen. *Form and Ideology in Crime Fiction*. London: Macmillan, 1980.

Todorov, Tzvetan. "The Typology of Detective Fiction." In *The Poetics of Prose*, translated by Richard Howard. Ithaca, NY: Cornell University Press, 1977.

11

"The Daughters of His Manhood": Christie and the Golden Age of Detective Fiction

Mary Anne Ackershoek

My title comes from a World War I poem, "A Father of Women," by the British poet Alice Meynell. It speaks of

> The million living fathers of the War—
> Mourning the crippled world, the bitter day—
> Whose striplings are no more.
>   . . . Come then,
> Fathers of women with your honour in trust,
> Approve, accept, know them daughters of men,
>   Now that your sons are dust. (Meynell)

These lines express two cultural attitudes that are of central importance in understanding the phenomenally successful production of detective fiction by British women in the 1920s: First, the perception that the world was crippled, that the Great War had irrevocably damaged, at least, that world of order and security England felt to be peculiarly its own.[1] The "golden summer" of 1914 was irretrievable. Signs of societal change were everywhere; "the old order had passed away, the halcyon days of the privileged classes" (Mowat 201). The other perception expressed by Meynell—a perception commonly spoken of by women—is that the deaths of so many men in World War I had left a gap in the structure of society that could, and must, be filled by women, including women acting in what had previously been male roles. The war years were to some extent emancipatory: Many women had been employed in traditionally male factory jobs during the war, and many others, such as Agatha Christie, found hospital work (Graves and Hodge 45). The passage of the 1918 Representation of the People Act, giving women over age thirty the right to vote; the Sex Disqualification Act of 1919, which admitted women to many professions, including the law; and the admission of women to full membership at Oxford in the same year emphasize the way in which the events of the war years "exerted powerful pressures in eroding the sex barriers which had restricted British women over the decades" (Kenneth Morgan 590).

At first glance, Agatha Christie's novels seem to reflect little of this societal change. The ordered world depicted in her texts seems untouched by the realities of postwar Britain; indeed, it has often been interpreted as a nostalgic recreation of prewar society, basking in the glow of the Edwardian sunset (Grossvogel 264). However, the Christie world is shaped by its postwar context in subtle but important ways, and it is into this context of crisis and change that the achievements of Agatha Christie and her female contemporaries must be placed.

Women had written detective stories before the 1920s—Conan Doyle's contemporaries Catherine Pirkis, L. T. Meade, and Baroness Orczy, for example[2]—but the postwar generation of authors represented a phenomenon that was in many ways new. It was not only the sheer number and commercial success of these women that made their achievements important. They transformed the genre not only by their presence but also by the new possibilities for female characters as the detectives, victims, and murderers they depicted. Also, as Stephen Knight points out in his study of Christie, they created popular types of male detectives quite different from the impressive, cooling masculine Holmes, detectives apparently far more appealing to a female audience. Christie's Hercule Poirot is a "fussy, unheroic figure . . . [w]hat is of value in him is not tied to masculine stereotypes" of power (107-8). Dorothy L. Sayers's Lord Peter Wimsey and Margery Allingham's Albert Campion begin their fictional lives as affected, somewhat irritating eccentrics with clear affinities to Harold Acton and his fellow "children of the sun," though both later become more viable romantic heroes.

It is important to realize, however, that this was not the first time detectives very different from Holmes had been created by women. Catherine Pirkis' female detective, Loveday Brooke, and Baroness Orczy's "Old Man in the Corner" had been created a generation earlier and enjoyed some popularity. But such figures never presented a serious threat to Holmes's position in the public imagination as the archetypal detective. Poirot, Marple, Wimsey, and Campion did; and the public's taste for a different version of the detective was shaped by social change, change in large part effected by the war.

The war not only changed behavioral norms and vocations for women; it also triggered a fundamental change in attitudes toward authority. The political "fathers" of Britain had led their country into a bloody and senseless war that decimated the ranks of their sons. Poems, fiction, and memoirs of the Great War insist over and over again on the image of the war as a fundamental betrayal of trust, particularly of a *paternal* trust.[3] The protective masculine authority figures had failed to protect their charges. This crisis of authority had an immediate impact on the detective story, whose structure depended upon the depiction of some person or agency capable of containing the threat of disorder.

Christie, Sayers, Allingham, and others responded by creating detectives whose abilities were not bound to traditional images of male power. The popularity of their work is at least in part due to the postwar public need it fed: to provide reassurance, at least for the length of a novel, that crises can be overcome and a viable, if different, social order be reclaimed from chaos.

The postwar legacy is clearest in Sayers's early depictions of Wimsey. He is a victim of the war, surviving, but psychologically wounded, no longer able to function within the traditional structures of his aristocratic family. He is nursed through traumatic battle flashbacks by his valet and former batman, Bunter, in a particularly vivid reversal of traditional class roles (*Whose Body?* 114-15). Allingham's Campion comes of uncertain lineage but is depicted as an aristocrat who has renounced his identity to turn detective, thus creating a role within society for himself and a kind of authority more viable than the hierarchical one he was born to.

But it is in Christie that the depiction of an alternative authority is most striking. Both Poirot and Marple draw their power from what were traditionally depicted—and often trivialized—as female attributes or activities: information-gathering through the homely means of gossip and observation of seemingly minor details of domestic life and of human behavior. The seemingly intuitive leaps to conclusions made by Marple and Poirot are, in fact, made through rational analyses of the patterns of information thus acquired, analyses that are "intuitive" only in that they differ from more authoritarian depictions of reasoning. Marple and Poirot do not so much arrange information in a sequence shaped by their own ratiocinations as allow the inherent patterns within the information they acquire to fall into shape (Knight 109). They differ from the other characters presented in their texts not in reasoning ability but in thoroughness; their function is to see the entire network of interconnected information, whereas the others see only isolated units. Paradoxically, they gain access to this network not through a Holmesian social empowerment but through disempowerment. It is because both Poirot and Marple are perceived as peripheral figures by the society they work within that the total pattern is revealed to them; they are given information because it is complacently assumed they have no way of making use of it. They are treated with affectionate condescension or outright contempt; above all, they are not taken seriously. It is this error that they turn to their advantage, triumphing not so much *over* their perceived shortcomings as *because* of them.[4] Thus, both Poirot and Marple represent a new form of empowerment for the detective, one deeply rooted in female experience.

Christie's detectives are clearly a product of the period of post–World War I social change. Yet the "Christie world" is usually described by critics as "cozy"—as an idyllic vision of country-house life, peopled by a stable, serene, leisured ruling class, secure in its power, amusing itself with the refined pursuits of tennis, croquet, and the occasional murder (Barnard 203). This world seems untouched by the trauma of the war; yet, in fact, the upper-middle and upper classes had been severely traumatized by the deaths of heirs and by the inflation and taxes that reduced their capital: "the glittering Edwardian days had gone forever. Great estates were being broken up, great houses sold . . . high taxes and death duties were doing the work of the redistribution of property. . . . For the first time a country house was a problem" (Mowat 203).

But if anxieties over such issues are present at all in Christie's texts, it has been argued they are present only to be safely and reassuringly contained by the structure. Grossvogel, for example, characterizes the murder plot of Christie's first novel, *The Mysterious Affair at Styles*, as a "trivial unpleasantness . . . contrived for the pleasure of ending it." The conclusion leaves "the upper-middle-class ritual . . . once again resumed. Law, order and property are secure" (265).

But such an argument is not only overly simple; it is also intimately bound to the way detective fiction encourages us to read. The process is typified by the classic detective metaphor of the maze and the clue of thread. However circuitous the reader's journey, however many times the string tangles, knots, even snaps, once arrived at the goal the reader looks back along what now seems to be an unbroken cord leading to an inevitable end. The ending, in effect, reshapes the entire text; not only do the knots in the thread untangle, but what we may have glimpsed hiding in the shrubbery along our journey vanishes. Not only does the resolution of the plot appear inevitable, but so does an interpretation of the text in which its resolution becomes the basis for analysis.

Christie's texts seem to privilege this goal-oriented approach. Yet they also provide another metaphor, which may represent another way of reading, in which the knots in the thread are as important as where it ends, in the image of Jane Marple's pink, fluffy knitting. Knitting is her perpetual activity, and it is surely not insignificant that Christie's favorite detective is symbolized by a process that is creative, that consists not of following a thread but of reshaping it into something, something warm, soft, and eminently reassuring but a made thing nonetheless, a fabrication with the potential to be unravelled.

For despite the fact that Christie's texts depict a detective process in which the detective is not a controlling figure, of course there is a control present, that of the narrative itself. Christie's critics have often fallen into the trap of assuming that the voice of the narrative is, in fact, the voice of Agatha Christie—the stolid, conservative Victorian matron depicting her own class and society in ideal terms.[5] Reading a preconceived notion of an author into her texts is always a dangerous pursuit and is particularly problematic in the case of Christie. Robert Barnard is one of the few critics who have been astute enough to realize this. In his 1980 study of Christie, *A Talent to Deceive*, he suggests that the publicity surrounding Christie's notorious 1926 disappearance caused her to choose to become a "disappearing author" in another sense, that is, "to give away nothing of herself" in her novels. Thus "not only is there no sense of her own personality in the books; she is equally elusive as to her own tastes and opinions. In fact, she sometimes lets us *presume* those, purposely to mislead us.

. . . Precisely similar things happen when we look at Christie's social and political attitudes" (55-56). Barnard cites as an example of this phenomenon the character of Alistair Blunt in Christie's *One, Two, Buckle My Shoe*. Blunt is

a conservative banker who apparently stands behind and is the principal prop of the government of Britain: a safe, steady, conventional figure. . . . Everything in the novel is directed towards building him up as a man after the average middle-class reader's political heart. . . .

In fact . . . [Hercule Poirot] says to Blunt, "You stand for all the things that to my mind are important. For sanity and balance and stability and honest dealing."

But that is just before he has Blunt arrested for murder. . . . [N]ot only has [Christie] fooled the reader—she has covered her tracks as well. The reader has been encouraged in his natural desire to commit himself to Alistair Blunt: He has dug his own trap, and fallen into it. And when he finds he has been misled, no opinion one way or the other, on politics or international finance, can be attribued to Agatha Christie. (57-58)

The end result of all this Christiean misdirection is that we do not have a reliable way of knowing what Christie's intentions as an author were. She had apparently absorbed the lesson her characters learn again and again: Those who reveal too much hang themselves. And, in life as in art, a little mystery is a popular thing; as Janet Morgan puts it, "reticence and restraint . . . only quicken public attention and serve to enhance her mystique. The more she eluded her devotees, the more firmly they appropriated her. The less she said about herself, the more they claimed to know" (162). This has been as true of her detractors as of her admirers.

What we do know of Christie's life does not always support the oft-cited image of her as a stereotypical woman of the leisured classes. We should not ignore the fact that she was a career woman, and a spectacularly successful one. She may have begun her career as a wife and mother who wrote detective stories as a pleasant and moderately lucrative hobby, but her traumatic divorce made writing necessary to her survival.[6] She was a self-made woman, not only in terms of her career but very probably in terms of her public persona. Whatever Victorian attitudes she may have expressed, she was a participant in the changing role of women in this century. And however nostalgically she remembered the leisured people of her childhood, she never chose to become one again; she continued to work, even long after she had ample financial means to retire. Her relationship to the class she was born into may well have been more ambivalent than she expressed.

Most important, her texts display ambivalence. If we resist a linear reading of the novels in which resolution of mystery automatically absolves and validates those characters not complicit in the plot's central crime, this is readily apparent. The country-house world depicted in many of Christie's best-known novels is not a "bucolic dream," as Grossvogel terms it (256), of England at its best, but a hazardous world in which no one is what he or she seems. The flat, generalized quality of these country-house settings reveals their unreality: They are more like theatrical sets than real estates. The characters who inhabit them are known to each other only by virtue of the roles they play, roles that they resolutely pretend are real, though most of them have "offstage" activities, carefully concealed from the other players. What these depictions indicate is not a securely powerful leisured class, but a class that is purposeless and doomed. Murder disrupts this world because it calls attention to its falseness; in the course of the investigation, the hidden failures of its inhabitants will be revealed. Once the disruptive force is removed, the society returns to its normal course; but this closure is less a confirmation of the society's essential validity than a confirmation of its static nature, its inability to change in response to changing times. Its members close ranks because that is the only response they are capable of; they must turn to each other, at least until they turn upon each other. This world can appear comfortable and comforting only from the audience's point of view; we, after all, know the curtain will fall and we will not have to stay there.

The society Christie depicts is ideally suited to producing murderers. It is materialistic; and its inhabitants, for the most part, believe there are only two ways to make money: By inheriting it or by marrying into it (the most enterprising, of course, combine the two). For one character to inherit money, another character has to die; at least one motive for murder is always present. Thus, as Barnard points out, "the coziness and the stability are only skin-deep . . . the reestablishment of apparent order at the end can never be entirely reassuring, except to the wishful thinker or the superficial reader" (30).

The Great War may have put an end to "the halcyon days of the privileged classes" (Mowat 201), but those members of the gentry who could afford to do so continued to attempt to live in their accustomed manner throughout the 1920s and 1930s. The problematic conditions thus created shape Christie's texts.

Most of the inhabitants of Christie's "country-house" murder novels of the 1920s and 1930s are not members of the working middle classes but of upper or upper-middle classes that live on accumulated capital. This distinction is an important one and provides a starting point for rethinking Christie's alleged validations of bourgeois values. After the war, some members of the country gentry were able to regain power by entering the competitive world of business: "The former 'ruling classes,' whose sons had gone into Parliament and the services as a matter of course, was now forced more and more into business . . . their political power lived on only insofar as they became influential in business" (Graves 65). But most "lived a quiet life," attempting to preserve as much as they could of their old estates (Graves 66). Most of Christie's characters are from this latter group, "the respectable and tenanted failures of the manor" (Grossvogel 258), who must rely on the past as a means of survival because they are unequipped to find another means. The trouble with living on capital is that sooner or later it runs out. This is a class on the verge of bankruptcy, in literal and figurative senses. Unable to function in any other society, the members of this group must use each other as a means of replenishing funds, through murder if necessary. They are not the competitive bourgeoisie; rather, they are trapped by their own unfitness to compete.

Christie was a great admirer of Dickens, and the static society depicted in her novels manifests a classic Dickens theme: When inertia takes hold, rot inevitably follows. Christie's country manors are collapsing as surely—if not quite so dramatically—as the propped-up buildings in *Bleak House* or *Little Dorrit*. The inhabitants of her houses, too, crumble. Unable to grow, these characters sink into progressive decay, as is indicated by their repetition of meaningless activities—they have nothing productive to do—and, especially, by their warped emotional responses.

Peril at End House, published in 1932, is one of Christie's finest elaborations of this theme. The story centers on Nick Buckley, the young and beautiful mistress of End House, a home that is, events prove, appropriately named. The somewhat melodramatic title of the novel seems perfectly suited to the early plot developments: Young Nick lives alone in her crumbling ancestral home, which is perched on the cliffs of Cornwall. A series of rather theatrical attempts on her life take place, including a heavy picture frame crashing down on her bed and a boulder crashing down on her path. Fortunately for Nick, Hercule Poirot is on the scene, determined to rescue her from her unknown enemy (one is tempted to say "dastardly villain"). What makes all this creaky melodramatic machinery plausible, to both Poirot and the reader, is that Nick is so determinedly not the Victorian damsel in distress the plot seems to call for; she is, rather, an extremely "modern" young woman: Hard-edged, bold, aggressive. She is not a prisoner in her isolated, gloomy home. She spends much of her time in London, running with a "fast crowd" of friends, including cocaine dealers and daring young aviators. She is not, Poirot concludes, the hysterical type who might fabricate a romance of danger in order to gain attention; indeed, Poirot has great difficulty convincing her to take her danger seriously. This helps to convince the reader that the threat is real. It materializes when Nick's cousin Maggie Buckley, wearing a distinctive shawl of Nick's, is shot, apparently by mistake.

But in this case, it is the *falseness* of the threat that is real; the attempts on Nick's life are as theatrical as they seem. Nick has stage-managed it all in order to disguise the fact that she herself is the murderer, and Maggie's death is no mistake, as it enables Nick to inherit a fortune.

Superficially, it seems that the ending of this text is a condemnation of the idea of the modern young woman that Nick represents. Tough and assertive, she is also amoral, and the masculine nickname (pun unavoidable) by which she is known seems a symbol of her lack of femininity. Yet if this ending is seeking to reinforce traditional standards of female behavior, it is strange that the last pages of the novel present in a positive light Nick's friend, a young woman who is also known by a masculine nickname, Freddie, who is also tough and assertive and who has the decidedly nontraditional attributes of being both a cocaine addict and an adulteress.[7]

In fact, to accept Nick as a representative of modernity is to fall victim once again to Nick's own stage management. Hastings, Poirot's "Watson," says of her, "What an actress the world had missed" (*Peril at End House* 160); and Poirot, "She staged a fine drama here" (170). Most of Christie's characters are actors, and Nick is a consummate one. Nick's vivacious and optimistic persona is entirely fraudulent; she is firmly wedded to the past. Her superficial modernity is a screen for her actual inability to move forward. Hastings, who can sometimes come close to the truth without realizing it, says early in the story that Nick's face contains "something haunting and arresting"(8). Actually, *haunted* and *arrested* describe Nick's situation. The dated quality of the fabri- cated attempts on her life, of her melodramatic depiction of herself as a damsel in distress, reveals this; she can apply a veneer of modernity to a stale story, but she cannot create a new one. She is also fundamentally traditionalist; it is typical of her that, prior to the murder, the only way she considers getting the money she wants is by marrying into it.

Nick kills for money, and she wants the money for one key reason: To keep and maintain End House. It has been in her family for three hundred years, and she is the last of her line. She is "passionately and fanatically devoted to her home" (169)—the home that is literally crumbling around her. Early in the novel, Poirot tells her, "You are young and beautiful, and the sun shines and the world is pleasant, and there is life and love ahead of you" (29). But Nick is concerned with nothing that is ahead of her, only with what is behind her, with an inheritance she will keep at all costs. In her dedication to the dead past, she shares the spiritual "dry rot" that afflicts End House. Ultimately, and ironically, Nick *is* trapped "in a dark mysterious mansion, haunted by a family curse" as Poirot jokingly remarks (7), but unlike the LeFanu heroines subject to such curses, Nick imprisons herself; no wicked relations confine her, except the dead ones she has bound herself to.

It is in this novel that a rather peculiar conversation takes place, between Poirot and Nick's housekeeper, Ellen:

"You see, sir," she said, "this isn't a good house." . . . Poirot . . . seemed to find the remark not in the least unusual. "You mean it is an old house." "Yes, sir, not a good house." . . . Poirot looked at her attentively. "In an old house," he said, "there is sometimes an atmosphere of evil." "That's it, sir," said Ellen eagerly. "Evil. Bad thoughts and bad deeds too. It's like dry rot in a house, sir, you can't get it out. It's a sort of feeling in the air. I always knew something bad would happen in this house, someday." (98)

What is odd about this exchange is its automatic equation of "old house" with "not a good house." While this point is not explicitly made in all Christie's country-house novels, the houses do generally seem to represent the dangerous influence the past can exert on the present and future. The past—like the old house—is not inevitably a bad thing in and of itself, but if it is not allowed to *become* the past, if it is kept unnaturally alive, it will stifle new growth.

The theme of a rotting society resonates through Christie's novels at all periods of her career. It is present in Poirot's first case, which takes place at the significantly named Styles House: Another home of conventionalism and false appearances. It is vividly illustrated in later works such as *Sleeping Murder* and *Nemesis*, whose murderers kill for twisted, incestuous love, love so resistant to change and growth that its inevitable outcome is killing its object.[8]

The danger inherent in believing in things and people that are not what they seem and of clinging to an illusory reality that does not adapt to change is central to Christie's work. It may well have had its roots in the dramatic changes World War I brought to British society and the responses she and other women writers help formulate. Whatever nostalgic impulses her texts may inspire, ultimately they insist on their own unreality, on their status as works of fiction, and on the necessity of social change and growth. Her 1965 novel, *At Bertram's Hotel*, provides the archetypal example of this pattern. Bertram's is a carefully recreated piece of the past—the past as we generally like to have it recreated, with all the modern amenities—and as such a work of art. But the danger of Bertram's is that it presents itself as real and thus can trap one into living out illusion as reality. Bertram's can be understood only by recognizing its status as a fiction, especially in the way it is constructed to produce a particular illusion. The same may be true of Christie's novels, whose design draws our perceptions away from the possibility that they are not what they seem.

NOTES

1. The classic exploration of this issue in terms of literature of the period is Paul Fussell's *The Great War and Modern Memory* (London: Oxford University Press, 1975). See especially 317.

2. These three authors produced many detective stories in the 1890s and early 1900s. Some of this fiction has been reprinted in Alan K. Russell's *Rivals of Sherlock Holmes*, (Secaucus, NJ: Castle Books, 1978).

3. The prime example is perhaps Wilfred Owen's "Parable of the Old Man and the Young."

4. Grossvogel describes Poirot as "the detective who triumphs, as he brings the action to a close, over even his own shortcomings" (264).

5. Grossvogel seems to take the validity of this technique for granted; even so astute a critic as Stephen Knight is occasionally guilty. To cite one example, Grossvogel, in his analysis of *The Mysterious Affair at Styles*, states that murder "darkens the vision of a pristine Devonshire belonging to two English girls" (257)—that is, that the text, *sans murder*, is Christie's fond portrait of the world she knew as a child. He offers no textual support for interpreting the novel's setting (which is Essex, not Devonshire) in this way, nor for inserting not only Christie but also her sister into a paragraph that began as a discussion of the text. The intentional fallacy seems to die a harder death in criticism of this genre than any other (55-56).

6. Even this may be debatable, since Morgan indicates (104-5) that Christie's attitude

toward her work had become very professional long before her divorce.

7. Christie's portraits of "modern" young women like Freddie are in fact usually favorable, as Gillian Gill points out in *Agatha Christie: The Woman and Her Mysteries* (85-87).

8. Christie's *The Mysterious Affair at Styles* was written during World War I and published in 1920. *Sleeping Murder* was written during World War II but published after Christie's death in 1976; *Nemesis*, the last Miss Marple novel to be written, was published in 1971.

REFERENCES

Barnard, Robert. *A Talent to Deceive: An Appreciation of Agatha Christie*. New York: Dodd, Mead, and Co., 1980.

Christie, Agatha. *At Bertram's Hotel*. London: Crime Club-Collins, 1965.

____. *Peril at End House*. New York: Pocket Books, 1942.

Gill, Gillian. *Agatha Christie: The Woman and Her Mysteries*. New York: Free Press, 1990.

Graves, Robert, and Alan Hodge. *The Long Week End: A Social History of Great Britain, 1918-1939*. New York: W. W. Norton and Co., 1963.

Grossvogel, David I. "Agatha Christie: Containment of the Unknown." In *The Poetics of Murder*, edited by Glenn W. Most and William W. Stowe, 252-65. New York: Harcourt Brace Jovanovich, 1983.

Knight, Stephen. *Form and Ideology in Crime Fiction*. Bloomington: Indiana University Press, 1980.

Morgan, Janet. *Agatha Christie: A Biography*. New York: Perennial Library/ Harper and Row, 1986.

Morgan, Kenneth O., ed. *The Oxford History of Britain* Oxford: Oxford University Press, 1988.

Mowat, Charles Loch. *Britain between the Wars: 1918-1940*. Chicago: University of Chicago Press, 1955.

Sayers, Dorothy L. *Whose Body?* New York: Perennial Library/Harper and Row, 1987.

12

"I am Duchess of Malfi still": The Identity-Death Nexus in *The Duchess of Malfi* and *The Skull beneath the Skin*

Carolyn F. Scott

The Duchess of Malfi, by John Webster, not only provides essential elements in the plot of *The Skull beneath the Skin*, by P. D. James, but it also contributes to the framework for the narrative and itself finally achieves a new resolution in the conclusion of the modern mystery. By discovering and exposing the murder of Clarissa Lisle, Cordelia Gray redeems both the Duchess of Malfi and Bosola. The murders of the Duchess and Clarissa Lisle result from a failure of their servitors, Bosola and Cordelia Gray. While Bosola cannot resolve the crime and loses his own life in the process of trying to atone for his actions, Cordelia Gray, caught in the crux of the identity-death nexus, not only learns the identity of the murderer but also arrives at a new understanding of her own position as both the Duchess and Bosola, as both victim and victimizer. Charles R. Forker analyzes the love-death nexus or the "dramatization of the ironic interplay between love and death" (237) in his study of Webster. Just as love and death are inextricably bound in Webster's plays, identity and death also operate in tandem. Only at the moment of death can characters truly recognize their identities; the moment of authentic self-recognition leads to death. The characters in *The Duchess of Malfi* must confront their identities and their deaths simultaneously. The characters in *The Skull beneath the Skin* face the same conjunction.

The Duchess of Malfi provides a fertile ground for writers of detective fiction. Agatha Christie reconsiders the play in *Sleeping Murder*, using it to furnish both a clue to the mystery and a motive for the murder. A production of *The Duchess of Malfi* and the line "Cover her face; mine eyes dazzle: She died young" (IV.ii. 255) awaken in Gwenda Reed the memory of a murder she witnessed as a child. As she and her husband delve further into the question of whether there was a murder and, if so, who the murderer is, Gwenda wonders if her "childish memory [is] the only link [the dead woman's] got with life—with truth?" (100). Their search becomes imperative "so that the truth will be known" (100). As in *The Duchess of Malfi*, suppressed incestuous desire is among the motives for the murder. Miss Marple observes of the murderer, "He wasn't normal. He adored his half-sister and that affection became possessive and unwholesome. That kind of thing happens oftener than you'd think" (165). In this case, the play acts as a thread that connects memory, motive, and murderer. Some deeper connections exist, however. *The Skull beneath the Skin* goes further by weaving the play into the novel as an inextricable web, expanding and explicating the characters and events.

The several layers of connection between the two works establish an association that goes beyond surface considerations. A production of *The Duchess of Malfi* provides the impetus and the context for the gathering of victim, suspects, and detective in the novel. Furthermore, specific lines from the play provide clues within the novel. Equally important, the play provides the outline of the book, with its five acts corresponding to the first five chapters of the novel. The sixth chapter supplies the resolution to the murders that the play fails to furnish.

Clarissa Lisle clearly associates herself with both the play and the character of the Duchess of Malfi. Sir George explains to Cordelia that "This performance is important to her . . . if she can regain her confidence she might feel that she can do [a revival of the play]" (17). Clarissa's power and identity as an actress hinge on her ability to play the role successfully. In fact, as an actress, Clarissa's identity depends on her skill in becoming someone else; acting continually risks confronting the identity-death nexus. Ivo Whittingham observes "how Clarissa could take on an almost luminous beauty, the power of that high, slightly cracked voice, the grace with which she used her arms and body . . . she did manage to convey something of the high erotic excitement, the vulnerability, and the rashness of a woman deeply in love. That wasn't surprising; it was a part she had played often enough in real life" (107). Clarissa is both a product and a producer of her roles, making her identity both more and less determinate. Insofar as her identity controls her characters, she has a sure grasp of who she is. To the extent that the parts she plays guide her actions and interactions, her identity becomes a construction.

The Duchess, like Clarissa, must also play different roles that both help and hinder her ability to know herself. Forker notes that "as a royal and necessarily ceremonial figure, the Duchess is by definition a player of roles; her acceptance of the tragic role forced upon her by her cruel brothers and by her own desire for emotional fulfillment is more a means of self-confrontation than a mawkish escape from reality" (327-28). Role-playing is inherent in the Duchess's character. In order to divert suspicion about her secret marriage to Antonio, she must play the part of chaste widow and dutiful sister. To Antonio she must be both sovereign and wife. The delicate balance she must maintain can be seen when she courts Antonio, a reversal of the usual roles. She explains, "We are forc'd to woo, because none dare woo us" (I.iii.151). Her love enables her to play multiple roles simultaneously. At the same time, she recognizes the danger implicit in loving and in ambiguous identity. Early in their flirtation, Antonio suggests that she give her "excellent self" (I.iii.98) to a husband. Her response is the query, "In a winding-sheet?" (I.iii.99). She indicates a connection among her self, marriage, and death. In spite of the threat of death inherent in giving herself to Antonio, the Duchess chooses to love and accepts the consequences. Although she must play many roles, she never loses contact with her true self.

Both Clarissa and the Duchess must cling to their identity in the face of ever-increasing threats to their lives. The poison-pen notes sent to Clarissa assault her ability as an actress. She loses confidence, "drying up" during crucial performances until she finally seizes one last chance to salvage her career in an amateur production of *The Duchess of Malfi*. Her life and livelihood depend on her successful presentation of this role. Clarissa explains to Cordelia the power and the terror that these notes contain. They focus on "Death. That's what I'm afraid of. Just death. . . . There never was a time when I didn't see the skull beneath the skin. . . . It isn't the death of other people. It isn't the fact of death. It's my death I'm afraid of" (141-42). As the threatening notes strip away her ability to act other roles, Clarissa is forced closer and closer to confronting her own identity. Instinctively she recognizes that such a confrontation will entail annihilation; death lies at the heart of authentic self-recognition. Clarissa's life emerges as one long struggle to avoid the final acknowledgment of who she is.

The Duchess encounters similar threats to her identity and her life. Her brother Ferdinand's incestuous infatuation with her prevents her from openly acknowledging her love for and marriage to Antonio. The scene where lover and brother suddenly change places leads the Duchess to an awareness of the proximity of death. The scene begins positively, even comically, with the Duchess, Cariola, and Antonio joking and laughing together. As the Duchess continues to tease, Antonio and Cariola steal from the room behind her back, leaving her talking to herself about her love for Antonio. At this point Ferdinand enters the room unseen. The Duchess prattles on and, when she gets no response from Antonio, declares "whether I am doom'd to live or die, / I can do both like a prince" (III.ii.73-74). Ferdinand shatters her complacency by demanding, "Die, then, quickly" (III.iii.74), and handing her a knife. His jealousy threatens her identity, her love, and her life. He cannot bring himself to kill her at this point, yet all his subsequent actions denote the mixture of love and loathing that motivates him. As Forker points out, "thus does Webster present Ferdinand's self-alienation as an aspect of his identification with the image of his sister. The confused feelings of love-hatred that he expresses toward her are dramatized as a transference, in part, of inadmissable feelings about the self" (308). Ferdinand seeks control of the Duchess's identity in order to control his own. Later he has her imprisoned and seeks to drive her mad in order to destroy her identity. He pretends to offer a reconciliation and gives her, instead of his own hand, the hand of a dead man, implying that it belongs to Antonio. The marble arm of the dead princess used to batter in Clarissa Lisle's face is clearly related to this macabre gift. The artificial figures of her dead family and the roomful of madmen further Ferdinand's efforts to drive the Duchess insane. Unlike Clarissa, however, the Duchess does not fear death.

The close identification between Clarissa and the Duchess culminates in their deaths. Cordelia senses the relationship between the two women as she enters Clarissa's room the night before the murder. As Cordelia looks into the room, "it was easy to imagine that she stood in the doorway of a bedroom in Amalfi with Webster's doomed duchess bright-haired at her toilet while horror and corruption stalked in the shadows" (134). The bed too is as "sinister and portentous as a catafalque" (133-34). Cordelia perceives an atmosphere of death surrounding Clarissa, particularly through her identification with the Duchess. Clarissa also provides an indication that she is marked for death, although she does so apparently unconsciously. She flippantly greets her husband, "here I am, Duchess of Malfi still" (157). In the context of the play, this declaration by the Duchess, "I am Duchess of Malfi still" (IV.ii.133), indicates both her triumph and her doom.[1] She affirms her identity, demanding respect from her tormentors, particularly Bosola. At this moment of supreme self-recognition the Duchess faces the knowledge of her death confidently. She orders Bosola, "Tell my brothers / That I perceive death, now I am well awake, / Best gift is they can give or I can take" (IV.ii.214-16). Identity and death merge as the Duchess accepts both. Clarissa invokes death by identifying herself as the Duchess. In her efforts to avoid both identity and death she enters the nexus that leads to her murder.

The job of solving or avenging the murders falls on the two servants, who both feel themselves responsible for the deaths, Bosola with good reason. Bosola struggles to accommodate his identity also. Ferdinand hires him "To live i' th' court here, and observe the duchess; / To note all the particulars of her haviour" (I.ii.164-65). Bosola understands that agreeing to do so will lead to a betrayal of his integrity. He argues with Ferdinand, observing "you would create me / One of your familiars . . . would make . . . me an impudent traitor . . . a villain" (I.ii.171-188); but in the end he acquiesces, declaring, "I am your creature" (I.ii.202). Bosola allows Ferdinand to determine his identity even as he recognizes that the self that they create is a false one. Throughout the remainder of the play Bosola makes declarations that indicate the ambiguity of his identity. Before he kills the Duchess, he tells her he is "a tombmaker" and "the common bellman" (IV.ii.138, 163). With each statement Bosola equates himself more and more closely to death until at last he becomes its personification by strangling the Duchess. Even as he completes this task, he regrets his actions as both a betrayal of the good and as a betrayal of his self. Bosola discovers, as Forker observes, that

reluctant but growing admiration for both the Duchess and her spouse quickens his conscience, and his perception of Ferdinand's ingratitude pushes him one degree further into a radical reappraisal of himself and of his entire situation. Coming at length to revere the Duchess almost as devotedly as Antonio, he renounces allegiance to his cruel master and attempts to ally himself with the persecuted husband. What loving the Duchess had done for Antonio, torturing and killing her does for Bosola. (329)

The victimizer finds unexpected strength in the victim and seeks to make it his own. He confronts Ferdinand with the deed, demanding acknowledgment of its offense against nature. Ferdinand denies both responsibility and Bosola. Bosola reminds him, "I serv'd your tyranny, and strove / To satisy yourself than all the world: / And though I loath'd the evil, yet I lov'd / You that did counsel it; and rather sought / To appear a true servant than an honest man" (IV.ii.214-18). Repudiated, Bosola confesses, "What would I do, were this to do again? / I would not change my peace of conscience / For all the wealth of Europe" (IV.ii.224-26). Filled with remorse, he attempts to atone for his guilt and to avenge the Duchess by protecting Antonio and by killing Ferdinand and the Cardinal.

Cordelia, while not directly responsible for Clarissa's death, experiences guilt over her failure. She is in the process of establishing her identity as a detective, a private investigator. The job of protecting Clarissa Lisle proves distasteful both because it casts her in the role of a servant and because she finds Clarissa personally abhorrent. She must remind herself that "She was here to protect Clarissa, not to judge her" (122). Later, when torn between obligations to Sir George and Clarissa, she decides "It was Clarissa who had sent for her, Clarissa who was her client, Clarissa she was paid to protect" (157). Unlike Bosola, Cordelia possesses a clear sense of what her job is and who she is in relationship to it. Her instructions do not require her to betray her identity, yet, like Bosola, she ultimately fails the woman she is meant to serve. She assumes responsibility for Clarissa's death. Sir George even believes momentarily that she is confessing her guilt until she explains, "You employed me to look after her. I was here to keep her safe. I should never have left her" (188). Cordelia loses a part of her identity through this failure. When Chief Inspector Grogran remarks, "So you call yourself a detective, Miss Gray?" (223), her response, "I don't call myself anything. I own and run a detective agency" (224), indicates the ambiguity of her identity. She both is and is not a detective; the rest of the novel involves not only her search for the identity of the murderer but her quest for her own identity as well.

Like Bosola, Cordelia desires to protect the innocent husband of the victim. In this case, Bosola fails again in his efforts. Rather than aiding Antonio, Bosola accidentally stabs "The man I would have sav'd 'bove mine own life" (V.iv.57). With the death of Antonio adding to his guilt, Bosola can only "solve" the murder by completing his atonement through the death of Ferdinand and the Cardinal. Cordelia, too, must solve the murder to save Sir George. She begs him to allow her to reveal evidence that would exonerate him. When he refuses, her only recourse lies in determining the true murderer. Since death has stripped them both of their identities, Bosola and Cordelia must confront death in order to regain their selves. They both meet with some degree of success, but Bosola loses his life in the process. As he dies, he confesses that he has been "an actor in the main of all / Much 'gainst mine own good nature yet i' th' end / Neglected" (V.v.87-89). His last statement of identity declares, "I am gone" (V.v.99). Just as he became the personification of death for the Duchess, in his own end he faces the conjunction of identity and death.[2] He achieves a degree of redemption for himself and the Duchess, but it falls to Cordelia to complete the process.

As she begins to unravel the mystery surrounding the death of Clarissa Lisle, Cordelia encounters this advice from Voltaire by way of Chief Inspector Grogan: "We owe respect to the living; to the dead we owe only the truth" (227). Obeying an imperative similar to that felt by Gwenda Reed in *Sleeping Murder*, Cordelia must determine the truth for the Duchess, Bosola, Clarissa, and herself in order to regain her identity. Her investigations lead her to the knowledge of Ambrose Gorringe's involvement in the murder of Clarissa. When Cordelia presents him with the truth, he reveals his own fear of annihilation. He explains "If you accept, as I do absolutely, that this life is all that we have, that we die as animals, that everything about us is finally lost irrevocably, that we go into the night without hope, then that belief must influence how you live your life" (386). Unable to accept death, he denies his humanity, manipulating the other characters for his own ends. He is prepared to extinguish all other identities in order to preserve his own, embodied in his possession of his island estate. Although Simon has committed the actual murder, Gorringe had already begun the process through the threatening notes that had effectively destroyed Clarissa. Gorringe can even be held indirectly responsible for the situation that led to Simon's actions since Gorringe creates the atmosphere that causes Clarissa to demand a quasi-incestuous sexual relationship from Simon, which leads, in turn, to the fatal blow struck in revulsion. Gorringe perceives his actions as reasonable in defense of his identity. When Cordelia declares that she must reveal the truth to the police, Gorringe replies, "Oh no, you don't, Cordelia! No, you don't! Don't try to fool yourself that you no longer have the responsibility of choice" (389). His response provides a new threat to Cordelia's identity as he casts her in the role of the Duchess, the victim of masculine aggression.

Once again Cordelia must attempt to save a relatively innocent victim when she discovers Simon handcuffed in the Devil's Kettle. Gorringe locks them both in as the tide rises, and Cordelia comes face to face with the reality of her own mortality. She frees Simon, and they attempt to swim through the underwater passage:

She knew that she was swimming for her life, and that was almost all she knew. It had been a moment for action, not for thought, and she was unprepared for the darkness, the icy terror, the strength of the inflowing tide. She could hear nothing but a pounding in her ears, feel nothing but the pain above her heart and the black tide against which she fought like a desperate and cornered beast. The sea was death, and she struggled against it with all she could muster of life and youth and hope. (403)

Like the Duchess, Cordelia asserts her essential self against the threat of annihilation. Struggling free at last, Cordelia muses, "So this was what it was like to be born" (403), and, recovering slowly, "then she knew who and where she was" (404). Her passage through death returns her to life and to clarity of identity. Cordelia overcomes death and, in doing so, redeems the Duchess as she ceases to be a victim and seizes control of her destiny.

Not only has Cordelia been a victim, she has also perceived herself to be victimizer like Bosola. As Forker observes, "like Cain and Abel, the persecutor and the persecuted are primordially linked" (304). Her feeling of culpability in Clarissa's death achieves mitigation when she wins through to a new life. While Bosola can only "solve" the murder through more deaths, including his own, Cordelia solves the murder by revealing the truth. She encounters Gorringe once again, and when he continues to deny reality, she explodes:

Suddenly she felt an immense and overpowering anger, almost cosmic in its intensity as if one fragile female body could hold all the concentrated outrage of the world's pitiable victims robbed of their unvalued lives. She cried, "You killed him and you tried to kill me. Me! Not even in self-defense. Not even out of hatred. My life counted for less than your comfort, your possessions, your private world. My life." (411)

Her outburst speaks for the Duchess and Bosola as well as herself. She asserts the value and worth of each individual and frees both victim and victimizer from the roles society forces upon them. Confident of her identity, Cordelia realizes that "Suddenly, she felt inviolate. The police would have to make their own decisions. She had already made hers, without hesitation and without a struggle. She would tell the truth, and she would survive" (416). After encountering the identity-death nexus, Cordelia emerges triumphant, transforming death into life and redeeming those identities trapped in the threat of annihilation.

With the conclusion of the modern novel, the mystery inherent in the Renaissance play finds resolution. Bosola's despairing cry, "I am gone," the negative echo of that ultimate self-identification, the epiphanal "I am who am" of Exodus, transforms into Cordelia's expression of cosmic certitude. The Duchesss, who calmly maintains her knowledge of her self, equally finds her essence in this manifestation. The sixth chapter of the novel provides a sixth act to the play that demonstrates the triumph of goodness and truth over death and despair. The reverberations of the assertion, "I am Duchess of Malfi still," ring on in the life of Cordelia Gray.

NOTES

1. Forker sets the Duchess's statement in the context of her growth to maturity as the play progresses. He comments, "This reaffirmation is more than a simple assertion

of the self as dramatized earlier in the lady's defiance of marital conventions. It implies spiritual enlargement and growth, deepened perception, indeed a fundamental readjustment of values" (326). Clarissa fails to achieve such growth.

   2. Gosola does not achieve the success in his search for identity that the Duchess does. Forker concludes:

At the deepest level Bosola is a man in quest of psychological and moral authenticity, but Webster presents his pursuit of identity as an intermittently conscious process involving much escapism and attempted self-deception. Because his fullest recognition of self coincides with his death, Bosola possesses tragic stature in his own right. But, he is also the catalyst by means of whom the Duchess achieves her own tragic self-realization. (334)

Only Cordelia, who is both the Duchess and Bosola, can complete the quest and achieve a life-giving self-knowledge.

REFERENCES

Christie, Agatha. *Sleeping Murder* and *The Murder at the Vicarage*. New York: Dodd, Mead, 1976.

Forker, Charles R. *Skull beneath the Skin: The Achievement of John Webster*. Carbondale: Southern Illinois University Press, 1986.

James, P. D. *The Skull beneath the Skin*. New York: Warner, 1982.

Webster, John. "The Duchess of Malfi." In *Six Elizabethan Plays*, edited by R. C. Bald, 297-389. Boston: Houghton Mifflin, 1963.

13

"An Unsuitable Job" for Anyone: The "Filthy Trade" in P. D. James

Marnie Jones and Barbara Barker

P. D. James was once asked if she thought her novels encourage murder. She must, by now, be used to the question. She replied: "The detective story is far more about the restoration of order out of disorder, far more about the application of human intelligence to a puzzle" (Lehman and Clifton 81). That may be true about the genre as a whole, but no British writer more insistently asks us to question the restoration of order than does P. D. James. Two months later, *60 Minutes*, in a segment entitled "Murder She Writes," could barely restrain the question, "What's a nice little old lady like you doing writing stories like these?" That unasked question seems to prompt her toward a more vigorous defense of murder mysteries than a close reading of her work would suggest. "I think detective fiction flourishes best in ages of pessimism rather than optimism, because it is a reassuring genre," she has said. "Detective stories help reassure us in the belief that the universe, underneath it all, is rational." Perhaps, but there is little comfort to be found in James's world, where even the police worry about the damage they inflict in the name of justice. Her novels disturb because she repeatedly calls attention to our own deep ambivalence toward the police who are authorized to invade our privacy.[1]

If *An Unsuitable Job for a Woman* (1972) asserts that detection is an equal opportunity profession, the body of P. D. James's work suggests it is not suitable for anyone.[2] Since her earliest novels James has been conscious of the price paid for police work; what began as passing recognition on the part of the detective has become the central theme of her most recent work. In her second novel, *A Mind to Murder* (1963), Adam Dalgliesh, surveying the crowd at his publisher's sherry party, muses: "Presumably they wanted murderers caught however much they might argue about what should happen to them afterwards; but they displayed a typical ambivalence towards those who did the catching" (20). The violent crime of murder sets off a chain reaction of contamination, with the police as the agents of infection. This is remarkable precisely because the criminals in her books commit ghastly crimes: brutal stabbings, strangulations, and mutilations. Yet, James explicitly links the work of the police to these acts of violence. In *Death of an Expert Witness* (1977), the Controller of the Forensic Service says to Adam Dalgliesh, "'You chaps usually bring as much trouble with you as you solve. You can't help it. Murder is like that, a contaminating crime. Oh, you'll solve it, I know. You always do. But I'm wondering at what cost'" (92). Thus, it is the nature of the profession itself that disturbs.

As T. J. Binyon observes in *Murder Will Out*, detective writers have often accorded their heroes some degree of amateur status—Dupin, Holmes, Poirot, Lord Peter—because they did not want readers to associate their fictional detectives with the professionals, whose work focused on exposing the "dirty linen of divorce cases" (7). Binyon's point can be pushed even further. One very good reason for separating detective heroes from professional detectives and the police is our own deep ambivalence toward these professionals. While British mystery writers so often avoid stirring such ambivalent feelings, P. D. James makes these feelings the subject of her recent work.

Her one work of nonfiction, *The Maul and the Pear Tree*, written in 1971 with T. A. Critchley, marks a move toward making this interest her central theme.[3] James and Critchley wrote the book to "solve" the Ratcliffe Highway murders, which Thomas DeQuincy had made famous in *On Murder Considered as One of the Fine Arts*. During the process of investigating this one-hundred-and-eighty-year-old case, the authors trace our ambivalence to the creation of the police force itself. In seeking to understand our fear of the police, James and Critchley pose this essential question: "How was an efficient system of police to be reconciled with traditional English liberties?" (181).

James and Critchley document the meager system at work in 1811. They note that, contrary to the impression that an organized police force however, rudimentary, existed in London prior to the establishment of the metropolitan police in 1829, no such force actually existed capable of responding to such events as the Ratcliffe Highway murders. In fact, one could hardly create a system less able to react. Crime was fought at the parish level and had been since the Middle Ages. Parish churchwardens, overseers, and trustees conscripted up to a dozen people to serve as constables, who were unpaid and parttime. The constables, after a hard day spent as tradesmen or artisans, performed a number of services, including setting the nightly watch, that is, if they did not get out of the work by paying the parish a ten pound fine or paying a deputy to work in their stead. James and Critchley note that "most of these deputies were corrupt, and many served on for years" (18).

Efficient protection of the population broke down further at the line of first defense. Constables and deputies oversaw the night watchmen, who seem to have been no more inclined to do the work than their supervisors. Thirty-five worked the parish of St. George's-in-the-East. A night beadle oversaw the watchmen, who were paid two shillings a night to arrest anyone who disturbed the peace. But James and Critchley note that the watchmen only were interested in the fourteen shilling salary. Old men were chosen because one parish that had experimented with young watchmen had been "'obliged to abandon it on account of the connection which subsisted between them and the Prostitutes, who withdrew them from their Duty while Depredations were committing'" (19).

Corruption was deeply entrenched in the system. A contemporary report documented one typical scam. The watchman accepted a bribe from a burglar, often a friend, to arrest an innocent stranger on some technicality. When the watchman took the man to the watchbox, he was kept busy arguing with the understandably incensed innocent man. While the argument heated, the burglar got to work. It was a doubly profitable scam: The altercation at the watchbox was often ended when money changed hands, the innocent victim paying to have the false charge dropped (20).

There were also at this time three local magistrates, who had the power to hire not more than eight police officers, who had no uniforms, badges, or equipment. They were retained for a fee of twenty-one shillings a week, but they made upward of one hundred pounds a year by taking jobs for private individuals. There was deep-felt antagonism between the two forces created to ensure public safety. Understandably, given the corruption among the night watchmen, they considered the police officers as spies. Independent units—such as the Bow Street Runners or Thames police—functioned throughout the city; none of them exchanged information when a crime was under investigation: It was "a point of honour." "Under this system—or rather lack of it—there was no regular focal point, and no one was answerable to anyone for anything" (24). Readers of detective fiction enjoy *The Maul and the Pear Tree's* foray into historical detection precisely because the authors do what Dupin and Holmes did so well: They show the police to be incompetent.[4]

The Maul and the Pear Tree dramatizes how dangerous the world was in 1811, when traditional liberties had not been comprised yet by a systematic and competent police force authorized to invade personal privacy. There were problems everywhere: Napoleon was blockading continental ports, King George III was now "irrevocably" insane, the harvest had been disastrous, and the Luddite Riots in the North of England had erupted in violence. Local residents had cause for concern closer to home. Ratcliffe Highway is a posh district today, in London's East End, but in 1811 it had had "an evil reputation" for two centuries. Ten thousand thieves worked the dock, stealing an estimated £500,000 a year (7). And in December that year, seven people, including a three-month-old boy, were "brutally clubbed to death" in two households in the neighborhood over the course of twelve days. The public was so terrified that they eventually would surrender some of their traditional liberty for the security offered by a system of police protection.

The Maul and the Pear Tree argues that it was the national notoriety this crime received that prompted the creation of a police force. It took eighteen years precisely because there was such vigorous opposition to the idea.[5] The

English feared taking this step, the authors note, because the idea of a police force called to mind in all Englishmen the French police, which were "notorious as an instrument of armed terror; and few were prepared to press for reform at the risk of introducing tyranny" (181).

As James and Critchley observe, at the end of the nineteenth century 14,000 Metropolitan policemen with the support of hundreds of detectives, hunted Jack the Ripper—without success. Despite their failure, the existence of a police force did provide some reassurance. In 1811, without a police force, the "panic was unbridled" (1). Thus, James and Critchley invite us to imagine a world utterly different from our own—a world before there was a police force. The "barbarity and ruthlessness powerfully gripped the public imagination. . . . Never before, even at the time of the Gordon Riots when London was brought to the edge of anarchy, had there been such a national outcry against the traditional means of keeping the peace, or a more vigorous and persistent demand for reform" (1).

If James is right that "detective fiction flourishes in pessimistic times," it should not surprise us that her books *A Taste for Death* (1986) and *Devices and Desires* (1989) have done so well. For our world seems much more violent than it did when she began publishing in 1962. Jeffrey Dahmer is one of the most horrific examples of barbarity that have become almost commonplace. Examples from other communities come to mind. In 1990, as students at the University of Florida prepared for the fall term, someone terrorized the community of Gainesville by killing and mutilating five college students. Consider James and Critchley's description of what the public feared in 1811:

The murders from the first exercised a unique power over the hearts and minds of Londoners. The emotion was compounded partly of horror at the cruelty and ruthlessness of the deed, and partly of a pity at the helplessness and youth of the victims, all under twenty-five years of age. . . . Timothy Marr had been poor, hardworking and respectable, living at peace with his neighbors, a good husband and father. Nothing had saved him; neither virtue nor poverty. He and his whole family had been annihilated in a brutal holocaust as if they were of no account, either to heaven or man . . . yet [in 1811] atrocious murder was comparatively uncommon. . . . Murder . . . was still the unique, the horrifying crime. The wiping out of the whole Marr family seemed to strike at the very foundations, not only of public order, but of morality and religion themselves. If this could happen, who could be safe? If decency and humbleness could not protect a man, what could? (37-38)

"If this could happen, who could be safe?" This is the fear that created the police force. This book only obliquely considers what James increasingly will focus on in her novels—that creating a police force compounds the fear.

The authors convincingly document that these crimes prompted people to perceive that something was wrong with society itself. They quote the poet Robert Southey, who noted that even from his perspective 300 miles away from London, everyone talked incessantly about the murders. He thought it brought "a stigma, not merely on the police, but on the land we live in, and even our human nature" (181). Prime Minister Spencer Perceval questioned whether any institution could guarantee public safety when he addressed Parliament after the Ratcliffe Highway murders. He sought to defend the institution of churchwardens, constables, night beadles, and night watchmen: "If such enormous guilt lurked in the human breast, no system of govenment could hinder it from endeavuring to effect its object." Fourteen thousand police officers plus one hundred detectives failed to catch Jack the Ripper. The prime minister continued, "It might be close to us; it might be in our houses" (186). The murderers in P. D. James's fiction can't be locked out—they are fathers, lovers, sisters, coworkers, respectable members of the community whom no one would reasonably fear.

There was considerable fear about the threat to liberty in the years before the police force was established. As James and Critchley inform us, parliamentary committees heard these concerns in 1816 and in 1818 and again in 1822. Once the Metropolitan Police Force was created by Sir Robert Peel in 1829, the vestry in the very parish where the Ratcliffe murders had occurred argued that the police force was unconstitutional. In early 1830, the parish vestry determined that the new "Bobbies" provided no answer to the problem of crime. Burglaries were on the increase, the streets "are in an intolerable state of riot and disorder at night," and citizens are so fearful that they hire private watchmen. The vestry was more deeply concerned, however, that "the present system is unconstitutional, and tends only to sap the foundations of our liberties" (193).

There was by no means uniformity of opinion against a police force however. While the hunt for the Ratcliffe murderer was at its peak, Robert Southey had felt for quite some time the need for increased protection. "The police laws cannot be too rigorous; and the usual objection that a rigorous police is inconsistent with English liberty might easily be shown to be absurd" (Gaskell 173). Southey's confidence in both policemen and the constitutional question can be linked to his status in the privileged upper class. But it is also worth noting that he has earned a kind of posthumous fame for wrongheaded predictions, for he was the one who advised the unpublished Currer Bell, guessing that Charlotte Brontë was a woman, that "literature cannot be the business of a woman's life and it ought not to be." Today, polls tell us most would agree with Southey about the need for rigorous enforcement of the laws. But James's popular novels continue to remind us that we also fear such rigorous enforcement. No mystery writer is more interested in the tenuous nature of our privacy than P. D. James.

Since the genre's inception, detectives have been notorious for their almost compulsive need for privacy. The most memorable of them have been invested with disturbing qualities. Generally, they have been in the tradition of the romantic hero: Poe's Dupin retreats from the world and the daylight, living in a gloomy mansion; Sherlock Holmes, preferring the company of his own mind, alleviates his boredom by turning to either detection or drugs. But if these detectives disturb, it is because of their personal characteristics, not their profession.

Like Dupin, like Holmes, Adam Dalgliesh is an intensely private person. P. D. James's interest in violations of privacy are evident even in her earliest novels, where she considers the question in terms of the personality of her detective. From the first novel on, James links Dalgliesh's impulse to protect his privacy to his wife's death. In *Cover Her Face* (1962), Eleanor Maxie, a woman who has murdered to protect her own son, says:

'Of course, I disapproved of this so-called engagement. Would you wish for such a marriage for your son?' For one unbelievable second Dalgliesh thought that she knew. . . . He wondered what she would say if he replied, 'I have no son. My own child and his mother died three hours after he was born.' . . . He could imagine her frown of well-bred distaste that he should embarrass her at such a time with a private grief at once so old, so intimate, so unrelated to the matter at hand. (93-94)

While this biographical fact may have been "unrelated to the matter" of Sally Jupp's death, it is centrally related to Dalgliesh's character—and his job. But James makes the connection between the two clear only in later novels. In the second novel, *A Mind to Murder* (1963), Dalgliesh hesitates to ask Deborah Riscoe out to dinner. There are good reasons for his hesitation: In the first novel, Dalgliesh had arrested her mother, Mrs. Maxie, for murder. However, he links his hesitation to his own psychological state: "Ever since the death of his wife in childbirth, he had insulated himself carefully against pain; sex, little more than an exercise in skill; a love affair merely an emotional pavanne, formalized, danced according to the rules, committing one to nothing" (*A Mind to Murder* 22). His emotional insulation still remains an enticing biographical fact; James does not yet explore the effect on his psyche.

In *The Black Tower* (1975) James explicitly links the personal trauma to his job as a police detective. Dalgliesh has the opportunity to consider his own emotional state because he is on leave recuperating from illness.

His grief for his dead wife, so genuine, so heartbreaking at the time—how conveniently personal tragedy had excused him from further emotional involvement. His love affairs . . . had been detached, civilized, agreeable, undemanding. . . . What, he wondered, had those carefully spaced encounters, both participants groomed for pleasure like a couple of sleek cats, to do with love, with untidy bedrooms, unwashed dishes, babies' nappies, the warm, close claustrophobic life of marriage and commitment. His bereavement, his job, his poetry, all had been used to justify self-sufficiency. (4)

His own words make it clear that his need for privacy predated his marriage: The deaths eventually became a convenient "excuse from . . . the claustrophobic life of marriage and commitment." This insulation extends not only to romantic involvements but to every other aspect of his life as well. The insulation both protects and paralyzes him emotionally. Dalgliesh realizes that it was too late to change now. "In the last fifteen years he hadn't deliberately hurt a single human being. It struck him now that nothing more damning could be said about anyone" (4).

In fact, the manner of his wife's death only underscores this particular detective's connection to criminals. As Richard Smyer has pointed out, Dalgliesh feels uncomfortable about his own responsibility in the deaths of Mrs. Maxie, in *Cover Her Face* (1962), Matron Taylor in *Shroud for a Nightingdale* (1971) and Grace Willison in *The Black Tower* (1975). The woman whose death he is most responsible for, however, is his wife. In his concern for these other women Smyer finds "at least a dim awareness that as the deceased wife's sexual partner, he helped set in motion the process that led to her death" (55). Certainly, James does not allow Dalgliesh to dwell on that connection, but he clearly feels his job links him with death. If murder contaminates, so does death. Dalgliesh was unintentionally partly responsible for his wife's death, and that death has come to contaminate his emotions.

His emotional paralysis has its advantages, given his job. If murder does, in fact, contaminate, then Adam Dalgliesh's neurosis helps to shield him from the contamination. His assistant in *Death of an Expert Witness*, John Massingham, notes that his superior has a more comfortable relationship with the bereaved than with his own colleagues. Massingham recalls watching Dalgliesh deal with the parents of a murdered child, and muses: "They seem to like him. . . . God knows why. At times he's cold enough to be barely human. . . . What, if anything, . . . would move Dalgliesh to spontaneous pity?" (178). There is proof, though, that he feels something, that he cannot entirely shut out the emotions of the world. In the same reverie, Massingham remembers a previous case involving the death of a child. Dalgliesh had "regarded the parents with just such a look of calm appraisal." However, after working relentlessly to solve the crime, his poetry bore evidence of the toll. "His next book of poems had contained the extraordinary one about a murdered child which no one at the Yard, even those who professed to understand it, had had the temerity even to mention to its author" (178).

In *Death of an Expert Witness*, James for the first time extensively probes the tenuous nature of privacy for all involved. Dalgliesh and Massingham read a series of tormented love letters in a relentless search for clues to the death of Dr. Lorrimer, the "expert witness" of the title. "It was the strangest part of a detective's job," muses Dalgliesh, "this building up of a relationship with the dead, seen only as a crumpled corpse at the scene of crime or naked on the mortuary table. The victim was central to the mystery of his own death. He died because of what he was" (88). P.D. James makes it clear that murder twice violates a person. The murderer ends Lorrimer's life, and he becomes a "victim"; yet Lorrimer is victimized a second time, when the police explore the details of his life. His affairs are now in the public domain. Massingham, reading Lorrimer's love letters, is surprised to feel shame at the invasion because, as he puts it, he was "accustomed to perusing the private pornography of murdered lives" (188). Both detectives are cast in the role of voyeur.[6]

Dalgliesh questions the standard justification for police intrusion: "Given the choice, Lorrimer would probably have preferred his murder to go unavenged than for any eyes but his to have seen these letters" (190).

The contamination extends beyond the victim and when it spreads—more harm is done. Those whose lives had touched Lorrimers, now suspects in his death, are as unable to defend themselves against the relentless police invasion of privacy as the dead man. For them, it is worse: They are alive to feel the pain. While guilty of no crime in the legal sense, everything about their lives becomes suspect. Consider just one example from the novel: Nell, the sixteen-year-old daughter of the murderer. She had accepted her father's guilt—even embraced it—because she felt he had done it for her—it proved he loved her. That illusion falls apart when she learns the true motive. As Dalgliesh watches her face, that truth he observes, "The case had been broken; except that it was never the case that broke, only the people." Moments earlier, watching the child "break," another suspect says, "'My God, yours is a filthy trade.' 'Not a trade. Just a job,' Massingham replies. 'And are you saying that it's one you don't want done?'" (339-40).

Dalgliesh recognizes the reality of violation, but he regards it as a necessary evil. There is no alternative if the machinery of justice is to fulfill its role by methodically seeking out the criminal at all costs. Dalgliesh appeals to readers because he is a detective with a conscience. He cares not only about the work he does but also about its effect on innocent people drawn into the contamination of murder by association. He notes that "Murder was always solved at a cost, sometimes to himself, more often to others. . . . It was a crime that contaminated everyone whom it touched, innocent and guilty alike" (92). He notes later, "It was possible to do police work honestly; there was, indeed, no other safe way to do it. But it wasn't possible to do it without giving pain" (340).

In *Devices and Desires* the Norfolk coast has been terrorized by a serial killer, known as "the Whistler." Miles Lessingham literally stumbles over "the Whistler's" most recent victim. Arriving hours late to a dinner party, at which Dalgliesh is a guest, Lessingham enthralls those present with the salacious details. Suddenly conscious that a teenage girl is standing in the shadows, Dalgliesh "said, hardly aware of the severity in his voice: 'Didn't Chief Inspector Rickards ask you to keep this information confidential?' There was an embarrassed silence. He thought, They had forgotten for a moment that I'm a policeman."

That single question, reminding them of who he was and what he represented, chilled the room and changed their mood from fascinated and horrified interest to a half-shameful unease. And, when a minute later, he got up to say his goodbyes and thank his hostess, there was an almost visible sense of relief. . . . But merely by being there, he increased their awakening fear and repugnance at this latest horror. On each of their minds was imprinted the mental image of that violated face, the half-open mouth stuffed with hair, those staring, sightless eyes, and his presence intensified the picture; brought it into sharper focus. Horror and death were his trade and, like an undertaker, he carried with him the contagion of his craft. (92-93)

Everyone present had the perfect alibi: They had been dining with Adam Dalgliesh when the crime was committed. As they are not personally at risk now, why does Dalgliesh's presence instill such discomfort? If P. D. James is right when she says that the detective story is reassuring, then he should inspire some comfort—if for no other reason than that they must be safe from suspicion. This scene dramatizes the deep suspicion people feel toward the police. James plays the scene so that the details of the crime do not contaminate but the presence of the tradesman who deals in death does. James links the police detective with the criminal; the guests draw back from Dalgliesh as they would from the psychopathic killer himself.

Lessingham's indiscretion becomes central to the plot. While Dalgliesh's presence gives them the perfect alibi for the murder that night, Lessingham's account makes everyone a prime suspect in the next, copycat murder of Hilary Robarts. Meg Dennison, present that night, has fled from the world to the isolated headland of the Norfolk coast. She proves that people can be hurt by such investigations: The past she had tried to flee is brought uncomfortably into the present again. Meg is tainted in another way, though. Not only is she a suspect, she is the one person in the novel who hears the criminal's "confession." Meg knows that she "shall never be able to unlearn, never forget" what happened that evening (444). This time, however, she chooses to embrace what she learns, buying the murderer's house, "Martyr's Cottage." The novel ends with Meg acknowledging that "'Terrible things have happened in the past to people living on this headland. . . . But, I still feel at home here'" (465). In this P. D. James novel, the detective and this suspect accept the terrible as a part of life.

It is because terrible things were done to Alice Mair in her youth that she commits murder. Dalgliesh describes Alice, the hostess of that ill-fated dinner party, as having "the absence of a spark of sexuality and . . . a deep-seated reserve" (22). The two traits are, in fact, linked. As a child, Alice had been forced into a sexual relationship with her father. Her brother Alex chooses to allow their father to bleed to death in order to end the abuse. Alice, in turn, thirty years later kills Alex's lover out of a sense of debt to her brother: She tells Meg Dennison, "'I owed [him] a death'" (448). The author is thus provided with a psychological explanation, and the character with a rationalization.

Alice Mair is remarkable because she articulates the P. D. Jamesian insight that the living pay a great price for conventional justice. It is perhaps surprising to find that both the criminal and the detective agree about what happens in the aftermath of wrongful death. But Alice Mair is more like Adam Dalgliesh than any other character in this or any other novel. Both are successful writers, published by the same press; Adam is a poet of some acclaim, seen by his publisher as "his newest candidate for media fame" (13). Both are intelligent, successful members of the elite professional class. Alice seems the least likely of suspects because James presents her as perfectly respectable. More important than these surface similarities, though, are the insights they share about the price paid for detection. "'The dead stay dead,'" she tells Meg. "'All you can do is to hurt the living in the name of justice or retribution or revenge. If that gives you any pleasure, then do it, but don't imagine that there's virtue in it'" (451).

In identifying Alice Mair as an important voice who cautions us not to "imagine there's any virtue in it," James does not endorse her behavior. While Alice is the most articulate criminal in all of P. D. James, she uses her intelligence to defend the indefensible. She believes there is justice to be had from murder: Her brother "deserved" a job, and she felt Hilary Robarts would have stood in his way. P. D. James does not give Dalgliesh the opportunity to argue with Alice's perverted justice, but Meg Dennison does exactly that: "'Nothing Hilary Robarts did deserved death.' 'I'm not arguing that she deserved to die. . . . What I'm saying is that I wanted her dead.' 'That seems to me so evil that it is beyond my understanding. Alice, what you did was a dreadful sin'" (444). The novelist, it seems, would agree. The title, *Devices and Desires*, comes from the "General Confession" in the Anglican *Book of Common Prayer*: "Almighty and most merciful father, we have erred and strayed from thy ways like lost sheep. We have followed too much the devices and desires of our own hearts" (*Order of Morning Prayer: Rite One*). Surely, Alice Mair followed too much the devices and desires of her own heart. But so has every other character in the novel. James does not mean us to accept her vision of justice, but there is much truth in her vision of life. She assures Meg that Hilary Robarts's death was easy—it was quick, she had no time to feel terror. "'It took courage [to kill her], but perhaps less than you would imagine. . . . It's what you do to the living that takes strong emotions, courage, hatred, love'" (444). That is the courage that Dalgliesh has not been able to summon. But this is also why we fear the detective's intrusion into our lives. Alice is right: What takes courage is what we do to the living. We feel the police are engaged in a "filthy trade" not because we have committed crimes the law has any interest in but because we commit "crimes of the heart" that take "strong emotion, courage, hatred, love."

None of this is particularly reassuring. In the concluding paragraph to the novel, Meg contemplates the nuclear power station that dominates the horizon, seeing in it a "symbol, too, of the intllectual and spiritual arrogance which had led Alice to murder, and it seemed to her for a second that she heard the echo of the last warning siren screaming its terrible message over the headland." That thought prompts her to think of future serial murderers: "And evil didn't end with the death of one evil-doer. Somewhere at this moment a new Whistler could be planning his dreadful revenge against a world in which he had never been at home" (465).

While James is right about the pleasure to be had from "the application of human intelligence to a puzzle," it cannot compensate for that pervasive sense of evil. It is true that Dalgliesh finds pleasure in his work, but he also knows it does not compensate: "Perhaps this was part of the attraction of his job, that the process of detection dignified the individual death, even the death of the least attractive, the most unworthy, mirroring in its excessive interest in clues and motives man's perennial fascination with the mystery of his mortality. . . ." Dalgliesh's optimism is immediately undercut. The sentence continues: "Providing, too, a comforting illusion of a moral universe in which innocence could be avenged, right vindicated, order restored. But nothing was restored, certainly not life, and the only justice vindicated was the uncertain justice of men" (161). Dalgliesh seems to echo Alice's feelings; it is not just virtue that is called into question, but justice as well.

NOTES

1. Interview aired with the dramatization of *Mystery's Devices and Desires*, October 1991; Erlene Hubly argues that critics are wrong in persistently placing James among writers of classic detective fiction, for her world "is finally one in which order cannot be restored, it having never existed in the first place" (519-20).

2. It is a barmaid who supposes Cordelia will give up the detective agency because "'It isn't a suitable job for a woman.' 'No different from working behind a bar,'" observes Cordelia. In her mind, she hears the mother she never knew articulate the novel's point of view: "her mother thought it an entirely suitable job for a woman." *Unsuitable Job for a Woman* 21.

3. Critchley, her coauthor, was a retired member of the Home Office staff.

4. See 196 and following for the summation of the catalogue of police "deficiencies and negligences" the authors find "incomprehensible."

5. The authors note that "Probably a vigorous Home Secretary could have pushed a radical Metropolitan Police Bill through the House of Commons in 1812" (183).

6. Dennis Porter, in "Detection and Ethics: The Case of P. D. James," argues "that in her fiction P. D. James turns out to be aware of the apparent 'unsuitability' of both activities—of detecting—and of reading about detection." She is, he notes, "highly self-conscious in recognizing how morally ambivalent" the work of detection is.

REFERENCES

Binyon, T. J. *"Murder Will Out": The Detective in Fiction*. London: Oxford University Press, 1990.

Book of Common Prayer: and Administration of the Sacraments and Other Rites and Ceremonies of the Church. New York: Frowd, 1989.

Devices and Desires. Dir. John Davies. *Mystery*. PBS, October 1991.

Gaskell, Elizabeth. *The Life of Charlotte Bronte*. 1857. Reprint. London: Penguin, 1975.

Hubly, Erlene. "The Formula Challenged: The Novels of P. D. James." *Modern Fiction Studies* 29, no. 3 (Autumn 1983): 511-21.

James, P. D. *The Black Tower*. 1975. Reprint. New York: Warner Books, 1987.

____. *Cover Her Face*. 1962. Reprint. New York: Warner Books, 1982.

____. *Death of an Expert Witness*. 1977. Reprint. New York: Warner Books, 1982.

____. *Devices and Desires*. 1989. Reprint. New York: Warner Books, 1991.
____. *A Mind to Murder*. 1963. Reprint. New York: Warner Books, 1976.
____. *Shroud for a Nightingdale*. New York: Scribner, 1971.
____. *An Unsuitable Job for a Woman*. 1972. Reprint. New York: Warner Books, 1987.
James, P. D., and T. A. Critchley. *The Maul and the Pear Tree*. 1971. Reprint. New York: Warner Books, 1987.
Lehman, David, and Tony Clifton. "A Queen of Crime." *Newsweek*, October 20, 1986, 81-82.
"Murder She Writes." *60 Minutes*. CBS, January 5, 1992.
Porter, Dennis. "Detection and Ethics: The Case of P. D. James." In *The Sleuth and the Scholar: Origins, Evolution, and Current Trends in Detective Fiction*, edited by Barbara A. Rader and Howard G. Zettler. New York: Greenwood Press, 1988.
Smyer, Richard I. "P. D. James: Crime and the Human Condition." *Clues* 3, no. 1 (Spring/Summer 1983).

14

Between Men: How Ruth Rendell Reads for Gender

Martha Stoddard Holmes

While detective fiction is frequently called a conservative genre, the fact remains that the heart of any detective story is a series of questions. Regardless of what stabilizing answers the end may try to deliver, the middle's search for what Peter Hühn calls "a hidden story inscribed in everyday reality" effectively transforms the fictional landscape into one in which "all phenomena may lose their usual, automatically ascribed meanings and signify something else" (454).

An investigation of persons is a significant component of the process of unearthing the buried story of the crime, and thus notions of individual subjectivity are actively questioned, or at least shaken, in the middles of detective stories. If we take the position that individual subjectivity as constructed within and by society is always gendered and that this "mark of gendering" cannot be voluntarily excluded from subjectivity, then detective fiction's destabilizing investigations of persons are inescapably investigations of gender as well. Accordingly, the genre invites scholarly inquiry into the ways in which criminal investigations both construct and question gender identities and, at the same time, gender (both concepts of gender and the gender of the investigator) constructs investigations.

On a more simplistic level, I might argue that any genre that reproduces the adage "*Cherchez la femme*" practically announces its participation in the social construction of gender and "social relationships based on perceived differences between the sexes" (Scott 94). If, as Myra Jehlen has suggested, "one has to read for gender; unless it figures explicitly in story or poem, it will seldom read for itself" (273), one might say that detective fiction routinely reads gender for itself and us.[1]

Different examples of the genre, obviously, offer different intensities of "reading for gender." A particularly vivid example of a structure marked by gender both "inside" and "outside" the narrative is that in which a woman writer creates a male detective in the business of investigating women (both corpses and suspects). *Cherchez la femme* takes on a whole new range of meanings when a woman is not just the object of masculine inquiry but also the creator of the whole project. The phrase can also transform itself into *cherchez la feministe*, as we frantically search for a feminist toehold in anything that looks like an ironic fissure in the masculine character's controlling point of view.

The structure just described is a frequent paradigm for twentieth-century British writer Ruth Rendell's Inspector Wexford novels. The objects of Wexford's investigations are a host of terrifying women, frequently mothers; and his official interrogations of their relations to crimes are frequently accompanied by a private interrogation of various issues of gender and sexuality, including feminism. As such, the novels are fascinating studies of Wexford's construction—sometimes criminalization—of femininity and, by implication, his notions about his own masculinity.[2]

In one of her early novels, however, *Shake Hands Forever*, Rendell transforms this model into one that reads for gender in different and more complicated ways. While Chief Inspector Reginald Wexford begins by observing Angela Hathall's corpse and speculating about sexual behaviors that may have led to her murder by a stranger, he gradually shifts his interest from Angela to her husband Robert, putting his career and sanity at risk through his attempts to prove Robert the real murderer. Concurrently, while Wexford's interrogation of his own gendered identity initially proceeds through his anxiously eroticized interactions with Nancy Lake, the dead woman's neighbor, the site of his self-location within a range of possible masculinities shifts to the men in his life and the case, including, finally, Robert Hathall.

Eve Sedgwick, Luce Irigaray, and others have argued that women function as currency in male transactions or as a bonding medium for male-male relationships.[3] This is not only true in situations in which two men are rivals for the affections of one woman: "The status of women, and the whole question of arrangements between genders, is deeply and inescapably inscribed in the structure even of relationships that seem to exclude women—even in male homosocial/homosexual relationships" (Sedgwick 25). Rendell's novel dramatizes graphically the presence and subsequent absence of the woman in the classic erotic triangle, as well as the single-gender relationships her absence facilitates. At the end, however, despite the provocative reappearance of women who have literally and figuratively disappeared, certain questions remain about at what cost—and whose—the novel produces its rich examination of the construction of Wexford's masculinity.

In the early chapters of *Shake Hands Forever*, Wexford moves between two narratives about the murder of Angela Hathall. One he bases on the fact of Robert Hathall's alibi and on previous assumptions about femininity: "Probably the woman had picked up a stranger and the stranger had killed her" (11). The source of the other narrative is his own strong feeling that Hathall has murdered his wife. Both stories are wrong—in fact, the dead woman is *not* Angela Hathall, but Angela's victim, a woman who discovered the Hathalls' embezzlement scheme—but Wexford is not yet capable of realizing this.

When Wexford comes home from his first day on the case (and the fact that he has a traditional home life, complete with spouse, children, and grandchildren, distinguishes him among detectives), his thoughts about the investigation blend into his "private" concerns. Wexford kisses his "placid . . . sensible" wife Dora with especial warmth because "another man's wife was dead, had died foully," a thought that makes him squeamish and activates "his small-hours sensitivity" even in the comfort of home (12). Another juxtaposition of work and home follows. Dora Wexford characterizes Nancy Lake, the Hathalls' pretty neighbor, as "very much one for the men"; the next moment finds Wexford looking at himself in the mirror, "drawing in the muscles of his belly" and reflecting that "in the past year he had lost three stone in weight . . . and for the first time in a decade he could regard his own reflection with contentment if not with actual delight. . . . If only there was something one could go without, some strenuous game one could play, that would result in remedying hair loss" (13). Although Wexford reflects before going to sleep that "he had taught himself not to dwell on work during the night, and work had seldom kept him awake or troubled his dreams," it already seems clear that any public/private distinctions will be disrupted in the course of the novel (14).

The passage prepares us to expect, as well, that Wexford's dealings with Nancy Lake, who later approaches him with information on Angela Hathall, will form a component of his gender identity in the course of the novel. Initially, this seems to be in the works. Wexford has a quick and complex response to the flirting of Lake, a woman who walks "confidently in the manner of one who has never known rejection" and is "one of those rare creatures whom time cannot wither or stale or devitalize" (22-33). He is uncomfortable, but flattered and attracted, asking himself, "How many years was it since a woman had flirted with him, had wanted to be with him and enjoyed the touch of his hand?" (28). Wexford thinks of his marriage vows, but also regrets that "work and convention and prudence prevented him from leading this woman to his car, driving her to some quiet hotel. Champagne and roses, he thought, and that hand once more reaching across a table to lie warmly in his" (28).

Instead of building as a significant subplot, however, Wexford's interactions with Nancy Lake only represent a few scenes in the middle of the novel. While their approach-avoidance encounters indicate Wexford's shifting feelings about himself as a probably attractive and possibly adulterous man, Wexford's articulation of his gender identity does not really have the *opportunity* to develop in direct response to Lake.

At the same time, Lake functions as a marker for the much more sustained group of relationships that are directly involved in Wexford's growth. Along with Wexford's concern with his weight, one of the "ongoing" dramas of the self we encounter in Wexford is that of his sense of inferiority in regard to other men. When he goes to interview Mark Somerset, who is Angela Hathall's cousin and a potential suspect, his impressions are much more than professionally incisive: "An athletic-looking man in his fifties, he wore neat black jeans and a tee-shirt, and Wexford detected his age only by the lines about his bright blue eyes and the veining of his strong hands. The man's belly was flat, his chest well muscled, and he had had the good fortune to keep his hair which, having once been golden, was now silver-gilt" (36). Much of Wexford's description of Somerset mirrors his own assessment of himself earlier in the book; a process of comparison is clearly suggested. Somerset becomes even more significant as a yardstick for masculinity, however, when Wexford discovers, several chapters later, that the other man is Nancy Lake's lover.

The relative weights of Somerset and Lake are indicated by the way that Lake drops out of the equation as soon as Somerset enters it. Wexford thinks "what an old fool he was to suppose Nancy Lake fancied him when she was going to marry Somerset" (150). He is suddenly compelled to discount his correct assessment of Nancy Lake's interest in him, not because she is previously involved (after all, so is he), but because her lover is his physical and class superior. Even an imagined relationship between Wexford and Somerset seems to take precedence over the real one between himself and Lake.

Wexford's insecurity about Mark Somerset is replicated in his relationship to his nephew, Chief Superintendent Howard Fortune, which forms a subplot of the novel:

For years Wexford had been in awe of him, his awe mixed with envy of this nephew, so aptly named, into whose lap so many good things had fallen, apparently without effort on his part, a first-class honours degree, a house in Chelsea, marriage to a beautiful fashion model, rapid promotion until his rank far surpassed his uncle's. And these two had taken on in his eyes the hard gloss of jet-set people, entering, although he hardly knew them, into that category of rich relations who will despise us from a distance and snub us if we make overtures to them. (57-58)

The final blow, predictable in light of the book's diet/weight trope, is Howard's ridiculously high metabolism.

While the above remarks are made retrospectively, Wexford and Fortune having since become friends, Wexford's insecurity about Fortune is hardly finished business. Fortune and his wife go out of their way to support Wexford in his unofficial investigation of Hathall, but when Wexford has to wait for an informational call from Fortune, he began to feel bitterly injured, and those old feelings he used to have about Howard reasserted themselves. True, he had listened sympathetically to all his uncle's ramblings about this case, but what was he really thinking? That this was an elderly man's fantasy? Country bumpkin rubbish? It seemed likely that he had only played along to humour him and had deferred that call . . . until he could spare the time from his more important metropolitan business. (97)

Similarly, when Fortune actually volunteers to watch Hathall, Wexford's reactions are conflicted:

The awe had gone long ago, giving way to love and comradeship. But that "I will do it," spoken so lightly and pleasantly, brought back all the old humiliation and envy and awareness of the other's advantages. Wexford felt a hot dark flush suffuse his face. "*You*?" he said roughly, "you yourself? You must be joking. You take rank over me, remember?" (123)

The most intense male-male relationship is that between Wexford and Hathall. The complexity of the hunter-hunted bond is a long-standing convention of crime fiction, from *Caleb Williams* to *Basil* to *Strangers on a Train*, to list only a few examples.[4] While these fictional relationships often begin with an attraction, Wexford's self-positioning in terms of Hathall, whom he finds ugly, paranoid, murderous, and generally repellent, is no less productive of growth. Through the successive and perhaps simultaneous stages of repulsion, obsession, and identification, Wexford achieves a balance of knowledge and distance that enables him not only to understand Hathall but also to understand himself.

After his initial sense that Hathall is a fake, Wexford grows curious about Hathall's "hidden story" on a number of levels, which by now should sound familiar:

Hathall, in spite of his grief, looked angry and resentful. His hard craggy features had the appearance of being carved out of roseate granite, his hands were large and red, and even his eyes, though not bloodshot, held a red gleam.

Wexford wouldn't have judged him attractive to women, yet he had two wives. Was it perhaps that certain women, very feminine or nervous or maladjusted women, saw him as a rock to which they might cling, a stronghold where they might find shelter? Possibly that colouring of his indicated passion and tenacity and strength as well as ill-temper. (32)

Wexford's perplexity about men, women, and attractions sends him fishing for all kinds of explanations; the string of possibilities from "very feminine" to "maladjusted" rings about as true as his earlier statement about Angela Hathall picking up a man. The paragraph dramatizes the lack of effective models for masculinity, femininity, and gender relations in Wexford's mind, as well as his awareness of this inadequacy.

In the midst of this confusion, however, Wexford remains convinced that Hathall, though not present at the murder, was responsible for it. After finding a new fingerprint at the scene of the crime, he develops yet another explanatory narrative: Hathall has a mistress who enacted the murder they planned together. When Hathall complains that Wexford is trying to entrap him, however, Wexford is ordered not to contact him again; the Chief Constable tells him, "'I will not have the reputation of Mid-Sussex sacrificed to your *feelings*'" (81).

Unable to forget Hathall—"he might be tedious but what he had done was not" (86)—Wexford decides to "go unofficial." He begins a private search for the woman accomplice, hiring an ex-con to tail Hathall. He begins to dream about him. He continues to construct, partly from his imagination and partly from interviews with Hathall's former employers and ex-wife, a picture of Hathall as a man who was married very young, who was faithful until middle age, and who suddenly became a womanizer. As his obsession with Hathall grows, Wexford moves from spying by proxy to stalking Hathall personally. He spends his vacation tracing the steps of Robert Hathall's present life, wondering, for example, as he rides the bus, "if Robert Hathall had ever sat on that very seat and looked out through this window" (111).

At last, in great excitement, Wexford follows Hathall and a woman to Hathall's flat—only to find that the woman is Hathall's daughter. Hathall's reaction, and Rendell's description of the two men, gives us a sense that not only Wexford but both men are conscious partners in an intimate and dangerous dance:

They were the same height and their eyes met on a level. Briefly, Hathall's showed white and staring around hard black irises in which that curious red spark glittered. They were at the head of the steep flight of stairs, and as Wexford turned to descend them, he was aware of a movement behind him, of Hathall's splayed hand rising. He grasped the banister and swung down a couple of steps. Then he made himself walk down slowly and steadily. Hathall didn't move, but when Wexford reached the bottom and looked back, he saw the raised hand lifted higher and the fingers closed in a solemn and somehow portentous gesture of farewell. (120)

Hathall believes, and Wexford fears, that in fact the game may be over. Hathall is about to move to Brazil, and extradition is unlikely on the evidence Wexford has of his past embezzlement. Wexford's obsession is such that it is unclear how he will live his life without Robert Hathall.

It is Wexford's last meeting with Nancy Lake that teaches him how to solve the mystery. Lake turns out to be the route not only to Mark Somerset but to Robert Hathall's hidden story as well. She tells Wexford that in a time of depression over Somerset, she made advances to Hathall and was turned down. After Wexford also turns her down, he finally asks himself, "Why had Hathall, who in middle life had come to enjoy sexual variety, repulsed such a woman as Nancy Lake?" (158).

Although for reasons of suspense we are not party to the moments in which Wexford works through this question, it seems clear that, instead of answering it, he must rewrite it. What is required of Wexford is that he acknowledge the similarity between himself and Hathall and proceed from there. Wexford doesn't believe that a man suddenly turns philanderer after a life of being faithful; after all, he himself refused Nancy Lake. If he extends his own experience to Hathall's, he can only imagine a man who went from one faithful marriage to a second equally faithful one. Thus, he is able to say to Howard Fortune, after the capture, "'Hathall was in love with his wife. Oh, I know we decided he'd acquired amorous tastes, but what real evidence did we have of that?' With a slight self-consciousness too well covered for Howard to detect, Wexford said, "If he was so susceptible, why did he reject the advances of a certain very attractive neighbour of his?'" (181).

It is the rewriting of the earlier question into "why does a faithful man who loves his wife kill her?" that solves the mystery, because Wexford can only answer, "He doesn't," and go on from there. He reconstructs Angela's murder of the woman who discovers the Hathalls' embezzlement and her assumption of the dead woman's identity in time to capture Robert and Angela hours before they leave England forever.

Wexford's reimagining of his gendered relations to women and men and his unravelling of the Hathalls' crime are inseparably linked in terms of his work as a detective. In a very literal sense, he can't solve the crime until he rethinks his own masculine identity.

Rendell's portrayal of masculinity as something constructed in relations between men is almost more interesting than the mystery plot, and her use of the detective as the man "under construction" is a worthy addition to the great tradition of women crime novelists, who seem always to have known that a case of shell shock or other "weakness" added sympathy and roundness to a sleuth.

To return to the notion of *cherchez la feministe*, however, the question remains, at whose expense is this examination of the construction of masculinity produced? As a feminist reader, I feel compelled to say that a parallel questioning of femininity is absent from the novel, as from all the Rendell novels I have read (Barbara Vine, Rendell's alter ego, presents a somewhat different story, especially in *The House of Stairs*). Most of the women characters are static, from Robert Hathall's frightening mother and his pathetic ex-wife, "one of those women who have been roses and are now cabbages" (73), to the "positive" characters like Dora Wexford, who are neither objectified nor given a subjectivity.

Nancy Lake looks like an exception. She is a beautiful middle-aged woman whose independent sexuality is paralleled by her unashamed consumption of cream-filled pastries, and Rendell gives her a strong and memorable voice, as well as the wit and intelligence to comment on the objectification in which she participates as a married man's lover: "'It gets hard, sometimes, alternating between being a queen and a—distraction. I shall get my crown back, this year, next year, sometime. I shall never abdicate'" (52).

Lake seems pathetically overwhelmed by sexual objectification, however,

the last time we "see" her, when she transforms herself into a gift for
Wexford, standing naked at the top of her stairway, "as he had seen her in his
fantasies—only better" (156). She never again *speaks* in the novel.

Angela Hathall, around whose supposed body circulate various narratives
of identity, presents another missed opportunity for Rendell to question
assumptions about femininity. Angela inspires some of Wexford's most
offensive remarks; thankfully, he never seems to *believe* his story of her as a
victim of her own sexuality, a lonely woman who "need not be desperate or
a nymphomaniac or on the road to prostitution . . . not even intend[ing]
infidelity" to pick up a strange man (14).

Like his investigation of Robert, Wexford's attempts to typify Angela
Hathall continually move him away from clichés and closer to the truth: That
she was a loving wife, a brilliant criminal, and the murderer instead of the
victim. All the same, partly because the plot prevents it, the novel fails to
capitalize fully on Angela as an opportunity to problematize myths of
femininity. While Wexford, at their first meeting, looks at Angela "long and
long, staring greedily as a man in love stares at the woman whose coming he
has awaited for months on end" (177), it is clear that he wants her only
because she is the key to Robert. Again, the really charged relationship is
between men; the women are neither desiring subjects nor sustained and
interesting objects of desire.

The concept of gender has meaning only as a description of difference; thus
there is in some sense always a man behind discussions of femininity and a
woman behind those of masculinity. While, as Joan Scott observes, gender has
often been used in recent years as a synonym for women, "gender as a substitute for women is often used to suggest that information about women is
necessarily information about men, that one implies the other" (84). We have
all seen, however, the dangers of assuming the reverse is true; the *femme* we
need to *chercher* in discourses of masculinity is not always legible.

Rendell is to be commended for literalizing the notion that there is always
a woman in relations between men and that women, in fact, create those
relations; in making the dynamics of triangular relations blatant, she makes
them readable. Both Angela Hathall, by (presumably) dying, and Nancy Lake,
by living, act as conduits for Wexford's desire for, and dread of Mark
Somerset, Howard Fortune, and Robert Hathall. Furthermore, both women
reappear at the end of the text, further dramatizing their existence—under
erasure—in what seem to be exclusively male relationships.

Because of the lack of full subjectivity granted these women characters,
however, the feminine resurfaces most engagingly in Wexford himself. He is
feminized from the novel's start by his habitation of not only a public,
patriarchal realm but also a private, domestic, matriarchal one, as well as by
the fact that the boundaries between these realms are disrupted throughout the
novel, culminating in the solution of the official investigation by the unofficial
one. Wexford's "feelings," a recurrent trope in the novels, add to his

feminization; in a later novel Wexford's superior actually calls them hysterical.

Among the many gender issues *Shake Hands Forever* dramatizes, then, is the idea that "masculinity imagines itself poorly, or imagines itself, at most, only by feminizing itself."[5] What is disappointing is that it illustrates this in a context in which femininity imagines itself not at all.

NOTES

1. Carolyn Heilbrun's observation that "the qualities, good, bad and maddening, which . . . detectives of either sex demonstrate, are remarkably difficult to assign by gender" made this point, through a different focus, two decades ago. See Carolyn G. Heilbrun, "Female Sleuths and Others," *Hecate* 2 (July 1976): 74-75.

2. The same narrative structure, with similar by-products, characterizes two nineteenth-century crime novels, Mary Elizabeth Braddon's *Lady Audley's Secret* (1862) and Anna Katharine Green's *The Leavenworth Case* (1878).

3. See Eve Kosofsky Sedgwick, *Between Men*, and Luce Irigaray, "Women on the Market," in *This Sex Which Is Not One*.

4. The movie *Black Widow* revivifies and expands this narrative model by extending it to two women.

5. Philippe Lacoue-Labarthe, quoted in Frank Lentricchia, "Patriarchy against Itself—The Young Manhood of Wallace Stevens," *Critical Inquiry* 13 (Summer 1987): 742, quoted in Elaine Showalter, "Introduction: The Rise of Gender," *Speaking of Gender* (New York: Routledge, 1989), 6-7.

REFERENCES

Hühn, Peter. "The Detective as Reader: Narrativity and Reading Concepts in Detective Fiction." *Modern Fiction Studies* 33 (Autumn 1987).

Irigaray, Luce. "Women on the Market." In *This Sex Which Is Not One*, translated by Catherine Porter and Carolyn Burke. Ithaca, NY: Cornell University Press, 1985. 170-91.

Jehlen, Myra. "Gender." In *Critical Terms for Literary Study*. Ed. Frank Lentricchia and Thomas McLaughlin. Chicago: University of Chicago Press, 1990.

Rendell, Ruth. *Shake Hands Forever.* Garden City, NY: Doubleday, 1975.

Scott, Joan W. "Gender: A Useful Category of Historical Analysis." In *Coming to Terms: Feminism, Theory, Politics*. Ed. Elizabeth Weed. New York: Routledge, 1989.

Sedgwick, Eve Kosofsky. *Between Men: English Literature and Male Homosocial Desire*. New York: Columbia University Press, 1985.

15

Class, Gender, and the Possibilities of Detection in Anne Perry's Victorian Reconstructions

Iska S. Alter

The fierce psychic landscape, the disrupted social universe, and the equivocal moral geography that constitute Anne Perry's bleak version of late-nineteenth-century London reconstruct a male-directed culture of authority and submission. Here the unavoidable intersections of presumably fixed categories of class, gender, and sexuality provoke the very transgressive acts that such configurations of separation are meant to contain, discipline, or perhaps, at the last, even deny. The complex, entangling network of "mutually agreed deceits" (*CS* 130) that defines a society whose continuation is sustained by the contradictory intricacies of isolation and dependence produced by class disjuncture and gender segregation insures an environment that "is all to do with what seems and nothing to do with what is" (*RR* 64). Throughout Perry's fictions, these patterns of evasion and secrecy, private duplicity and public artifice, emerging from the "icebound rules" (*RP* 27) of decorum and propriety negotiated by the dominant culture to regulate the inchoate energies of the marginalized and the powerless, create the conditions that name criminal behavior. The illusory, if placid, arrangement of surface generated by the ideology of division, which would establish order through hierarchical control, certainty through willed ignorance, and serenity through passional repression, simultaneously engenders its own subversive counterparts—a jungle of Darwinian reciprocity:

"I know perfectly well there is a world of criminal classes whose standards are totally different . . . at least from mine!"

"Oh, very different. . . . Although whether you are referring to moral standards or standards of living you didn't say. But perhaps they are not so far apart as the words imply. In fact, I have come to think they are usually symbiotic. . . . Each dependent upon the other. A relationship of coexistence, of mutual feeding." (*CSH* 76)

The inevitable attempt of the aggrandizing bourgeoisie and the privileged aristo-cracy to manipulate the disparities of power, in order to objectify further those who are not and to exploit those who have not, necessarily leads to violence, violation, and death.

Crime, in the author's representation of the late Victorian past, dissolves the structural distinctions dictating the terms of compliance that govern personal conduct, gender identity, and class behavior and are encoded in systemic patriarchy. These distinctions remind the empowered as well as the outsider of the instability of those characteristics of rule and obedience believed to be inherent, sanctioned by biology. The presence of murder disturbs this ironic world of masks, as Charlotte Pitt observes, "stripp[ing] off the facade so we saw all the weak and the ugly things we had learned to hide from ourselves and others" (*RR* 53).

And in such a world, crime is "seldom a single act, or the fault of a single person" (*HR* 47). The violence that initiates Perry's narratives is invariably offered as a paradox of discrepant activity. A matter of the wrong body (for example, a sixteen-year-old aristocrat in the early stages of syphilis) found in an unsuitable location (in this case, the sewers of Bluegate Fields, a slum of "seething, grinding poverty" [*BF* 3]), suffering an inappropriate death (drowned in his bath and dumped in the sewers to avoid discovery), prompts an extended investigation into the nature of the particular social anomaly. This introductory violation, usually sexual (often perversely so) as well as brutal, proves to be the culminating act in a tangled series of transgressions, both cultural and criminal, that exposes the dark, disordered heart of Victorian society. Indeed, over the course of eleven novels, the solution to one instigatory puzzle becomes secondary, overwhelmed by the dynamics of revelation that implicate all the major institutions that have determined the ideologies of late-nineteenth-century class and gender performance—the family, the legal system, the medical establishment, Parliament, the church—in the unraveling fabric of wrongdoing. However, it must be noted that in many of the texts the detectors self-consciously withhold the darkest secret, the ultimate outrage—infanticide, incest, unwilled but deadly rage, even deliberate homicide—from public judgment in order to shield the victimized or the otherwise protected social obloquy.

Policing such ambiguous territory, then, is a complicated and dangerous business because the process—investigation, discovery, prevention, solution, enforcement—is designed to question the primary assumptions that order and organize this civilization. Given the permeable boundaries that uncertainly mark the phagic sites of influence and impoverishment, detection must perforce become a collaborative effort incorporating the professional and the heterodox. The participants in this cooperative venture consist of Inspector Thomas Pitt, the formal representative of the Law, as well as an informal gathering of uncommon women—Charlotte Ellison Pitt and Emily Ellison Ashworth Radley, aptly named after those other Victorian sisters; the Lady Vespasia Cumming-Gould; and the group's most recent member, Grace, Charlotte's maid of all work—whose various and flexible class allegiances provide entry into the troubling regions hidden by convention to which Pitt has only limited, if informed access. These detectors—individuals who uncover the extent to which cultural presuppositions call into being the kind of atrocities committed rather than those who merely wish to ascertain the identity of a single guilty culprit and dismiss as irrelevant the ramifications of his or her crime—have themselves in some way deliberately eluded, deflated, or subverted the power of unrelenting propriety to create disorder.

Thomas Pitt is the individual embodiment of the problematic status occupied by the police during the Victorian historical moment, resented for what their very necessity asserts about the actual consequences of hierarchy and the presumption of order. The authority invested in the institution not only threatens the entrenched weight of position but also overrides the corrosive distinctions embedded in society's hypocritical decorum: "'I was under the misapprehension that we were to prevent crime or arrest criminals whenever possible and that the social standing or the moral habits of the victim and the offender were quite irrelevant—that we should seek to enforce the law—something about "without malice, fear or favor"'" (*BF* 219).

Because their professional function so clearly undermines the jurisdiction of control claimed by the dominant culture, the middle and upper classes seek to renegotiate the social terms of the warrant under which the police are permitted to operate, naming them as vulgar, tainted in their view of human nature by the crimes whose solutions they are required to discover. They are to be regarded as the disturbers of bourgeois and aristocratic peace whose presence in the neighborhood, at the front door, or within the drawing room comes to signify the possibilities of communal failure: "One reported a break-in, of course, and that was regrettable enough, but at least a break-in was an outside affair, a misfortune that could happen to anyone with goods worth the taking. Domestic crime was different; it was something that might involve the questioning, and resultant embarrassment, of one's friends, and, therefore resorting to the police was unthinkable" (*RP* 23). More frighteningly, however, for whose who inhabit the closes, the squares, and the crescents of well-to-do London, the policeman is "an intruder, a reminder of the darkest possibilities, the ugliest explanation" (*RP* 50).

The possessors finally wish to transform the police into instruments of repression and denial, an extension of their own exploitative power—a metamorphosis to which the police frequently concede as their own insecurities of caste demand, creating a reflexive identification with the governing classes whose public values construct the idea of order they are asked to enforce. Young Harcourt Gillivray prefers "the investigation of robbery, particularly robbery from the wealthy and the lesser aristocracy. The quiet, discreet association with such people when he was assisting was rather a pleasing way to advance his career" (*BF* 13). His superior (and Pitt's) observes with considerable satisfaction that, although Gillivray is ambitious, "he accepted that one must climb the ladder rung by rung, everything in order, each advance earned" (*BF* 161). Gillivray smugly endorses a system of justice that reinforces the status of things as they are:

Each arm of the machinery had its proper function: The police to detect and apprehend; the barristers to prosecute or to defend; the judge to preside and see that the procedures of the law were followed; the jury to decide truth and fact. And in due course, if necessary, the warders to guard, and the executioner to end life rapidly and efficiently. For any one arm to usurp the function of another was to put the whole principle in jeopardy. This was what a civilized society was about, each person knowing his function and place. (*BF* 152)

It should not surprise, then, that he is willing to manufacture evidence to serve the tyranny of such a meticulous design.

Within this equivocal terrain of shifting institutional expectations, Thomas Pitt is the one exemplary professional, a model of personal and investigatory rectitude. Although admired in the ranks—"the sergeant had heard Pitt's name and spoke with some respect" (*SHC* 1)—he nevertheless is mistrusted and misused by supervisors, themselves wishing "to rise high enough in [the] profession to become socially acceptable" (*SHC* 2), as one who "had ideas above himself," proven by his offensive and incomprehensible marriage, with "no respect for position" (*BF* 9), until he gains the safety of a superintendent possessing "sufficient family background and private means to care about neither" (*BF* 27).

Even his physical presentation disturbs. His substantial height imposes an uncomfortable presence, for it allows "a way of meeting the eyes" (*BF* 181) that decreases the social distance hierarchy requires. The untidiness by which he is described from first, in *The Cater Street Hangman*—"the man who came was tall and looked large because he was untidy" (62)—to last, in *Highgate Rise*—"scruffy, ill-clad . . . pockets bulged with nameless rubbish, his gloves were odd" (3)—reflects "a suppressed energy . . . that was hardly decent" (*PW* 38) and encodes a disorderliness of experience that eludes the neat classifications that arrange the appearance of Victorian bourgeois society. And in a social universe where "a man's origins could be distinguished by the turn of a vowel in his mouth" (*SHC* 3), Pitt's extraordinary voice, the product of the dislocating education of a gamekeeper's son to be the companion of a young heir to a large country estate, "sort of surrounds you like warm treacle, and his diction and grammar are excellent." His gestures (kissing the hand of Lady Vespasia Cumming-Gould), "ridiculous . . . from a policeman, who after all was more or less a tradesman" (*PW* 35), his personal behavior (the inappropriate marriage "considerably above himself" [*SHC* 3] to Charlotte Ellison), and his professional decorum (the consistent refusal to use the tradesmen's entrance as policemen were supposed to do) are ironic testimony to the transparency of all such presumably immutable status designations.

Supporting these external signifiers of status discomfort is Pitt's valuation of the essential meaning of police work—"un-tangling the threads of mystery and discovering the truth — some-times an ugly truth" (*BF* 248). His recognition that "murder is no respecter of persons, or of social distinctions" (*CSH* 127), his certainty that "morality is universal," not contingent on whether one is a servant or a gentleman, circumstances only "alter[ing] the degree of blame, but not that an act is wrong" (*CSH* 128), not only frees Pitt from imprisoning vocational definitions but would annul the insistent categories of class and power that describe the environments in which he must act.

His experience of the parasitic nexus between use and indifference, between evasion and exposure, between those who own and those who do not, which creates the economic conditions under which crime must of necessity flourish, permits him to reveal the false order of Victorian England and its human cost: "the filthy, teeming rookeries squatting behind stately streets" (*PW* 33); the slums of London barely containing "poverty so intense; rotting tenements stood stacked against each other, fifteen people to a room living and dying together" a stone's throw from "the sumptuous and elegant heart of Empire" (*CC* 3); the fortunes made by Lord Edward St. Jermyn from the whorehouses of Resurrection Row; or Bertie Astley collecting rents in the Devil's Acre, while "his family kept their fine drawing rooms and their soft white ladies on the profits of our filth" (*DDA* 265); or sainted Bishop Worlingham, whose wealth came from the poor of Lisbon Street, "the keepers of brothels, the distilling in gin mills, the masters of sweatshops and the sellers of opium" (*HR* 326).

Pitt also is aware of the personal hypocrisies inevitably present within the elaborate system of manners and propriety that are meant, on the one hand, to inhibit the possibilities of transgression while, on the other, to provide the screen behind which they can be enacted and justified: "Without the discipline of work, they had invented the discipline of etiquette, and it had become as ruthless a master" (*PW* 4). Because Pitt has learned that violence and outrage emerge from that area of duplicity that can no longer contain the "outward act born from inward selfishness, greed or hate that had grown too big inside, the dishonesties suddenly without restraint" (*PW* 29), he is able to manipulate those same conventions in order to unearth the widespread corruption of class, to disclose individual or collective guilt, and to assign responsibility.

However, it is Pitt's empathetic responsiveness that ultimately renders him not only a particularly effective detector but also a subversive alternate to right behavior in a culture built on the arrogant discrepancies of hierarchy and dependence, whose models of gender expectations refuse to acknowledge, much less accept on trust, the shared authority of feeling, preferring instead its negation by naming emotion as vulgar or, worse yet, as hysteria. As Pitt himself understands, to have to admit the autonomous value of emotion, to have to concede the principle of the shared authority of feeling, is to insure the eventual disintegration of the dehumanizing classifications that have nourished the structures of Victorian inequity. Notwithstanding Pitt's objectifying function as an agent of regulation and enforcement, he has retained his sensitivity in the face of violence: "I have seen death many times, but I hope I never find myself accepting it without shock, or a sense of grief for those who cared" (*RP* 59), and he continues to be "shocked by the savagery of crime . . . the pain of the individual still had power to move him" (*CC* 3). Institutional disinterest still enrages: "He wanted to shout at the rich, at Parliament, at anyone who was comfortable, or who was ignorant of these tens of thousands who clung to life by such a frail and dangerous thread, who had not been bred to afford morality expect of the crudest sort" (*SHC* 48). To his own surprise, he is able even to muster sympathy for "the rich as for any of the poor. Some of them were as pathetic, as imprisoned in the hierarchy—welded to their function or lack of function in it" (*PW* 166).

But Pitt's undeniable sympathies, his anger and his pain, are products of an external, willed identification, for he stands outside the rookeries, outside the workhouses, and, most important, outside the jails—the final site of his fulfilled duties. No matter the depth of his concerns or the vividness with which he can reconstruct the experiences of those for whom "crime was the road to survival" (*PW* 33), he is the instrument of the Law, and they are the Other. It is only when Pitt himself is unjustly imprisoned to protest a crime of class and reputation that he knows with literal truth the weight of power; that he experiences the actual consequences of his vocational imperative; that, finally, he loses the last separating designation of Inspector, the sign of deference and occupational power, and becomes the Other:

Prison life was unlike anything Pitt had imagined. At first the sheer shock of his arrest, of being suddenly and violently thrust from one side of the law to the other, had numbed his feelings, robbing him of all but the most superficial reactions. . . . Days went by, and Pitt became accustomed to the routine, the wretched food, always being cold except when labor made him sweat. . . . He hated always being dirty, he loathed the lack of any privacy even for essential functions. He was lonelier than he had ever been in his life; and yet never alone. Actual physical solitude would have been a blessing, a chance to relax the tension, the awareness of enmity, and to explore the thoughts crowding inside himself without prying, cruel eyes watching. . . . Then through small acts, glimpses of pain, he was reached . . . a stupid and pointless tragedy involving Raeburn jerked Pitt violently out of his self-pity. . . . From hating the other men, he surprised himself by managing to forget . . . all the world of difference between himself and them, and felt only the pain they had in common. (*SHC* 292-300)

Yet even the exemplary Pitt is confused by the limits of his official identity to the careful examination of the detailed surfaces that describe public behavior. Not only does "the swarming population" of the slums "regard the police [as] the natural enemy" (*DDA* 46); so, too, do the possessors regard him as an unfortunate, if necessary, evil and attempt to curb or control or eliminate entirely access to concealed landscapes of other lives. As Charlotte observes to her mother, explaining the need for feminine involvement:

"Thomas can find facts, but it may take you or me to understand them. After all, you cannot expect the police to know the feelings of someone like Mina. Something that would seem trivial to them might have been overwhelming to her."

It was not necessary to explain all the differences of class, sex, and the whole framework of customs that lay between Pitt and Mina. Both Charlotte and Caroline understood that all the sensitivity or imagination he was capable of would not guide him to see with Mina's eyes or recognize what it was that had accomplished her death. (*RP* 68)

Given the power of female desire to deconstruct forms of patriarchy, the male-directed order of Victorian cultural dominance must, through informal networks of custom and contention and the legitimate machinery of the law, devalue a woman's need for an authentic identity, enclose the feminine within an acceptable institution of regulation, and disallow her access to modes of public experience. The gathering company of women in Anne Perry's fictions who become increasingly necessary to the process of detection represent and then exploit the various skills required to manage that territory, defined by marriage, the home, and, in covert fashion, by respectable society itself, conceded to limited female sovereignty by the repressive agents of social control: Observation, interpretation, role-playing, and moral exemplification, alternative sources of knowledge denied authority by men, but important to solving puzzles and uncovering mysteries.

Because the decorum of hierarchy effectively silences women and prevents their entry into the masculine world of significant action, they are enforced observers:

"What acute observation! Did you learn it from being married to the police, or is it a natural gift?"

"I think it comes from being a woman. . . . When I was single, I had so little to do that observation of other people formed a large part of the day." (*HR* 129)

Pitt questions women particularly carefully, much to the resentment of fathers and husbands, for whom his presence dramatizes emasculating disorder and loss of ascendancy, because he has learned to trust their capacity for watchfulness:

"I do require to speak to your wife and daughters. Women are very observant, you know. And women observe other women. You would be surprised how much might miss your eye, or mine, but not theirs."

"My wife and daughters have more to interest them than the romances of Lady Mitchell." Edward's face was growing redder and his hands were clenched. (*CSH* 66)

Furthermore, in order to find areas of freedom within the governing codes of conduct, women must read carefully the nuances of behavior lest they be excluded from respectability, reinventing the terms of intelligence in the process:

"Most women have perfectly good intelligence for the things that matter, such as the conduct of one's daily life" (*CS* 87).

Perry's sisterhood of detection also bears the significance of marginal language, that is, speech that has been trivialized and dismissed because of its association with women's worlds, women's work, and women's wants—gossip, servants' talk, and the subversive rhetoric of political reform—but that often provides indispensable relevatory information about context and motive. Most important, however, is the gradual recognition among the detectors that women possess subtle, if unacknowledged, power to disrupt the imprisoning ideologies of restraint and propriety: "Subtle though it was, a very great deal of society was governed one way or another by women. Men might do all manner of things if they were sufficiently discreet, indulge tastes they would not acknowledge even to their fellows. But publicly, and in the domestic tranquillity of their homes, they would deplore such affronts to the fabric of a civilized people" (*HR* 45).

The complementary Ellison sisters—Charlotte who marries below her station and Emily who marries above it—are the core of the detecting sisterhood. Each possesses qualities that the other lacks, then envies, eventually respects, and finally incorporates into the particularities of her own conduct. For both, the existence of an initial domestic puzzle or tragedy becomes the method of entry into the deeper mysteries that taint and corrupt culture.

Charlotte begins as and remains throughout a Victorian anomaly. With her height, her strong features, and "her heavy mahogany-colored hair that was difficult to keep tidy" (*CSH* 6), she is a powerful physical presence, although she is far from the era's ideal of deliberate, childlike beauty. We first see her in *The Cater Street Hangman* indulging in a series of minor rebellions—reading a newspaper, discussing politics, asserting her interest in military history—singularly inappropriate behavior for the well-bred Victorian woman—that bespeak a profound dissatisfaction with the emptiness of acceptable feminine expectations: "Would it always be like this? Endless days of needlework, painting, house chores and skills, Papa and Domenic coming home? What did other people do? They married, raised children, ran houses" (*CSH* 17).

Her willful, unconventional marriage to Thomas Pitt frees her from the constraints of class and exchanges the insecurity of deference for a relationship of equals. Her liberation from a fixed definition of a woman's role and a female self is reflected not only in her continuing desire to see human existence whole without the oppressive, confrontational distinctions embedded in notions of late Victorian hierarchy or in her ability to assume other identities in the pursuit of unravelling secrets but also in her ability to move relatively unencumbered through the ironic geography of London, from the enclosed rooms and hidden gardens of the bourgeoisie and the upper classes to the nearby slums of the Devil's Acre and Lisbon Street. With "no ambition to make her curb her tongue and seek to impress" (*PW* 43), she questions the worth of social conventions and trusts the very instincts convention would domesticate and so is able to see clearly into the center of the Victorian psychic and communal darkness.

Emily Ellison Ashworth Radley, who has married into the aristocracy, understands of necessity the formulae that govern social activity and therefore owns "a disconcertingly acute judgment of most people, both about what they wanted and, even more uncomfortably, why they wanted it" (*RP* 116). She certainly accepts the utility of these formulae as a way of organizing conduct; and, initially, she may even have believed in the values they supported. But ambition once achieved, she admits "that the fashionable life lacked something, a certain bite for which she was increasingly developing a taste" (*CS* 29) and which detection supplies. It begins for Emily as a game, a counter against boredom, an energizing testament to her skill at reading the texts of class and explaining the contexts of crime. She feels little for those who are hurt by these texts and contexts until violence occurs among her circle, because to feel deeply is to acknowledge that "the discipline of etiquette" to which she has been committed is a lie. Only when she is accused of her husband's murder is she able to recognize the false coherence of constructed hierarchy as a method of arranging experience. She learns to shrug off the predictable but unstable prescriptions of order in the service of justice as she chooses to play the lady's maid in the collective effort to rescue Pitt from the gallows. When she marries a second time, it is for love, not for business or ambition, and to a man who is himself ambiguously situated within the haute bourgeoisie.

Ironically named after the Roman emperor Vespasian, whose reign was known for order and prosperity, and "about as delicate as a steel sword," the Lady Vespasia Cumming-Could becomes the matriarchal guardian of Perry's sisterhood of detecting women. Liberated by age, position, memory, and a formidable will, a reformer and a feminist whose oldest friend, Zenobia Gunne, is an African explorer, she simply can afford to disregard the claims of the polite rules of social practice. She refuses to wear a watch or to wear black for mourning, and she is "odd enough for it not to matter any more what company [she is] seen to keep" (*RR* 27). Perhaps because she has been situated within the social process, she is the embodiment of "all the substance of the past" (*PW* 127).

What is finally even more significant about these seekers after truth (and yes, they all believe in an autonomous ideal of truth as worth pursuing) is that they all share the faculty of imagination (even the newly enlisted Gracie). Thus, each is capable of escaping the external classifications of propriety and the insistent psychic demands of the interior self to envision sympathetically another's life or to enter with compassion another's pain. Indeed, it is this will to sympathy that confronts and then controls the despair that darkens so much of the action in this reconstructed landscape that is Anne Perry's London.

REFERENCES

Perry, Anne. *Bethlehem Road*. New York: St. Martin's Press, 1990.
_____. *Bluegate Fields*. New York: Ballantine Books, 1984.
_____. *Callander Square*. New York: Ballantine Books, 1980.

____. *Cardington Crescent*. New York: Ballantine Books, 1987.

____. *The Cater Street Hangman*. New York: Ballantine Books, 1979.

____. *Death in the Devil's Acre*. New York: Ballantine Books, 1985.

____. *Highgate Rise*. New York: Ballantine Books, 1991.

____. *Paragon Walk*. New York: Ballantine Books, 1981.

____. *Resurrection Row*. New York: Ballantine Books, 1981.

____. *Rutland Place*. New York: Ballantine Books, 1983.

____. *Silence in Hanover Close*. New York: Ballantine Books, 1988.

16

A Suitable Job for a Woman: Sexuality, Motherhood, and Professionalism in *Gaudy Night*

Jasmine Y. Hall

> Thou blind man's mark, thou fool's self-chosen snare,
> Fond fancy's scum, and dregs of scattered thought,
> Band of all evils; cradle of causeless care;
> Thou web of will, whose end is never wrought:
> Desire! Desire! I have too dearly bought
> With price of mangled mind, thy worthless ware.

(Sir Philip Sidney, quoted in Sayers 1)

The quotation that opens Dorothy L. Sayers' *Gaudy Night* sets up an opposition between heart and mind that is central to the dialogue, plot, and even genre of the novel. From the first "gaudy night" that Harriet Vane spends contrasting the relative happiness of intellectual and emotional women, to the near fatal gaudy night in which Harriet is struck on the head and Miss de Vine has a heart attack, this conflict is repeatedly emphasized as having a special meaning and danger for women. As Gayle Wald has suggested, the genre of the novel itself reenacts the conflict by breaking one of Sayers' golden rules: It grafts the genre of the heart (the love story) onto the genre of the mind (the detective story) (98).

Wald correctly points out that Sayers expresses a fear of excess here, an excess that will not be fully controlled by the formulaic detective plot. That excess is the detective's desire, which in *Gaudy Night* drives both the detective and the romance narratives. Sayers wrote of the challenge she had set herself in combining these two stories of desire that "the new and exciting thing was to bring the love problem into line with the detective problem, so that the same key should unlock both at once" (Sayers, quoted in Wald 106). Sayers imagined, then, a "key" that would paradoxically lock up the excesses of love and crime by unlocking a common element between the two stories. I would suggest that such a key does exist—one that serves to lock up the excessive desires of the aristocratic detective, Peter Wimsey, and the poison-pen writer, Annie Wilson, at the same time that it unlocks a whole new set of problems revolving around issues of class and gender roles.

This key is contained in the economic image that ends the opening quotation: Desire does not merely injure the mind; the mind's energy is expended in buying desire's worthless ware. The solution to the heart/mind conflict will be found in a proper channeling of energy into valuable pursuits: "It's the work you are doing that really counts" (9). "After all, work's what one's here for" (143). "I don't see why proper feeling should prevent me from doing my proper job" (29). The "proper job," the new ideal of professionalism, was of increasing importance after World War I. Harold Perkin describes this emergent ideology in *The Rise of Professional Society* and locates its institutionalization in Oxbridge: "The whole system came to be aimed not at socializing a leisured class for a life of cultured idleness and aristocratic sport . . . but at forming an active, responsible, physically fit, self-disciplined elite of professional men and administrators for public service in church and state, the empire and liberal professions" (365).

Peter Wimsey is, in many of the novels, seen by other characters as a member of the "leisured class" who is in need of just such a system of socialization. He is a "chattering icicle in an eyeglass" (*Busman's Honeymoon* 5) who keeps himself from dying of boredom through his "hobbies"—collecting criminals, rare books, and "Viennese singers" (*Gaudy Night* 167). All of these hobbies signal an excessive desire expressing itself through repeated acts of pursuit and possession. One of the first questions raised about him by the dons of Shrewsbury College is whether or not the first of these pursuits, his detective investigations, is merely an example of "aristocratic sport." Harriet's answer, that it is "every citizen's obligation" (30) to help the police maintain law and order, helps establish a contrast between private desire and public duty. While the dons focus on Peter as an individual, highlighting his private interests in investigation, Harriet's response redirects the conversation to elaborate on a rule-governed society that his actions support. When Miss Barton refuses to follow Harriet's lead and continues to investigate Peter's motives, Harriet snaps at her, an emotional response that again shifts the focus of the conversation, this time to Harriet's own interest in Peter. Sayers raises the issue of the excess of desire represented by the detective's "pursuits"; then justifies those pursuits as public, professional service; and finally draws our attention away from the detective's motives to those of the women who are discussing him. Harriet's reaction, in fact, covers up for her knowledge that one of the other things Peter "does" is expend his time and energy proposing to her. This structure—that initially raises the threat of male sexual energy, resolves that energy in professionalism, and relocates the threat of private desire with women—is repeated in the novel as a whole when the actions of the female villain are represented as an overvaluing of the private at the expense of the public.

A summary of the emergent ideology of professionalism serves to illuminate the ways in which Peter's desire is reassuringly recast as the "proper job," while Annie's desire remains threateningly outside the new system. The elements of this ideology are:

1) high valuation on personal skill and training rather than class difference;
2) consequent deemphasis on material power in capital or land and an emphasis on human resources as capital;
3) insistence on personal skills being used in the service of the public good; and
4) strategies of exclusion governing membership in these professions. (Perkin 2-9)

The valuation of learned skill vs. class is highlighted by one of the central errors Harriet makes in her investigation: She assumes that none of the scouts (the college maids, including Annie) can be responsible for the poison pen notes because one of the notes is written in Virgilian hexameters. The ideological message of this mistake is that Harriet has based her assumption on outmoded notions of class distinction; now any person of any class has the opportunity to acquire a highly academic style. Harriet's error is interestingly related to Annie's motivation for composing the poison pen letters: Harriet sees academic knowledge, skill with language, and writing ability as belonging to one class, while Annie's attack on the dons is driven by the belief that such accomplishments rightfully belong only to the male gender. Significantly, Peter does not repeat Harriet's error. His ability to see through Harriet's class prejudice reinforces the idea that the power of language is equally available to all classes and genders, while at the same time the fact that the well-educated aristocrat is the only one with the ability to come to this conclusion is suggestive of a cause and effect relationship between the new hierarchy of talent and older systems of prestige.

The same valuation of professional skill over class standing is established in the love story through a comparison of the two most aristocratic characters: Peter and his nephew, the Viscount St. George. While both men share the good looks and good taste of the aristocracy, it is St. George who bears the brunt of the aristocratic vice of fast living, most particularly in his car accident. Peter's driving is just as fast, but, as Harriet speculates, his speed is controlled through superior skill (201). Similarly, while Peter may be tempted to dominate women because of the "six centuries of possessiveness" in his background, that possessiveness is "fastened under the yoke" (409) of culture and education. Gerry, on the other hand, examines the female students as if he were "a young Sultan inspecting a rather uncompromising consignment of Circassian slaves" (354).

The threat of the dilettante gentleman is not just his sexual pursuit of women, then, but his sexual possessiveness. It is this particular form of desire, not desire in general, that is transgressive in the novel. Harriet and Miss de Vine discuss modern society's "doctrine of snatching" (174) as an unsound moral principle, and decide that the most dangerous people are those "who make some other person their job" (175), not only possessing the other person, but violating the ideal of the impersonal job in the service of the public good. Possessiveness is recast as the novel's central threat in Sayers' characterization of Annie, whose most "fundamental passion" is the "fiercely possessive" attitude she takes toward her children (222). Peter's description of Annie's motive in attacking the college, "devoted love" (395) of her dead husband, also suggests that her actions are not only criminal, but also break with the fundamental moral precept of the novel.

The Victorian ideal of the "Angel-in-the-House," with its focus on the private sphere of husband and children, is here reversed into a criticism of women who treat children as property and who put loyalty to husband above the more abstract loyalty to the truth. Annie's husband had committed the crime of suppressing evidence in an academic paper. His crime not only places personal interest above the search for truth, but also undermines the evaluation of professional skill: He breaks the rules that establish professional membership in academia. After his exposure by Miss de Vine, one of the faculty at Shrewsbury College, he does not meekly accept the truth, but kills himself rather than live with the humiliation. Annie's attack on Shrewsbury College and on Miss de Vine in order to avenge her husband's suicide continue this overvaluation of private loyalties and interests over public good. Maternal protectiveness and spousal devotion, not aristocratic fast-living, are shown to be *Gaudy Night's* most significant danger.

Billie Melman, in her study of *Women and the Popular Imagination in the Twenties*, finds that the maternal instinct is also represented as the most dangerous aspect of women's sexuality in descriptions of "superfluous women." Quoting the *Daily Mirror*, she connects the fear of loose sexual mores in the flapper with an unchannelled maternal drive: "There is a large proportion of physically attractive girls with strong reproductive instincts and they are ever vying and competing with each other for the scarce and elusive male" (19). Like Peter's possessiveness, the energy of these reproductive instincts is represented as most easily controlled through professionalization. Peter's own investigative institution, The Cattery, puts the energy of superfluous women, spinsters like Miss Climpson as well as "Bright Young Things," (*Strong Poison* 44) to productive use. Similarly, a different attitude toward motherhood was developing at this time, one that saw the mother's role extended to include protection of the state: "Earlier in the century, motherhood and domesticity were presented as being desirable in themselves. . . . But now the notion acquired an additional emphasis. Domestic harmony . . . was presented as desirable, even essential, for the defense of Britain against her rivals overseas, indeed for the defense of the whole British empire" (MacKay 191-229).

Maternity at the service of the state is directly criticized in the novel in the several references to Germany's relegation of women to the care of "Kinder, Kirche, and Küche," and in the satiric portrait of Miss Schuster-Slatt's plans for arranged marriages between intellectually suitable breeding partners. However, the professionalization of motherhood is more subtly and more positively rendered in Harriet's friend Phoebe Bancroft whose attitude to her children provides a stark contrast to Annie's: "It would have been such a bore to be the mother of morons, and it's an absolute toss-up, isn't it? If one could only invent them, like characters in books, it would be much more satisfactory to a well-regulated mind" (14). Annie's fundamental passion becomes, in Phoebe, a laissez-faire attitude that fantasizes producing children not through the somewhat chancy method of biological reproduction but rather through the well-ordered method of writing fiction.

Writing is the profession that *Gaudy Night* presents as the one most able to mediate between private desire and public expression, both in the work of the academic and the detective novelist. And transgressive acts against writing threaten to unleash the destructive powers of that desire against the community. As stated above, the "original sin" of *Gaudy Night* is Annie's husband's suppression of an important piece of evidence in a scholarly text. Annie's own poison pennings are motivated by possessiveness, and her vandalism continues the attack on academic writing in defacing the library, in making use of Virgilian hexameters to attack the scholarly writers, in marring the proofs of Miss Lydgate's book, and in tearing out sections of Miss Barton's. A further comparison with Phoebe illustrates another fundamental error in Annie's relation to writing. Phoebe's role in her partnership with her husband is to correct and restrain the emotions of his writing. She explains to Harriet that her husband is writing a paper that "contradicts all old Lambard's conclusions, and I'm helping by toning down his adjectives and putting in deprecatory footnotes" (13). Woman's place in the family, while "professionalized," still retains the stereotypical elements of passivity and politeness; the calming and protecting influence of domesticity, but directed at the adjectives of the more combative male. Annie has failed in this new role of wife as editor—failed to protect her husband from his own competitiveness. It is here that the more subtle class criticism of Annie is made. The landlord's daughter, a girl of little education, Annie was the incorrect choice of helpmeet for a scholar. Though the novel is critical of the ready assumption that a member of the lower classes could not learn Virgilian hexameters, it reinforces these class stereotypes in the representation of Annie's marriage. As Perkin notes, "Professional society is based on merit, but some acquire merit more easily than others" (4).

While Peter initially represents the threat of sexual power and domination, professionalizing the love story in *Gaudy Night* serves to remove that threat and place the blame for the misuse of private energy again at the feet of a woman, Harriet Vane. If Annie's writing is poisoned by sexuality and its attendant possessiveness, Harriet suffers from being too detached from her sexuality—a detachment that does not allow her full use of her professional abilities. Rereading her own detective novels, Harriet feels that "they had been written with a mental reservation, a determination to keep her own opinions and personality out of view" (62). The energy that in Annie has not been properly harnessed for the public good in Harriet has been completely repressed. Harriet's difficulty, with both the narrative of the case and the narrative of her novel, is that she rigidly separates her sexual concerns from her professional ones. Her fear of her own sexuality colors her reading of the events of the detective narrative; she is convinced that the crime is the result of the kind of sexual repression from which she is suffering, and so most strongly suspects Miss Hillyard. Conversely, she continues to have problems writing her own novel until she follows Peter's suggestion and gives her main character the "violent and lifelike feelings" (302) of a pathological sexuality.

Harriet, unlike Annie, eventually learns to correctly harness sexual energy through the profession of writing. Earlier in the novel, however, sexuality is seen as a direct threat to writing. As Harriet attempts to write poetry for the first time in a number of years, she reflects on her sexual relationship with Philip Boyes (the murder victim in *Strong Poison*). She connects the many years in which her poetic voice had been "throttled into dumbness" with her "unhappy, contact with physical passion" (220). Peter is implicitly compared with Philip when he tells Harriet that the delicacy of her throat is "in itself a temptation to violence" (376). The threat that is posed by Peter—both his sexual interest and the possibility that that interest will again silence Harriet—is removed, however, when Peter teaches Harriet how to meet and overcome the attack of a strangler. Though this scene can be easily interpreted as a sexual encounter, finished off by the requisite smoking of a cigarette, physical contact with Peter is sanctioned by the context of the investigation: He is training her in a skill necessary for her to continue her detective work at Shrewsbury. Wrestling with Peter also serves another of Harriet's professional concerns: She immediately considers rewriting the event as a scene of seduction in her latest novel. But here again, the threat of Peter's sexual energy is channeled into a professional pursuit, Harriet's writing. Peter's mock strangulation wards off not only actual strangulation, but also the silencing of language which is the result of her relationship with Philip. Sexuality becomes properly regulated by writing, while writing becomes fueled by sexual energy.

Harriet's view of Peter continually shifts through the last third of the novel between a perception of him as a male sexual presence, and a more androgynous colleague (symbolized, for example, by Harriet and Peter's exchange of academic robes). What happens as these two perspectives merge is that the threat of domination that Harriet initially finds implicit in Peter's sexuality becomes absorbed by their seemingly equal status as professionals. Harriet is then able to acknowledge her own sexual desires in return.

Through professionalism, Harriet learns the lesson that Annie never did: The proper channeling of the human capital, desire. Both women misdirect that energy towards the private sphere—Annie in absorption with husband and children, Harriet in sexual repression. But by the time Peter presents the evidence that convicts Annie, Harriet has securely taken her place at his side as one who has learned to correctly make use of that energy.

Annie's response to Peter's evidence clearly points to that professional alliance. She accuses both the women in the room and Peter of never having done "a hand's turn of honest work" (445). By "honest work" Annie means menial labor which the dons, Harriet, and Peter do not do. What seemed to be a division along gender lines—Annie's attacks motivated by her feeling that women shouldn't work—thus is resolved as a division along class lines: The professional vs. the unskilled worker. The relative guilt or innocence of Annie, and, for that matter, Peter and Harriet, thus seems to rest entirely on the extent to which one believes in the professional ideology of the "proper job": That each person has a proper way of serving society whether it be scrubbing floors or being an Oxford don. That being an Oxford don, a writer of detective fiction, or an aristocratic sleuth might have more attendant power and prestige is ignored by this ideology. Instead, each person has a "natural" place in society just as a generation earlier had imagined that each gender had a "natural" role in the family.

In fact, the novel's continued emphasis on "possessiveness" as a valuation of private, familial relationships over public, professional ones serves to obscure class difference in an important way. Though Annie is labelled the most possessive character, she is, in many ways, the character who actually has the fewest possessions. She does not possess the education of the dons or the land, wealth, and power of the Wimseys. Treating another person as "one's job," the correct role for the Victorian Angel, is thus represented as a criminal source of power and domination in the lower-class, poorly educated woman, while the real sources of power in an Oxbridge education and in the male gender position are obscured by "proper" channeling into public service.

Professionalism seems to eradicate the inequalities of gender at the same time that it maintains a "suitable" and "proper" inequality of class. However, the equal status of colleagues that Peter and Harriet share at the end of the novel is illusory as suggested by a comparison of the imagery of fire that appears at the ending of both detective and love story. At the moment of her confession, Annie makes one last statement of transgressive desire: "I wish I could burn down this place and all the places like it—where you teach women to take men's jobs and rob them first and kill them afterwards" (443). Annie is, of course, prevented from fulfilling this desire, and so women, it seems, are freed from the oppressive and archaic ideology she represents, one that would keep women out of the workplace and tied to home and children. Three pages later, Harriet is also making a confession: "If I once gave way to Peter, I should go up like straw" (447). The independence that Harriet has worked through three novels to maintain is, then, about to go up in smoke. There is no suggestion in these last pages that this conflagration can, or even should, be avoided. One is left to wonder whether any of the "straw" that Harriet likens herself to will survive the flames of her marriage.

The moments immediately preceding the proposal do suggest, yet again, the possibility of a balanced and equal partnership rather than a consumption of straw by fire. When Peter and Harriet spend their last "gaudy night" together listening to a performance of a Bach Concerto, Peter likens their relationship to that of two equally talented musicians, each playing counterpoint to the other, with neither playing the role of "autocratic virtuoso" or "meek accompanist" (456). However, when Harriet describes her own and Peter's musical abilities, it is clear that these are exactly the roles that they will play. Harriet's "more slowly moving wits" (288) are not the equal of Peter's, and so she can only "feel" while he can "hear the whole intricate pattern . . . ravishing heart and mind together" (455). Only in the professionalized aristocrat, then, do heart and mind finally meet. The professional woman is still securely placed in the realm of the heart—approaching that ideal "ravishing" only through her admiration of the professional man's skill. To be a meek accompanist, it seems, is a suitable job for a woman.

REFERENCES

MacKay, Jane and Pat Thane. "The English Woman." *Englishness: Politics and Culture 1880-1920.* Ed. Robert Colls and Philip Dodd. London: Croom Helm, 1986. 191-229.

Melman, Billie. *Women and the Popular Imagination in the Twenties.* New York: St. Martin's Press, 1988.

Perkin, Harold. *The Rise of Professional Society: England Since 1880.* London: Routledge, 1989.

Sayers, Dorothy L. *Busman's Honeymoon.* New York: Harcourt Brace, 1937.

____. *Gaudy Night.* 1936. Reprint. New York: Harper and Row, 1986.

____. *Strong Poison.* 1930. Reprint. New York: Harper and Row, 1987.

Wald, Gayle. "Strong Poison: Love and the Novelistic in Dorothy Sayers." *The Cunning Craft: Original Essays on Detective Fiction and Contemporary Literary Theory.* Ed. Ronald G. Walker and June M. Frazer. Macomb, IL: Western Illinois University Press, 1990. 98-108.

17

The Bureaucrat as Reader:
The Detective Novel in the
Context of Middle-Class Culture

James E. Bartell

As has often been noted, of all the popular literary forms in the twentieth century, detective fiction has been by far the most fully developed and the most widely read. The genre that became widely popular at the end of the last century is many times more popular a hundred years later. Three key questions for the student of popular culture are presented by the unprecedented popularity of detective fiction: Why has the mystery attracted such a large international audience, why does this audience continue to grow, and what does this popularity tell us about our culture? Put in more personal terms: What does the reader of detective fiction get from the habitual reading of mysteries; what pleasures does a detective novel give that are not provided by other popular literary forms? These are the questions that give direction to the following discussion.

Briefly stated, my thesis is this: The hero of detective fiction is an idealized bureaucrat who speaks directly and deeply to the needs of readers, who themselves function as bureaucrats in their jobs or some other aspect of their lives. I would expect many of the readers of this chapter to bridle at such a suggestion since "bureaucracy" and its derivatives are commonly used pejoratively, usually in tones of high moral outrage. Even those who study bureaucracy seldom have anything good to say in its behalf. The tone of the following description by Henry Jacoby is typical:

The term *bureaucracy* refers to the fact that man's existence is directed and controlled by central agencies; not only is he unable to escape from the regulation and manipulation, he seems to depend on it. The overpowering anonymity of the control and the impenetrability of large powerful administrative machines produce fear and discontent. In spite of universal education and increasing use of the printed word and electronic media, the individual finds it increasingly difficult to understand the machinery. He has less influence on what happens in society now than before, because he lacks the means of making his will known. Man's alienation from his own world is expressed in his dissatisfaction with bureaucracy.[1]

This passage probably catches the feelings that most people have about bureaucracy, but I would suggest that such an analysis is inaccurate in an essential way as a description of how bureaucracy now works in Western culture, and it serves to distort investigations of its history.

The truth is, Western civilization has become so complex, so highly organized, so multileveled that essentially all of us function as bureaucrats in important aspects of our lives. It is bureaucracy that provides us not only with our livelihoods but with our identities and our self-worth as well. Even those whom we generally think of as living outside the electronic, information economy of the late twentieth century must often take on the role of bureaucrat. Workers on assembly lines become members of union committees: They analyze and solve problems; they mediate disputes; and they make speeches and write reports—all things that bureaucrats have been doing for centuries. Even farmers are tied into computer networks that provide planting advice, market quotations, and information on various government programs. Artists, supposedly the last holdout of romantic individualism, support themselves by teaching in universities—whose main function has always been the training of bureaucrats—or they spend great chunks of their time applying for private and government grants to support their art.

In the twentieth century, whether we like it or not, anyone who survives in our complex culture must serve, at least part of the time, as a bureaucrat. Through a long and complex process, we have only begun to understand that what was once a small but powerful aspect of government has become a pervasive force that includes and to a considerable degree defines us all.

If Western bureaucracy is, in fact, one of the central institutions of modern life, then one would expect the role of the bureaucrat to be represented at some point in a positive, mythical form accessible to a large audience. I would like to suggest that the detective of literature is just this apotheosis. In other words, the detective is the good bureaucrat in disguise. The detective offers the bureaucratic reader a figure with whom he can identify to offset the negative image of the bad bureaucrat that so occupies the public imagination. To restate from another perspective: The *reader* of detective fiction is himself the good bureaucrat, through he (or she) might violently reject such a title. The reader unconsciously identifies with the detective who represents, in slightly disguised form, the essential virtues of competency and integrity that he believes structure his own professional life. Since no one speaks up publicly for the bureaucrat, the job has been left largely to the writers of formulaic mysteries, who portray, through the vivid personality and professional competence of their detectives, those qualities that make our society function. The readers of detective fiction are good bureaucrats who must, all too often, stand by helplessly as others corrupt the system. Reading detective fiction serves the cathartic purpose of allowing the good bureaucrat to participate vicariously in the defeat of those who would malign and belittle bureaucracy even as they use it to serve their own unbounded ambitions.

Insight into why bureaucracy has become the dominant institution in Western culture and why the virtues of the ideal bureaucrat should come to be represented in the form of the detective of the formulaic mystery can, I think, best be understood from the perspective of a school of anthropology called *cultural materialism* by its best-known proponent, Marvin Harris. Stated in the simplest terms, the key assumption of this school is that human culture is the result of the interaction of primary human needs with the basic physical forces of the environment in which a society develops.[2] Following this strategy, I offer a less pejorative definition of bureaucracy: Bureaucracy is a necessary aspect of any society that has grown large and complex enough to require an institution to stimulate and organize the production of food, goods, and information and to oversee their collection, protection, and redistribution.[3] The bureaucrat, in other words, is the individual who serves as intermediary between producer and consumer. The bureaucrat is an organizer, a go-between, a distributor, an overseer, a mediator, a problem solver, a regulation writer. Such a description allows us to think about the social function of bureaucracy without the negative connotations that generally weigh down such discussions.

Part of the reason for the bureaucrat's bad name might be the long history of oppressive bureaucracies in ancient non-Western civilizations such as those of Mesopotamia, Egypt, India, and China; but as Karl Wittfogel has shown, the environmental forces that produced bureaucracy in these "hydraulic" cultures of the Orient were fundamentally different from those forces that produced bureaucracy in the West.[4] While there have been despotic regimes in the West that have for a time ruled through tightly controlled bureaucracies, larger cultural forces have always worked to overturn these states and their tyrannical institutions. The recent collapse of Soviet communism could be taken as a case in point. From the perspective of the cultural materialist, the long trend toward individualistic democracy and its accompanying institutions of independent-minded, semiautonomous bureaucrats should not be considered merely the result of happy historical happenstance. Western institutions have gradually evolved into their present form in response to basic environmental forces that have existed from the very beginning of Western history.[5]

The system of bureaucracy that slowly evolved in Europe during the Middle Ages was the result of the gradual consolidation of a highly dispersed economy. This economy was founded on an agricultural system made possible by a plentiful supply of water in the form of regular and widespread rainfall.

Once the forest had been cleared and the land broken to the plow, crops flourished. The great problem in a culture based on rainfall agriculture is not the need to stimulate food production but the need to find ways to distribute goods from areas of excess production to areas of need. In the earlier hydraulic civilizations of Mesopotamia, Egypt, India, and China, the great economic problem had never been the distribution of goods, for the extensive irrigation and flood-control networks that made these civilizations possible also provided extensive distribution and communication systems. The key factor responsible for the type of hierarchical and despotic social organization that evolved in these hydraulic cultures was the need to stimulate food production to provide for an ever-growing population. The creation, operation, and maintenance of a large irrigation and water-control system cannot be achieved through the initiatives of individual farmers and local officials. It requires centralized planning and management. The bureaucracy appropriate to such a system will be one that is completely subservient to the central authority, an authority that often arrogates to itself godlike attributes. The bureaucrats in a hydraulic culture serve essentially as extensions of the ruler's will. They carry out his policies without question and feel no inclination to initiate policy on their own.

The bureaucracy that is appropriate for a society based on a rainfall agriculture spread over half a continent will have markedly different qualities from those needed in a hydraulic culture. The central problem in Europe was not the stimulation and control of production as it was in ancient Egypt or China. Instead, it was the collection and redistribution of goods over a vast geographical area. It can be argued that Western culture developed so slowly because it took so long to create a central means of communication and transportation. Though there were river systems in Europe that were large enough to serve as the center of an irrigation-based culture, with all of Europe north of the Alps receiving abundant rainfall there was no incentive for the development of such a labor-intensive agriculture and the centralized government that goes with it. Without a large network of waterways linking north and south, east and west, communication and transportation were difficult (Braudel Vol. I, 415-30).[6] In fact, these problems were not finally solved until the nineteenth century and the development of the railroad, paved highways, and the telegraph.

If the considerable resources of Europe were to be made available for the support of a much denser population, an entirely new form of bureaucracy had to develop. Rather than depending on a network of waterways along which an imperial bureaucracy carried out the dictates of a god-king, European culture came to depend upon another kind of network, a network of semiautonomous bureaucrats made up of merchants and their operatives, officials attached to various princely houses, and the numerous functionaries of the church.[7] These groups had two crucial qualities in common: Members of each group had opportunity to develop perspectives of a more than local nature, and members of each group needed at least a rudimentary education. The members of the clergy tended to owe their allegiance to other than local powers, and early on the church came to serve as the basis of a trans-European communications network.

Over the centuries there grew up a class of people, drawn from the aristocracy, the clergy, the merchant families, the guilds, and even the peasantry, whose duties were to provide kings and other powers with information and advice and to serve all the other bureaucratic functions that go along with large mercantile and governmental operations. These individuals were sometimes unimportant servants, but at other times they acquired considerable influence and power. Often they would sell their services to first one organization and then another; thereby, they gained an independence of perspective, a sense of self-worth, and a view of the world that went beyond the region and class of their birth.

Of these groups, it was the class of merchants and their agents who had the greatest opportunities for acquiring a trans-European perspective; and it was the members of this group who, over the centuries, were most directly responsible for the growth of a continent-wide society; it was to this group that the individualistic bureaucratic ethic of present-day Europe and North America owes the most. It was, after all, the merchant who was directly responsible for the growth in the volume of goods distributed across Europe in increasingly complex trade networks. It was the merchant and the trader who made the steady growth of population possible through the ever more efficient distribution of foodstuffs and manufactured goods. By the very nature of his social role, the merchant tended to be more independent, more individualistic, and more aware of natural and social forces beyond his own immediate realms than most others in his culture.

The crucial qualities shared by the members of this new kind of middle-class bureaucracy in late Medieval and Renaissance Europe (and *middle* is the most appropriate term in that it clearly suggests the class's function as that of social go-between) are these: A relative independence of mind, a sense of self more strongly developed than in members of other social groups, and an identity derived more from the nature of their professional responsibilities than from the powers they served. Out of these traits gradually evolved a variety of bureaucrat who is quite unlike the earlier bureaucrats of despotic hydraulic cultures. The key quality of the Western bureaucrat is his well-developed confidence in his own abilities and his willingness and preparation for independent decision making. This characteristic is in marked contrast to the slavish nature of bureaucrats in highly centralized hierarchical cultures.

The Western bureaucrat needed to be semiautonomous because he functioned as the facilitator at the heart of a complex system of interregional trade and governmental interaction. Often there was neither time nor the opportunity for the bureaucrat to check back with the person he represented for authorization of a purchase of goods, the terms of a trade agreement, or a treaty between powers. The bureaucrat in Western culture was often in a distant city representing himself or someone else for extended periods without recourse to any council other than his own. If anything was to be achieved, the envoy had to be capable of forceful, imaginative, often courageous responses; he had to be able to act as if in his own behalf rather than that of someone else. Often enough, of course, the envoy was seduced by his independence and would work more for his own profit than that of his employer, but what is remarkable is how often over the centuries the semiautonomous bureaucrat was faithful to his charge. In fact, it is important to recognize that the bureaucrat of Western culture, at his best, is one whose strong sense of self-worth is derived from his living up to a highly refined, idealized standard of professional behavior. What is truly remarkable about the Western bureaucrat is the degree to which self-interest can be subordinated to a highly idealized sense of professional responsibility. The importance of this professional idealism is indicated by the scorn that is heaped upon the bureaucrat who violates this professionalism for a purely self-serving behavior. It is this wonderful mixture of independent self-interest and fidelity to an abstract code of behavior that distinguishes the Western version of the bureaucrat.

It is this paradoxical mixture of traits that has been a key, though often hidden, issue in the novel, the literary form that has been the most fully developed voice of Western bureaucracy. In such novels as those of Defoe, Richardson, Balzac, Dickens, and Dreiser, the world of the merchant-bureaucrat is often penetratingly treated. Very often at issue in these novels is the conflict that inevitably confronts the bureaucrat whenever he tries to balance the imperative to aggrandize himself and the imperative to disinterestedly serve society. In the detective novel this conflict is not just a regularly occurring issue but the very skeleton upon which the meat of character and plot are formed. Demonstrating this thesis is the purpose of the remainder of my essay.

Students of detective fiction generally recognize three basic sub-types, all of which derive from Poe's famous trilogy of stories, "The Murders in the Rue Morgue," "The Mystery of Marie Roget," "The Purloined Letter," and the even more widely known Sherlock Holmes stories of Arthur Conan Doyle. The first sub-type to develop after the initial period of experimentation is the classic story of ratiocination best exemplified by the novels of Agatha Christie and Dorothy Sayers. This sub-type flourished between 1915 and 1945, though numerous works that fall within this tradition are still being written. Writers of other nationalities have written in this tradition—Rex Stout and Amanda Cross are two from America—but I will refer to it as the English, country-house school, for reasons to be outlined in a moment.

The second sub-type of the detective novel, the hard-boiled, private-eye tradition, is essentially an American form, though again, writers from other countries have tried their hands at it. This sub-type developed in the pages of the pulp magazine *Black Mask* in the 1920s and was quickly made into a substantial literary form by Dashiell Hammett and Raymond Chandler in the 1930s and 1940s. It probably reached its zenith in the novels of Ross Macdonald in the 1950s and 1960s, though there are a number of good writers now writing in this tradition, most notably Sue Grafton and Robert Parker.

The third sub-type, the international police procedural, has its roots in the earlier forms but took recognizable shape after World War II in the works of Georges Simenon of France, J. J. Marric of England, and Ed McBain of America. This form probably has not yet reached its fullest development and widest popularity.

Though some students of detective fiction might consider all three sub-types as having equal claim on present-day writers and readers, there are good reasons to argue that evolutions in bureaucratic, middle-class culture during the century have made it progressively more difficult for authors to write convincingly in the first two forms, and these forms may be somewhat less culturally relevant for their readers than they once were. But, though my thesis applies even more obviously to the highly bureaucratized worlds of the private-eye novel and the police procedural than it does to the more bucolic world of the country-house mystery, I must confine my discussion to the English school because of the limitations of space.

The first sub-type of detective fiction can be meaningfully termed the English, country-house school because the setting for numerous stories in this tradition is a weekend party at a rural English estate. There are certain significant aspects of this typical situation that are to be found even in works that have ostensibly different settings, an excursion on the Nile, for example, a trip on the Orient Express, an island off the English coast, or the English Department of Harvard University.

The crucial fact in the novels of this school is that the action always takes place in an environment that physically and socially isolates a group of individuals from the surrounding society; this is a formal element that has profound thematic implications. The basic given of this school of detective fiction is that the world of murder is a closed one. Murder is a momentary expression of the breakdown of the rules that tie a social class together. It is assumed that the principles that govern this class are generally viable and work to produce a basic social harmony, though on occasion, violence results when individuals forget the importance of group solidarity and begin acting solely for their own benefit. Whenever an individual in a group begins thinking only of himself, he inevitably violates the rights of others and threatens the unity of the group as a whole. This violation is symbolized in the English, country-house mystery by the act of murder.

What sorts of people make up the group assembled for a weekend of formal dinners, gentlemanly sport, and emotionally loaded conversation and romantic assignations? Though there are almost always representatives of the working class in the background of these social gatherings, the servants of the manor, the villagers who serve it, and the enclosing rustics generally function only as elements of setting and devices of plot and as an unofficial Greek chorus. The murderer almost never comes from this class; in other words, the butler doesn't do it. The people who are caught at the focal point of the novel are almost invariably members of a landowning leisure class. Each has either inherited income-producing property, has acquired it through success in the professions or in commerce, or has been raised to expect this way of life as a birthright. Though this tight little group often includes members of the professions who must work during the week for a living, it is clear that essentially all of them feel daily labor a grave injustice that surely time and perhaps a little bit of murder will rectify. That attaining an independent income and the leisure and status that accompanies it is an all-consuming issue in this world is indicated by the number of plots that turn on wills and disputed inheritances.

It is from this closed group, a group made up of remnants from a decaying aristocracy, individuals from industry who have purchased or married into an old rural squirearchy, and upper-middle-class professionals, that both murdered and murderer come. In general, the motive for murder in this relatively tight world is the fact that it is at once too tight for some and not quite tight enough for others. The symbolic power of murder in the country-house mystery can be better understood if I return momentarily to the issue of class in the development of Western middle-class culture.

The numerous opportunities for acquiring wealth made possible by the gradual expansion of trade during the Middle Ages, the Renaissance, and the industrial age that followed placed great strains on the early, rural-based, two-class society formed of peasant and aristocrats. As the new, increasingly bureaucratic middle class of merchants, lawyers, manufacturers, and skilled craftsmen gained wealth and power, it became envious of the privileges reserved for the aristocracy. This became increasingly the case when time after time it was the bureaucratic skills of the middle class that saved the aristocracy from its own follies. Over the centuries, individuals from this upstart class of merchant-bureaucrats used their considerable manipulative skills to gain admittance to the realms of privilege and power.[8] Though the individual *parvenu* is angered by his exclusion from the charmed circle of the aristocracy, if he is clever, lucky, and patient enough to maneuver his way in, he becomes the most excluding of the exclusive. By the end of the nineteenth century, however, the circle of the select was no longer very exclusive, and only in the loosest sense of the word could it be termed aristocratic. Membership changed rapidly; and though having connections with the remnants of the older upper classes helped in establishing one's place in the pecking order, this new class was largely drawn from highly successful merchants, government functionaries, and professionals.

The great problem for this new class of would-be aristocrats was giving over the intensely aggressive, competitive, and independent behavior essential for success in middle-class bureaucracy for the more communal mode of living appropriate for a class that has inherited or pretends it has inherited its wealth, power, and social position. Ideally, the aristocrat is one whose individual identity is subsumed within the name and rank he has inherited. Having done little or nothing in his own person to earn his place in society, his allegiance is not to his own personal history but to those from whom he inherited and those who sustain him in his privileges, his lineage and his class as a whole. To shift in one or even several generations from an aggressively individualistic mode to a communal mode would be, psychologically speaking, impossible, even if it were clear that the communal mode of behavior were still socially viable. Even when successfully brought off, the aristocratic behavior of the new bourgeois aristocracy was only a matter of skillful play acting. (Perhaps this offers an explanation of why the English provide us with so many fine actors.) Underlying the elaborately modulated manners that people of this class were supposed to follow were repressed aggressions that can be expected to erupt occasionally in acts of violence. The threat of this latent aggression to the stability of society is the chief subject of and motivation for the country-house murder mystery.

For the middle class, murder is a particularly heinous crime, but not, as we often complacently assume, because our culture believes in the sacredness of life. (The threat of other cultures and other life forms by Western colonial societies puts the lie to this notion.) Murder is for us a terrible crime because it deprives the victim of his individuality, his right to compete for success.

Murder is a terrible crime from a middle-class perspective, but it is also a terrible crime from an older, more communal point of view as well. For a group that is not sure of its solidarity, the murder of one member by another is a grave threat to everyone. In the country-house murder mystery, this threat is suggested by the fact that everyone immediately becomes a suspect as well as potentially the next victim. Everyone in the country house at the time of the murder has not only the opportunity to commit the murder but, as the detective discovers, each has had a motive. In addition, the detective uncovers facts from the past of each that call into question the right of some or all of them to be considered members of this select group. At the same time he discovers behavior in each that suggests the capacity for murderous violence.

It is clear that one of the chief purposes of the country-house school is to reveal the fundamental fragility of this privileged class. Underneath its aristocratic facade are essentially middle-class impulses. The revelation of this hypocrisy is, no doubt, one of the pleasures enjoyed by the millions of Agatha Christie's readers. Clearly, only a few of Christie's original readers and perhaps none of her present ones could realistically consider themselves to be members of this privileged class, and it would be natural for a good bit of envy and resentment to accompany their vicarious enjoyment of the aristocratic way of life evoked in the novels. And yet, the essentially conservative writers and readers of this genre clearly could not imagine doing away with the *idea* of aristocracy. Though the country-house mystery uncovers the creaky structure underlying the pretensions of this class of would-be aristocrats, it is nevertheless at equal pains to paper over the flaws. This is the function of the second crucial ingredient of the country-house mystery, the detective himself.

The detective and the murderer form an emblematic contrast. The murderer is a member of the neo-aristocratic circle who continues to apply the rules of aggressive, middle-class individualism in an older, communal context. In his inability to conform to a new ethic he endangers the whole class and also the surrounding society, which needs a privileged class to provide a vision of the potential rewards of ambition and hard work. The detective is an idealized bureaucrat who serves society with a completely selfless and uncompromising dedication. While others are driven toward a ruthlessly competitive aggrandizement of the self, the detective is one who has found the inner resources to balance a highly refined sense of self-worth against an equally developed sense of professional idealism.

What differentiates him from the bourgeois aristocrats of the manor house, particularly the murderer, is his belief that validation of the self comes not through the external material rewards that society can bestow, but from doing a job as well as it can be done. The ideal middle-class bureaucrat can be motivated merely by the knowledge that a task needs doing, and he may be the only one who is qualified and disinterested enough to do it well. Such paragons of bureaucratic selflessness may not dominate real-life bureaucracy, and yet the success of our complex, independent society must be due, at least in part, to the fact that much of the time the average bureaucrat lives up to this ideal of selfless professionalism.

Because the detective is a self-defining professional who has foresworn social ambition, he is free to mediate the crisis within the select circle of bureaucrats *cum* aristocrats. The role of mediator was the original function of the bureaucratic middle class in Western society. From the outset the bureaucrat earned his bread by serving as a go-between between various segments of the culture. The detective, who reestablishes order out of the social chaos of the manor house in which murder has been committed, serves the function of reminding the bureaucratic reader of the vital social role of the good bureaucrat. In spite of the fact that his ability to manipulate both the physical and social aspects of life occasionally makes it possible for the entrepreneurial bureaucrat to gain great wealth and power, and though the stimulation of excess productive capacity and the accumulation of great masses of wealth is of actual and symbolic importance in our culture, only a few people can become truly wealthy and powerful. All other bureaucrats must be content to work hard largely for symbolic private rewards.

Thus it is that one of the great problems for the average bureaucrat is learning to balance the contradictory imperatives of ambitious self-aggrandizement and selfless professionalism. To give oneself completely to ambition can leave one open to destruction by a cleverer, more ruthless, or luckier competitor, or it can lead to a conspicuous success that makes one a potential scapegoat for a jealous and threatened society. On the other hand, to give oneself too timidly to the contest for power opens one up to exploitation and produces in the individual a deep sense of failure.

The detective represents these issues in quite dramatic terms. When the detective of the English country-house school such as Christie's Hercules Poirot or Dorothy Sayers's Lord Peter Wimsey comes into the scene of the crime, the social structure embodied in the manor house is about to collapse. If murder is committed in a group closed off from outside society, everyone becomes suspicious of everyone else; whenever the individual murderer cannot be found, all must participate in the guilt. This produces an intolerable state of paranoia. The detective, who represents the key virtues of middle-class culture, enters the scene as an objective, scientific observer. With a rigorous application of logic, intuitive sense of character and a finely tuned sense of middle-class motivations, he discovers the culprit. In the process he brings to light examples of obsessive, self-centered behavior in the lives of the other members of the charmed circle, and in doing so he renders this behavior harmless, at least momentarily.

The issue that provides the country-house novel with its suspense is not the search for the identity of the killer; it is, instead, the detective's efforts to break through the barriers of social pretension that the select circle in which murder has taken place has created around itself. If, through the sheer effectiveness of his professional method and the elemental strength of his sense of self, the detective can overcome the considerable social defenses of those in the aristocratic circle, then the murderer can be unmasked and the fragile bourgeois aristocracy saved in spite of itself. If he is unable to break down social barriers that would exclude him, then the mystery will not be solved.

This issue is set up for us very neatly at the outset of one of Christie's most famous novels, *Murder on the Orient Express*. The first character to spot Poirot on the train platform before the start of the train journey that provides the setting for the story states the challenge: "The little man removed his hat. What an egg-shaped head he had! In spite of her preoccupations Mary Beneham smiled. A ridiculous-looking little man. The sort of little man one could never take seriously."[9]

Not being taken seriously is the greatest insult and threat imaginable for the ambitious bureaucrat. Reciprocally, the bureaucratic reader likes to believe that not taking the bureaucrat seriously is the greatest mistake anyone of an exclusive clique can make. Underestimating Poirot is a repeated error of villains in Christie, and one suspects that identifying with the undervalued bureaucrat as he proceeds to outwit those who have tried to exclude him is one of the chief motivations for reading this kind of mystery.

The key scene in almost all mysteries of the English school is the one at the end, when the detective proves his own superiority by revealing the self-serving and self-defeating egotism of all involved while simultaneously reminding us through the explication of his investigative method of the true value of middle-class professionalism. This scene of revelation often takes place in the manor library with everyone including the murderer in attendance. The fact that this scene is staged so often in the library is suggestive: Books have always been the single most important vehicle of middle-class power. Without books the middle class could never have come into being or become the dominant class of Western culture. In staging the scene of revelation in a library, all, including the reader, are subtly reminded of the real strength and purpose of middle-class life. With everyone present, the detective—momentarily at the center and the leader of the circle of chastened murderers and would-be murderers—reminds us of the Puritan minister of old chastising his flock for straying once again into selfish materialism. The detective, preaching by example, reminds all of the true strengths and values of middle-class life.

When he leaves the manor house to return to his self-contained, unpretentious living, order has been restored. The possibility that excessive self-interest can bring down the whole system of middle-class bureaucratic culture is threat enough to frighten everyone into a more cooperative mode of behavior. The traditional country-house novel is a cautionary tale that ends usually on a positive note. There are dangerous undercurrents in middle-class culture, it is true, but when we are reminded of our responsibilities by a selfless bureaucrat, these tendencies, it is suggested, can be controlled.

This issue of disinterested professionalism is a complex one. The ideal that the good bureaucrat is motivated primarily by professional pride is deeply rooted in the necessities of Western culture. To work solely for one's own aggrandizement is frowned upon even by apologists for laissez-faire free enterprise. It is argued that the entrepreneur—a freelance bureaucrat—benefits society by generating jobs through the creation of new enterprises. The self-obsessed individual is a threat to everyone. The murderer in the mystery novel is just such a person. The detective involves himself in the investigation, even if there is no possibility of reward or recompense, because he realizes that egotism of this magnitude, if left unchecked, can destroy society. Whenever the bureaucratic principle of selfless professionalism falls under attack, the true bureaucrat feels compelled to act. This public altruism is motivated, no doubt, by a very personal sense of threat. The bureaucrat feels secure only so long as he believes that everyone else is abiding by the same principles of self-restraint and professional service. Whenever one person begins to ignore these restraints, there is great temptation for all to abandon them. The survival of the system and one's own hard-won career depends upon rapidly isolating and punishing the unrestrained egotist.

The system of bureaucracy in our culture provides opportunities for each bureaucrat to aggrandize himself at the expense of his profession and society. Even the most selfless professional cannot be trusted to remain that way. Constant vigilance is essential. This truth is symbolized in the fact that, by the time of the library scene of the typical English mystery, the detective has become the center of the charmed circle. The detective has displaced the squire who should rule at the center of an aristocratic world. The detective is, in an ultimate symbolic sense, the real murderer. He is, for the space of one scene, the archetypal parvenu who has usurped the aristocrat's throne and threatens the opportunities of all other bureaucrats who lust after power.

As the representation of such usurpation produces great anxiety in our society, it is presented in the country-house novel only symbolically and only momentarily. The detective remains at the center of the charmed group only long enough to point out the corruption of each member and to demonstrate the superiority of his own middle-class skills and morality. At the deepest level of the self, the middle-class bureaucrat knows that aristocracy is not aristocracy if its center is a bureaucrat. To lose the dream of ascension to the aristocracy is far worse than having to give up one's own momentary place in it. The middle class has meaning and security only so long as it can work hard to escape itself. This means there must be a class to escape to which it is not, but as soon as it becomes a part of this other, superior class, it is no longer other or superior. Therefore, the only way to return meaning to a disrupted middle-class society is to deny the possibility of attaining real aristocratic status. It must always remain only a symbolic possibility, a dream. In airing the charmed circle's dirty linen, the detective hero makes membership in the circle seem much less desirable for the moment. Once the murderer has been apprehended, the detective, along with the reader, can withdraw back into his own isolate, professional self with a mingled feeling of regret and earned moral superiority.

Detective fiction exists to help conserve the present values of culture by reminding us of what we are all supposed to believe and by showing us that these beliefs do, in fact, work. Whatever paradoxes exist in a mythology will not be recognized as such in its popular, formulaic art. In fact, the greatest artistic dilemma for the formulaic artist is to find ways of making the duality of paradox seem singular.

As we have seen, the paradox that must be finessed in the detective novel results from the conflict between the imperative of our bureaucratic culture toward individualistic self-assertion and the equally strong imperative toward altruistic professionalism. The problem of the writer of murder mysteries is to remind us of the importance of disinterested professionalism through the example of the detective without allowing his selfless behavior to call seriously into question the imperative toward self-aggrandizement. There is as much danger to Western, middle-class culture of passive self-abnegation as there is from an out-of-control self-centeredness. The health of our society depends upon keeping both imperatives in careful balance.

The writers of English country-house fiction paper over the paradoxical nature of middle-class mythology by treating one aspect through plot and the other through characterization. The detective's selfless professionalism is demonstrated through the methodical procedures through which he investigates every aspect of the crime. The detective is tireless and uncompromising in his pursuit of the truth. He gives no thought to his own comfort, and though there are ways he could turn the situation to his own benefit, the thought never occurs to him. His only concern is solving the puzzle of the crime. The detective's commitment to professional rigor and honesty is emphasized by the highly stylized ordering of the plot. This is particularly true of Agatha Christie's books, but the same quality is to be found in other works of this type. In *Murder on the Orient Express*, for example, the undeviating thoroughness of Poirot's investigation is underscored by the organization of the book into three parts: "The Facts," "The Evidence," and "Hercule Poirot Sits Back and Thinks." Poirot's method is further underscored by Christie's giving over the second and largest section to interviews with each of the thirteen suspects, a chapter being devoted to each.

To keep their detectives from seeming too selfless and passive, writers in this school rely on characterization. They ritually portray their heroes as highly eccentric and egotistical, a strategy invented by Poe in his treatment of Auguste Dupin. Hercule Poirot, like Dupin and Sherlock Holmes, shows through highly individualistic dress, speech, behavior, and style of living that he is the quintessential individualist whose altruistic devotion to the public good is the result of willed, independent choice rather than passive obedience to authority. By using two aspects of technique to present the two aspects of the bureaucratic paradox, writers in the English school manage to assert both simultaneously without calling attention to the fact that they are contradictory principles. The rigorous application of bureaucratic values by a detective characterized by small vanities rather than a grand egotism always returns society to its former healthy state. The basic bureaucratic skills that have led to middle-class ascendancy are triumphantly asserted by novel's end.

As in other types of formulaic literature, the impact on the reader of any detective novel will be only temporary. It is all to be experienced again the next evening with a book that is essentially the same as the one read the night before. Like other formulaic genres, detective fiction is a kind of ritual incantation. It exists to help conserve the present survival strategies of our culture by reminding us of what we are all supposed to believe and by showing us that these beliefs do, in fact, work. The good bureaucrat, in the guise of the detective, who has dedicated years of learning how to carry out a task requiring great craft and knowledge, acquires an aura of quiet power, a power that, when represented fictionally, can provide others with a deep, reassuring pleasure. This is the source of our affection for the great athlete or the great musician. This pleasure, perhaps as much as any other, may explain the wide appeal of detective fiction. It is a pleasure that is doubled by the solid craftsmanship of most mystery writers. Watching the good bureaucrat-writer perform his craft with dedication and calm, efficient assurance is bound to have a soothing effect on the unappreciated, much-maligned, overworked, and underpaid bureaucrat-reader.

NOTES

1. Henry Jacoby, *The Bureaucratization of the World*, 1.

2. For a systematic description of the principles of cultural materialism see Marvin Harris, *Cultural Materialism: The Struggle for a Science of Culture*, particularly 55-76; for illuminating applications of these principles see Harris's *Cows, Pigs, Wars and Witches: The Riddles of Culture* and *Cannibals and Kings: The Origins of Cultures*.

3. For insight into the conditions that necessitate the creation of bureaucracy see Harris, *Cannibals and Kings*, 69-82.

4. Karl A. Wittfogel, *Oriental Despotism: A Comparative Study of Total Power*, 50-59, 302-7, 331-43, 365-68. This is the seminal treatment of the environmental causes of centralized despotic power in "hydraulic" cultures (cultures whose population growth is accommodated through the development of an agriculture based on large irrigation and water control systems); Harris, in *Cannibals and Kings*, 155-63, gives a concise summary of Wittfogel's argument.

5. Harris gives an enlightening comparison of the origins of Western democratic institutions in an environment of rainfall agriculture (agriculture made possible by widespread dependable rainfall) with the despotic institutions of hydraulic cultures in *Cannibals and Kings*, 167-77.

6. Fernand Braudel, *The Structures of Everyday Life: The Limits of the Possible*, translated by Sian Reynolds, Vol. 1 of *Civilization and Capitalism: 15th-18th Century*, 415-30.

7. For a comprehensive survey of the development of European commerce and the culture that it necessitated see Braudel, *The Wheels of Commerce*, translated by Sian Reynolds, Vol. II of *Civilization and Capitalism*, 15th-18th Century, particularly 138-54; see also Robert S. Lopez, *The Commercial Revolution of the Middle Ages*, 950-1350; Joseph and Frances Gies, *Merchants and Moneymen: The Commercial Revolution*, 1000-1500; R. Burr Litchfield, *Emergence of a Bureaucracy: The Florentine Patrician*, 1530-1790; J. W. Gough, *The Rise of the Entrepreneur*.

8. Georges Duby, *The Early Growth of the European Economy: Warriors and Peasants from the Seventh to the Twelfth Century*, translated by Howard B. Clarke, 257-58; George Hupert, *Les Bourgeois Gentilshommes*, 174-77; Lawrence Stone, *The Crisis of the Aristocracy: 1558-1641*, 12-15.

9. Agatha Christie, *Murder on the Orient Express*, 4-5.

REFERENCES

Braudel, Fernand. *The Structures of Everyday Life: The Limits of the Possible*, translated by Sian Reynolds. *Civilization and Capitalism: 15th-18th Century*. Vol. 1. New York: Harper and Row, 1979.

_____. *The Wheels of Commerce*. Translated by Sian Reynolds. *Civilization and Capitalism: 15th-18th Century*. Vol. 2. New York: Harper and Row, 1982.

Christie, Agatha. *Murder on the Orient Express*. 1934. Reprint. New York: Pocket Books, 1975.

Duby, Georges. *The Early Growth of the European Economy: Warriors and Peasants from the Seventh to the Twelfth Century*, translated by Howard B. Clarke. Ithaca, NY: Cornell University Press, 1974.

Gies, Joseph and Francis. *Merchants and Moneymen: The Commercial Revolution*. New York: Thomas Y. Crowell, 1972.

Gough, J. W. *The Rise of the Entrepreneur*. New York: Schocken Books, 1969.

Harris, Marvin. *Cannibals and Kings: The Origins of Cultures*. New York: Random House, 1977.

_____. *Cows, Pigs, Wars and Witches: The Riddles of Culture*. New York: Random House, 1974.

_____. *Cultural Materialism: The Struggle for a Science of Culture*. New York: Random House, 1979.

Hupert, George. *Les Bourgeois Gentilshommes*. Chicago: University of Chicago Press, 1977.

Jacoby, Henry. *The Bureaucratization of the World*, translated by Eveline L. Kanes. Berkeley: University of California Press, 1973.

Litchfield, R. Burr. *Emergence of a Bureaucracy: The Florentine Patrician*. Princeton, NJ: Princeton University Press, 1986.

Lopez, Robert S. *The Commercial Revolution of the Middle Ages*. Englewood Cliffs, NJ: Prentice-Hall, 1971.

Stone, Lawrence. *The Crisis of the Aristocracy: 1558-1641*. Oxford: Clarendon Press, 1965.

Wittfogel, Karl A. *Oriental Despotism: A Comparative Study of Total Power*. New Haven, CT: Yale University Press, 1964.

Index

About the Editors and Contributors

MARY ANNE ACKERSHOEK received her Ph.D. from Brown University where she was an adjunct lecturer when she wrote Chapter 11.

ISKA S. ALTER is an associate professor of English at Hofstra University, where she teaches courses in American literature, American drama, and Shakespeare. She has written about Agatha Christie, P. D. James, and Anne Perry.

BARBARA BARKER is a doctoral student in English education at the University of South Florida. She is a fiction writer who teaches at Tampa Technical Institute.

JAMES E. BARTELL earned his Ph.D. in American literature at Washington University, St. Louis, in 1971 with a dissertation on narrative patterns in the novels of Theodore Dreiser. He began his teaching career in 1967 at Northern Arizona University, Flagstaff, where he has remained. In this time he has taught a wide range of courses in the American and British tradition and in popular literary genres, most particularly detective fiction.

TIMOTHY W. BOYD (instructor, Harvard Extension School, and teaching assistant, Harvard University) works in two fields: Epic traditions in Greek, Latin, and Old Irish and Victorian-to-modern British and American poetry. He has published articles on the transmission and performance of Homeric poems as well as on the Pre-Raphaelites. He is under contract to Southern Illinois University Press for an edition of the selected letters of William Allingham.

JOHN G. CAWELTI is a professor of English at the University of Kentucky and has written a number of books and articles about detective fiction, popular genres, and popular culture. Among his books are *Adventure, Mystery, and Romance; The Six-Gun Mystique*; and *Spy Story*.

JEROME H. DELAMATER is a professor of communication at Hofstra University, where he teaches courses in film studies and production. A specialist in the films of Gene Kelly, he is the author of *Dance in the Hollywood Musical* and has also written articles about the musical for the *International Encyclopedia of Dance* and about the Western for the *BFI Companion to the Western*.

JASMINE Y. HALL is an assistant professor in English and women's studies at Elms College, Chicopee, Massachusetts. Her work on narratives of investigation in Victorian literature has appeared in *Studies in Short Fiction* and *Dickens Studies Annual*. She is currently working on a study of the interplay among professionalism, consumerism, and gender identity in the Victorian and modern British novel.

INA RAE HARK is a professor of English and an associate dean of the College of Liberal Arts at the University of South Carolina. She is the author of *Edward Lear* and coeditor of *Screening the Male: Exploring Masculinities in Hollywood Cinema*. Among her numerous articles on literature and film, studies of mystery and suspense have appeared in *Studies in the Novel, New Orleans Review, Literature/Film Quarterly, Hitchcock's Re-Released Films*, and *Cinema Journal*.

CAROLYN HIGBIE (assistant professor, Department of the Classics, Harvard University) is interested in archaic Greece, both its literary and its archaeological remains, and has published three articles in her field. Her current research is on the Greek understanding of their own past; she is drawing on both written and archaeological evidence in this project.

MARTHA STODDARD HOLMES received her Ph.D. in English from the University of Colorado in 1996. She has published articles on contemporary poetry and Victorian fiction and is currently working on a book on physical disabilities in Victorian culture.

PETER HÜHN is a professor of English literature at Hamburg University and was a visiting professor at Purdue University in 1984-1985. He has published articles and books on British poetry, most recently a *History of English Poetry* and "Postmodern Tendencies in British Poetry" (1995). His other field of interest is British and American mystery fiction and narrative theory. He is currently working on a study of the crime novel.

MARNIE JONES is an associate professor of English at the University of North Florida where she directs the Honors Program. She has written *"Golden Rule" Jones: Contract of the Heart*.

JANICE MACDONALD received an M.A. in English from the University of Alberta, where she was a part-time lecturer. She now lectures at Grant MacEwan Community College in Edmonton, Alberta. She has taught non-credit mystery literature courses and writing courses in the genre. Her works include *The Next Margaret*, an academic mystery novel, and *Sticks & Stones*, another Randy Craig mystery, awaiting publication. She is at work on a third in the series. A children's book, entitled *The Ghouls' Night Out*, is due out in the fall of 1998.

ROBERT MERRILL is Foundation Professor of English at the University of Nevada, Reno. He has published books on Norman Mailer, Joseph Heller, and Kurt Vonnegut. His articles have appeared in journals such as *American Literature, Modern Fiction Studies, Modern Philology, Critique, Studies in American Fiction*, and *Texas Studies in Literature and Language*. He is currently editing a book on Raymond Chandler and writing a critical study of modern detective fiction.

KATHLEEN BELIN OWEN is a graduate student in the Ph.D. program in English at George Washington University. She has presented papers at conferences on Irish Studies on Clare Boylan and Julia O'Faolain and has also given a paper on Jane Austen.

TIMOTHY R. PRCHAL is a Ph.D. candidate at the University of Wisconsin, where he is completing a dissertation on American realism. His essay on fictional detectives and asceticism is scheduled to appear in an anthology forthcoming from Scarecrow Press, and an article on mystery author Anna Katharine Green is to appear in *Nineteenth Century American Women Writers: A Bio-Bibliographical Critical Sourcebook*, forthcoming from Greenwood Publishing Group. He also has had his own short fiction published.

RUTH PRIGOZY is professor of English at Hofstra University where she teaches courses in American literature and film studies. She has published many articles on F. Scott Fitzgerald, as well as on Hemingway, Salinger, and such filmmakers as Billy Wilder, DeSica, and Griffith. She has edited Fitzgerald's *This Side of Paradise* and *The Great Gatsby*.

CAROLYN F. SCOTT is an adjunct instructor of English at the University of St. Thomas in St. Paul, Minnesota. She received her Ph.D. from Indiana University. Her major field of study is Shakespeare and Renaissance drama, although she has published articles on Dante's *Inferno*, Edmund Campion, and Shakespeare's sonnets. Her current work examines issues of identity in Renaissance drama.

ANN THOMPSON and her husband John O. Thompson are coauthors of *Shakespeare, Meaning and Metaphor*. She is a professor of English at Roehampton Institute, London, and is the author of *Shakespeare's Chaucer* and of *"King Lear": The Critics' Debate*. She is one of the general editors of the Arden Shakespeare, third series, and is coeditor with Neil Taylor of *Hamlet*, forthcoming in that series. Most recently she has coedited, with Sasha Roberts, *Women Reading Shakespeare, 1660-1900*.

JOHN O. THOMPSON and his wife Ann Thompson are coauthors of *Shakespeare, Meaning and Metaphor*. Like Margaret Millar a Canadian expatriate, he lectures in film and television in the Centre for Journalism Studies at Cardiff University of Wales. He is the author of *Monty Python: Complete and Utter Theory of the Grotesque* and coeditor, with Antony Easthope, of *Contemporary Poetry Meets Modern Theory*. He has also published a book of verse, *Echo and Montana*.

ROBIN WOODS is an associate professor of English at Ripon College. She has published "'His Appearance Is Against Him': The Emergence of the Detective" in *The Cunning Craft: Original Essays in Detective Fiction and Contemporary Literary Theory* (*Essays in Literature*, 1990). Her current research interests are in crime literature and the popular ballard.

ISBN 0-313-30462-9

HARDCOVER BAR CODE